a visitor's guide

COSTA RICA'S

National Parks and Preserves

a visitor's guide

COSTA RICA'S

National Parks and Preserves

Second Edition
JOSEPH FRANKE

Color Photographs by
Gregory Dimijian

THE
MOUNTAINEERS

This book is for my parents,
Irving and Suzanne Franke

Published by
The Mountaineers
1001 SW Klickitat Way, Suite 201
Seattle, Washington 98134

First edition 1993. Second edition: first printing 1999, second printing 2001

Published simultaneously in Great Britain by Cordee, 3a DeMontfort Street, Leicester, England, LE1 7HD

Manufactured in Canada

Edited by Brenda Pittsley
Maps by Brian Metz/Green Rhino Graphics, Jerry Painter
All black and white photos by Joseph Franke, unless otherwise noted
Cover and book design by Kristy L. Welch
Layout by Kristy L. Welch
Cover photo: *Roman Urbina Biking the Cahuita National Park Trail, Costa Rica*
© Spiker Stock Photography
Interior color photography: Gregory Dimijian
Frontispiece: *Vegetation in Curú Wildlife Refuge*, photo by Joseph Franke

Library of Congress Cataloging-in-Publication Data
Franke, Joseph.
   Costa Rica's national parks and preserves : a visitor's guide /
Joseph Franke.—2nd ed.
      p. cm.
   Includes index.
   ISBN 0-89886-560-3
   1. National parks and reserves—Costa Rica—Guidebooks. I. Title.
   SB484.C8 F73 1999
   917.28604'5—dc21   99-6308
                                                                          CIP

CONTENTS

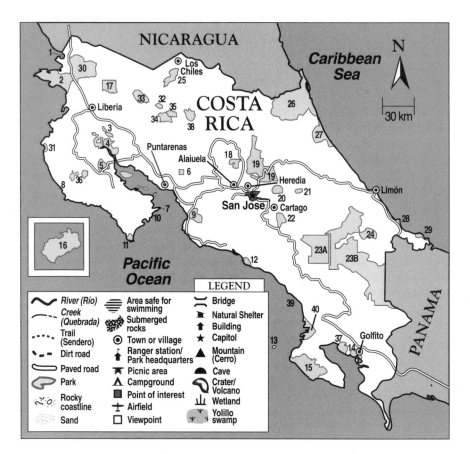

COSTA RICA'S NATIONAL PARKS AND PRESERVES

1. Isla Bolaños Wildlife Sanctuary
2. Santa Rosa National Park
3. Lomas Barbudal Biological Reserve
4. Palo Verde National Park
5. Barra Honda National Park
6. Peñas Blancas Wildlife Refuge
7. Guayabo, Negritos, and Los Párajos
   Islands Biological Reserves
8. Ostional Wildlife Refuge
9. Carara Biological Reserve
10. Curú Wildlife Refuge
11. Cabo Blanco Biological Reserve
12. Manuel Antonio National Park
13. Isla del Caño Biological Reserve
14. Golfito Wildlife Refuge
15. Corcovado National Park
16. Isla del Cocos National Park
17. Rincón de la Vieja National Park
18. Poás National Park
19. Braulio Carrillo National Park
20. Irazú National Park
21. Guayabo National Monument
22. Tapantí Wildlife Refuge
23. Chirripó National Park
24. Hitoy-Cerere Biological Reserve
25. Caño Negro Wildlife Refuge
26. Barra del Colorado Wildlife Refuge
27. Tortuguero National Park
28. Cahuita National Park
29. Gandoca-Manzanillo Wildlife Refuge
30. Guanacaste National Park
31. Las Baulas National Park and Tamarindo
    Wildlife Refuge
32. Arenal National Park
33. Tenorio National Park
34. Monteverde Forest Preserve
35. Children's Eternal Rain Forest Preserve
36. Diriá National Park
37. Esquinas National Park
38. La Amistad National Park
39. Ballena National Park
40. Mangrove Forest Reserve

Acknowledgments

The author would like to thank the following people: Maria Consuelo Lopez of Horizontes Tours, Lynne Rosselli of the Monteverde Conservation League, Claude Tremblay of WWF Canada, Luis Diego Gomez, Gail Hewson, and Annie Simpson de Gamboa of OTS, Jorge Mora (Man of the Mangroves), Mike Stiles of Sierpe Lodge, and Michael Schnitzler. Last but definitely not least, I would like to thank the many rangers and field staff actually working in the parks and refuges for continuing to hold the system together on so little.

Readers should feel free to write the author in care of The Mountaineers Books with suggestions for future editions of this guide. Thanks.

INTRODUCTION

Epithet after epithet was found too weak to convey to those who have not visited the intertropical regions, the sensation of delight which the mind experiences . . . . The land is one great wild, untidy, luxuriant hothouse, made by nature for herself.

Charles Darwin, *Voyage of the Beagle*

Costa Rica's territory covers 51,032 square kilometers. It is bordered by Nicaragua to the north and by Panama to the south. The human population numbers 2.9 million, with an annual growth rate of 2.7 percent. Unlike other Central American countries, the indigenous population is small—about 1 percent of the total. Thirty percent of the population is of African ancestry (concentrated primarily on the Atlantic coast), and the remainder is of Spanish descent. There are pockets of people with other European ancestry. The San Vito area, for example, boasts a population of Italian descendants. Because of the historically small indigenous population, there are relatively few *mestizos*, people of mixed indigenous and European heritage.

The Central Valley region, in which San José, Cartago, and Alajuela are located, contains roughly 60 percent of the population. You might think that this leaves much of the country sparsely populated, but keep in mind the relatively small size of Costa Rica. It is now widely recognized that the nation has a population problem. Unfortunately, the constant electoral changes from one political party to the next leave little room for a consistent planning policy, and the population continues to rise. This puts a tremendous strain on the country, both ecologically and socially.

Costa Rica's last large frontiers for settlement disappeared in the 1950s with the construction of the road from San José to San Isidro and the road from Guapiles to Limón in the 1970s and 1980s. Now, most of the land is settled or privately owned, leaving wilderness only in the parks and reserves and in reservations for indigenous peoples. If Costa Ricans hope to keep their traditionally high standard of living in place, there needs to be a coherent plan for monitoring and containing population growth.

The economy, like that of most Latin American countries, relies heavily on agricultural exports. The three biggest moneymakers are coffee, bananas, and tourism. Costa Rica's economy is starting to diversify, but in the past, reliance on agricultural export earnings created problems when prices for these commodities fell.

Costa Rica has an extremely high foreign debt, and the interest payments

Forest stream, Zona Protectora Las Tablas

sometimes have not been met. The country's economic problems really started to build in 1978, when a fall in coffee prices was compounded with a doubling in the price of oil the following year. Costa Rica borrowed heavily from the World Bank and other lenders to maintain the country's infrastructure. Unfortunately, developing countries are often forced to liquidate their natural resources in order to make their payments. Costa Rica has little in the way of exportable materials outside of the protected areas and reservations. But despite the country's problems, many Costa Ricans from all walks of life have managed to maintain a strong conservation ethic, of which the park and reserve system is a strong manifestation.

ABOUT THE PARKS

If you have never been to a tropical forest, you might be able to appreciate the trouble that even the likes of Charles Darwin had in adequately describing it when he wrote: "Epithet after epithet was found too weak to convey to those who have not visited the intertropical regions, the sensation of delight which the mind experiences."

Consider that tropical forests cover less than 7 percent of the earth's land surface, but contain more than 50 percent of all its species. Tropical forests serve as a huge storehouse of biological wealth, and are regarded as enormously important regulators of climate. They are also, as Darwin attempted to point out, sources of continuous intellectual and aesthetic stimulation for the visitor. In the forests of the American neotropics, a visitor can experience such wonders as iridescent blue morpho butterflies as big as a human hand, brilliantly hued poison dart frogs, and gigantic buttressed trees so covered with orchids, bromeliads, and other plants as to appear to be a forest inside a forest.

Costa Rica has become a mecca for naturalists and outdoorspersons interested in the tropics. It's not hard to see why everyone from backpackers to kayakers to research scientists is drawn to this country with its peaceful, completely demilitarized democracy, breathtaking scenic beauty, and remarkable biological diversity.

Still, it's Costa Rica's forty national parks and reserves, which cover more than 12 percent of its total area, that cinch the country as a natural-history-minded tourist's paradise. The parks have been well planned to incorporate the full spectrum of the country's natural diversity. On the Atlantic coast, they contain steamy lowland rain forests and canals, wetlands, and nesting beaches for turtles. In the central plateau region, there are forested volcanoes shrouded in mist, and the cold, eerily fascinating subalpine *paramo* grasslands. The southwest has the magnificent forests of Corcovado, probably the most species-rich in the country. The northwest offers pristine beaches and the fascinating dry tropical forest, which turns from a leafless brown and gray to vibrant green almost overnight with the coming of the summer rains.

Given the number of parks and reserves in the system and their remarkable diversity, it may surprise you to learn that just four parks get more than 75 percent of all foreign visitors. Why? Certainly not because Tortuguero, Poás, Cahuita, and Manuel Antonio are deserving of all of the attention, but because of the lack of easily available information about the others. This book has been written to fill that need.

I hope that this book gets you off the beaten track, not only so you can benefit from the wealth of experiences that await you, but also so the parks can benefit from your visit. Please keep in mind that while Costa Rica is committed to preserving a large part of its natural heritage, it is also saddled with one of the largest per-capita foreign debts in the world. Servicing this debt could someday push the government into budget cutbacks for new park acquisitions or even for basic operations. It is likely there will be pressure to open some protected areas to timber and mining development.

You can help ward off these potential threats by hiking in the magnificent forests of Hitoy-Cerere or by paddling the lakes and marshlands of Caño Negro. After your trip, write to the tourist board and the department of natural resources to tell them how much you enjoyed your visits to these areas and that you will recommend them to other visitors. Letters containing this sort of information can be used in arguments against cutting a budget for a particular park. Unfortunately, a park's value as a reservoir of biodiversity does not pay the rent. Tourism ranks as the third-largest generator of foreign exchange in Costa Rica, after bananas and coffee. If the undeservedly lesser-known parks are perceived as being a real or potential "draw," then their survival will most likely be assured.

With that said, open your heart and mind to the natural wonders contained within the protected natural areas of this diverse, lovely, and justifiably proud country known as the Rich Coast.

HOW TO USE THIS BOOK

Part I contains chapters on planning your trip, the different life zones you are likely to encounter during your stay, Costa Rica's conservation history, and the ethics of ecotourism.

Part II consists of chapters for each of four regions and includes the park descriptions. Each park description begins with an information block that details the park's size, its distance from San José, whether camping is permitted, if there are trails, recommended maps, when the dry season occurs, and public transportation to the park. Included in each park description are its location and directions to it, visitor facilities, and detailed descriptions of each trail and river route within it.

The trail descriptions also begin with an information block listing the hike's distance, the time required to hike it, elevation gain, and a recommended map. The trails included in this book range in length and difficulty from 1-kilometer morning hikes to 50-kilometer backpack trips. A map of each region is provided, as well as maps detailing all hikes described within each park.

Appendices include a list of support services such as guides, white-water companies, and air shuttles for independent hikers and naturalists; a list of conservation and sustainable development organizations working in Costa Rica (for those travelers whose experiences move them to action); and a list of suggested reading.

SPANISH GLOSSARY

aguas thermales	hot springs
arribadas	mass turtle nestings
bahia	bay, harbor
ballena	whale
bananillo	bananalike plant
barricadas	mass turtle nestings
baula	leatherback turtle
boca	bar snack
bosque	forest
cabinas	cabins
calzados	cobbled roads
camino	path, trail
campesino	farmer
cativo	type of forest plant
colmenar	apiary
colón, colones	Costa Rican currency
cordillera	mountain range
cuesta	hill
estero	estuary
finca	farm, ranch
garrobo	ctenosaur
gomba	buttress of tree trunk
gringo	foreigner, esp. English-speaking
gringo rico	rich foreigner
guano	dung
hacienda	large ranch, farmhouse
holillo	raffia palm
hornillas	kitchen stoves (also, small steam vents)
huevos de caballos	"horse's testicles" (a fruit)
invierno	winter
isla	island
juaragua	grasslands
lago	lake
laguna	lagoon
lancha	motorboat, foot-passenger ferry

llanuras	extensive plains
manzanillo	tree with caustic, poisonous sap
montículos	stone mounds
naranja	orange
olla	pot, kettle
paramo	high, cold plains
parrujas	biting midges, no-see-ums
pensión	boardinghouse
pilas de barro	mud pots
playa	beach
poza	swimming hole
puerto	port, harbor
pulperia	general store
punta	point, tip
quebrada	creek, small river
refresqueria	refreshment stand, soda stand
refugio	mountain hut, shelter
río	river
sendero	path, trail
supermercado	supermarket
tepisquintle	agouti
terciopelo	fer de lance viper
tico	citizen of Costa Rica
tigre	jaguar
tigrillo	margay
tortuga	tortoise, turtle
tortuguero	turtle catcher
verano	summer
volcán	volcano

Owl butterfly displaying false "eyes" used to frighten potential predators

Part I

Palm trees in old pasture, Curú Wildlife Refuge

I
PREPARING FOR YOUR TRIP

Travel in the tropics, particularly in the backcountry, presents some challenges that may be unfamiliar to a traveler from more temperate climes. The culture, weather, terrain, and biotic components of Costa Rica's environment should all be taken into consideration before you set out on your trip. This chapter gives you information about what activities are available and where, the best times to go, what to expect in the way of accommodations and food, how to get around, what to bring, and how to stay healthy and have a safe trip.

WHAT TO DO

There are a wide variety of outdoor activities you can pursue within the boundaries of Costa Rica's parks and reserves. This tropical country's beauty can be explored through terrestrial pursuits such as hiking and caving, as well as by aquatic sports such as scuba diving and kayaking. The following should help you decide what activities you want to undertake and what specialized equipment to bring beyond the essentials, which are detailed later in this chapter. Route descriptions for each type of activity listed below are given in the four chapters in Part II, with the exception of birding and wildlife watching, which are covered in Chapter 2, in the Flora and Fauna sections.

Hiking and Backpacking

Costa Rica's parks and reserves offer diverse day hikes and backpacking trips. The visitor can hike steamy lowland forests, long, deserted beaches, and along strenuous mountain paths. Almost all the parks have at least a few reasonably maintained short trails, and some, such as Santa Rosa, have excellent trail systems. In general, there are fewer well-maintained, long backpacking trails than you may have come to expect in North America. There are exceptions in Corcovado, Monteverde, and Santa Rosa, but most long trails were either there before the area became a park, or exist for utilitarian purposes for park personnel. This means that trails are almost never marked with tree blazes or other markings, and you need to be a little vigilant so as not to stray off main paths. For some areas, such as the largely unexplored La Amistad National Park, map and compass skills are a necessity. This is changing, and as more Costa Ricans and foreign tourists have shown interest in extensive backpacking trails, there has been serious discussion about the creation of trails that cross the country both north–south and east–west. Hopefully, a future edition of this book will have a description of a Costa Rican version of the Pacific Crest Trail or the Appalachian Trail.

Whatever the length and difficulty of the trails you hike in Costa Rica, remember that the intensity of the sun and humidity are more than you might be used to. Take it easy at first, and remember to carry and drink lots of water. It is not uncommon to need to drink three liters a day in the hot lowlands.

Mountain Biking

There are some excellent opportunities for mountain biking in some of the parks. Palo Verde, Lomas Barbudal, Peñas Blancas, and Ballena all have dirt roads that are untraveled save for the rare four-wheel-drive vehicle or horseback rider. Be prepared for a variety of surface conditions, as trails here can produce rim-bending rocks, mud up to the chainstays, and tire-puncturing thorns. You should bring all tools, tires, and spare parts with you.

Snorkeling and Scuba Diving

Costa Rica has two true coral reefs, both located off the Caribbean coast. The first, in Cahuita National Park, is the more mature and extensive of the two, but was badly damaged by the 1990 earthquake; it is still worth snorkeling around. The second is farther to the south in Gandoca-Manzanillo Wildlife Refuge. It's a younger and less extensive reef, but seems to be more biotically intact. There is also good snorkeling in Manuel Antonio National Park on the Pacific side.

Scuba diving is a relatively new sport in Costa Rica, but the newly created

Tributary of the Río Cerere, Hitoy-Cerere Biological Reserve

Ballena National Park and Isla del Caño feature some very attractive situations for experienced deepwater divers. The remote Isla del Cocos National Park is becoming world-renowned for its diving, but it is remote and expensive to get to. If you are going to dive without a guide or tour, you should bring all of your equipment with you, as no one rents it yet. You may be able to refill tanks through some of the dive tour operators out of Playa Hermosa or in Limón on the Caribbean side.

Sea Kayaking

Opportunities for sea kayakers exist on the Tortuguero canal on the Atlantic side, and in the Nicoya Peninsula and the Golfo Dulce region on the Pacific side. Each of these areas requires you to be experienced at weather prediction and dealing with tides. Kayaking in the side channels and creeks of the Tortuguero region further requires the use of topographic maps and a compass, as it is very easy to become disoriented in some of the backwater areas. Seas on the Pacific side are more predictable during the dry season. Tour operators out of San José offer package trips, or you can bring your own equipment.

Caving

Experienced cavers have opportunities in the limestone caverns of Barra Honda National Park, covered in Chapter 5, Northwestern Region. All caves in the park require specialized equipment, although it is possible to arrange a trip to one of the caverns with park rangers. Recently, a large cave system was discovered in the vicinity of La Amistad National Park, and this has yet to be explored.

WHEN TO GO

Weather and Climate

Costa Rica has a remarkable range of climatic conditions for such a small country. Sharp contrasts in topography create a variety of weather conditions, from torrid lowlands to cool upland valleys to high mountains, where subfreezing temperatures have been recorded.

Costa Rica's climate is also characterized by wet and dry seasons. Many visitors become confused when talking with Costa Ricans about the seasons; they seem to be reversed in relation to those in the Northern Hemisphere. When Costa Ricans talk about *verano* (summer), it refers to the hot dry season between December and May, and *invierno* (winter) refers to the wet season between May and November. This corresponds with seasons in Spain and is a carryover from the Spanish Mediterranean region from which the first colonists arrived.

Along with the rest of the world's climate, these seasons are becoming increasingly erratic, but the following generalities can be made.

The Atlantic or Caribbean side is driest from February through April, and wettest from November through January. However, you should be prepared for rain at any time during the year in this part of the country.

Coconut palm grove near Manzanillo, Gandoca-Manzanillo Wildlife Refuge

The Pacific side and central parts of the country are driest from January through March. Guanacaste Province, which includes Santa Rosa and Rincón de la Vieja National Parks, has a dry season in which virtually no rain falls in the lowlands for the duration. During the dry season in Guanacaste, it's a good idea to check with park personnel or local people about the availability of water on backcountry trips before setting out. During the dry season from December to March, the more popular parks can become quite crowded, particularly during Costa Rican school holidays.

The rainy season is from the end of May to November. The change in the landscape is quite spectacular with the coming of the first rains, shifting from browns and grays to vibrant greens virtually overnight. A major consideration for backcountry travelers is that access to Corcovado National Park is very limited during the rainy season on the Pacific coast, and the muddiness of trails and intensity of biting insects make hiking over long distances unpleasant. However, if you are not planning on visiting any of the more remote parks, and particularly if you would like to visit the popular ones such as Manuel Antonio and Chirripó, try to do so during the rainy season. The parks are surprisingly deserted during this period. You might be more likely to get wet, but the solitude can be worth it.

Holidays

You may want to plan your trip around Costa Rican holidays, because the entire country shuts down for certain holidays. Obviously, if you're on an extended backpacking trip during these times, you won't be affected. However, in urban areas the buses, shops, and government offices become nonoperational and hotel rooms can be more difficult to find. Banks are also usually closed. All of this can mean frustrating delays or require unexpected changes in travel plans. To help you anticipate and avoid such problems, the official holidays are listed below.

December 30 and January 1—New Year's
March 19—Saint Joseph's Day
Palm Sunday to Easter Sunday (late March to mid-April)—Holy Week
April 11—Juan Santa Maria Day
May 1—Labor Day
June 29—Day of Saint Peter and Saint Paul
July 25—Guanacaste Annexation Day
August 2—Virgin de los Angeles Day
August 15—Mother's Day
September 15—Independence Day
October 12—Columbus Day
December 8—Day of Immaculate Conception
December 25—Christmas

WHAT TO EXPECT IN COSTA RICA

To the North American or European traveler, Costa Rica feels the least culturally different of all the Central American countries. Yet there are some differences that a visitor to the parks and backcountry away from San José will encounter. Things happen more slowly. If the bus or plane is late, don't panic. Costa Ricans are generally very friendly people who are eager to please, so don't be insulted if someone in the countryside gives you directions that turn out to be wrong. It's possible that they did not know the answer to your question, and were trying to give you an answer that they thought you wanted to hear. Sometimes people in the countryside are so taken aback at the sight of a foreigner popping out of the forest onto their isolated farms that they just point without thinking. It's always a good idea to try to strike up a little bit of pleasant conversation before asking logistical questions, to let them get over the shock.

Foreign visitors coming in by plane first encounter what is commonly termed the Meseta Central or Central Valley. This has been the center of Costa Rica's population since colonial times, at least. Today, more than half of Costa Rica's 3 million people live there. The region actually encompasses two intermountain valleys. The lower and larger one contains the capital city of San José, as well as Alajuela and Heredia; the higher, smaller valley contains Cartago and the smaller cities around it. Although densely populated and largely deforested, the Meseta contains some very interesting parks such as Braulio Carrillo and Poás.

The Meseta is located within the mountain ranges that comprise the "spine" of the country. Farthest north is the Guanacaste Cordillera, which gives way to the Tilaran and Central Cordilleras progressing southward. Farthest south is the Talamanca Cordillera, in which the nation's highest peak is located: Chirripó (elevation 3,821 meters), in the national park of the same name.

To the east of the mountains lie the plains or *llanuras* of Guatuso, San Carlos, Tortuguero, and Santa Clara. In their natural state, these are plains only in the sense that they are quite flat; they were once covered with forests and wetlands, with remnants protected in such places as Tortuguero National Park and Caño Negro Wildlife Refuge. In contrast, the Pacific coast is punctuated by a number of hilly peninsulas, including the Nicoya in the north and the Osa in the south. This gives the Pacific coast considerably more coastline than the Atlantic—1,254 kilometers compared with the Atlantic's 212 kilometers.

Accommodations

If you are not going to be camping within the park boundaries, you have a wide variety of hotels and other accommodations to choose from. Starting from the bottom, *pensión*, or the word *tipico*, indicates a low-priced establishment. These tend to be frequented by Costa Ricans more than by tourists, and range in quality from abysmal holes to spartan, but quite comfortable, accommodations. You can meet a good cross section of Costa Rican society in these places, with a range that is similar to the quality of the accommodation. The rule is to take a look at the room before putting any money down. If there is a bar connected to the establishment, choose a room well away from it. In even the smallest towns, bar life can be quite loud and rowdy.

Other options include *cabinas*, which usually indicates something similar to a motel. It can also mean cabins that are separated from each other. In coastal areas, they can range in quality from terrible, hot-tin-roof convection ovens to luxury places that cost more than $80 a night. Private nature reserves provide good potential bases to explore the parks, and these vary widely in quality and price.

Food

One way to avoid potential illness or stomach problems when eating out in Costa Rica is to follow this rule of thumb—never eat in a place where the sanitary conditions are obviously so bad that you would not eat there if the place were in your home city. Some general restaurant guidelines follow: Request that meat be well done and avoid raw salads that you don't prepare yourself. The most bang for your colón (meaning the Costa Rican currency, although for those with a really weak stomach, it could be the other kind) are *casados*, mixed plates that combine rice, beans, chicken, meat, or fish, and sometimes potatoes and vegetables. After one of these, you can hike all day.

Refrescos or sweetened fruit drinks are also highly recommended. They are less sweet than the now ubiquitous soda pop, and they actually have some nutritional value. Bear in mind, however, that these drinks are made with local water. It's probably best to avoid buying them at roadside establishments.

Unless you are planning an extended backpacking trip into one of the more remote parks and want to cut down the weight with freeze-dried food, there is little if any need to bring any food supplies with you to Costa Rica. Costa Rica's markets have a tremendous variety of lightweight trail foods at very reasonable cost. Dried fruits such as mangos, bananas, and figs are easy to find, as are peanuts, cashews, and macadamia nuts, all considerably cheaper than in the United States. (Macadamias are particularly rich and can give you an upset stomach if you overindulge, so go easy on them.) Several varieties of beans and rice are available at the smallest village store. Prepackaged dairy and canned products are all safe here, unlike Mexico and Costa Rica's neighbors.

A couple of good places to do pre-trip shopping in San José are the Mercado Central, an indoor market located at Calles 6/8 in San José with stalls selling everything imaginable, or *supermercados* such as Mas X Menos, in San José and Alajuela.

Transportation

Getting around in Costa Rica to the parks and reserves is generally not very difficult, and usually you have several options for each. Renting a vehicle is obviously the most efficient way to get around, but there are some drawbacks. One is the expense. Costa Rican rental rates are as high or even higher than in the United States, and insurance, which is mandatory, adds to the cost. Many credit cards offer free insurance if you use them to rent a car, but if you get into an accident, you may have to hang around until the credit card company provides you with an attorney, sometimes a matter of days. Be advised that there is also a $750 deductible with all Costa Rican car insurance, and you will probably be forced to pay this even if it was the other driver's fault. (This is an obvious gouge on tourists and it would be nice if the system were changed.) An increasing number of private citizens rent their vehicles to tourists, usually at a rate cheaper than the rental companies. If you decide to try this, make sure their insurance policy covers *all* drivers of the vehicle.

Driving in Costa Rica, while not quite as rigorous as in Mexico, still should not be undertaken without serious thought. The main highways, while usually in good shape, are mostly two lanes and heavily trafficked with both private vehicles and eighteen-wheel trucks. Costa Ricans traditionally pass on blind curves to get around trucks and are generally pretty macho when it comes to their potential demise behind the wheel; consequently, the country has one of the highest traffic mortality rates in the world. And, please, avoid driving at night, particularly in cattle grazing areas.

You also should be advised that speed limits are very low all over the country, and there are plenty of traffic cops equipped with radar awaiting the arrival of a *gringo rico* as he or she races to catch the last ferry out of Puntarenas. Getting

Birding from a boat on the Tortuguero Canal

a ticket can be a real hassle, and the police have the right to take your license and hold it hostage until you show up at the local court to pay the fine. Lately, there have been many reports (and my personal experience as well) of police forcing speeders to pay outrageous bribes in order to avoid this process. Should this happen to you, ask the policeman for his identification badge and take down the number located in the lower left-hand corner. If he refuses, write down the location and time of the incident and report it to the Dirección de Transito (Transit Directorate) in San José. Eventually, the authorities might be embarrassed enough to do something about the situation. They are considering doing away with the tourist license plates currently required on rental vehicles, and this would help. The best way to avoid trouble, however, is to drive the speed limit and always wear your seat belt.

Luckily, there are some good alternatives to renting a vehicle. You can get taxis, including four-wheel-drive vehicles, from almost any village in the country. Taking a taxi and arranging for it to pick you up at a designated time and place is almost always cheaper than having a rental car sitting unused for several days while you are exploring. You also don't have to deal with the hassle of driving and the expense of gas, which is about four times the cost of fuel in the United States.

Buses go just about everywhere and are very reasonable. They vary tremendously in quality, however. Some, such as the cross-country San Isidro bus from San José, are gleaming, comfortable, and modern, while local buses are often ancient relics, loud and hot. Buses are owned and operated by private companies, some of which run on only a few routes. Schedules are prone to change and it's a good idea to call ahead (if you speak Spanish) to get the latest arrival and departure times, or call the Instituto Costarricense de Tourismo (ICT) or Costa Rican Tourism Institute at 222-1090 for information.

The bus "terminals" are located in different parts of San José. The relevant address and telephone number for each is provided in the introduction of each park description. Construction of new central terminals has been discussed for many years, but no progress had been made on this project as of early 1999. Many buses leave from the "Coca-Cola" bus terminal—so called because of a bottling plant that used to be there—located in the western part of the city between Avenidas 1 and 3. This is one of the rougher areas of the city with many pickpockets and baggage thieves on the prowl. Be particularly wary at night and don't walk around in this neighborhood after dark. Take a taxi from the terminal to your destination.

It is also possible to fly within Costa Rica. Travelair and SANSA, the two internal airlines with regular routes within the country, offer reasonable rates and are a lot faster than the bus. You should always go to the airline offices at the airport and prepay your ticket, preferably several days in advance, or they will not hold your reservation.

Flying SANSA can be a real adventure. I once sat next to a retired U.S. Air

Force pilot who told me excitedly that the plane we were flying on was of the type that he had flown early in his career, a 1943 DC-3. But the level of service has improved somewhat since Travelair began giving SANSA some competition in the last few years. Travelair's planes tend to be newer, but their fares are more expensive. Travelair will make reservations over the telephone (232-7883). Call SANSA (233-0397) for the latest schedules and ticket policies.

There are also a couple of privately run small airlines that fly little Cessnas seating up to four people and gear to some of the more remote areas such as Corcovado from San José or such places as Golfito. These are not cheap, but may be worth it if split between three or four people. One such company is VETSA (232-1010) in San José.

Telephones

All telephone numbers within Costa Rica have seven digits. Long-distance calls within the country do not require an area code, but cost more than local calls. Pay phones can be a bit daunting for the uninitiated. Pay phones take 5, 10, and 20 colón coins. You should be ready with a handful of them, particularly if you are calling to somewhere more than 25 kilometers distant. To make a call at a pay phone, place a few coins in the slot and dial your number. When the party at the other end answers, the phone will consume your coins and, depending on how much you put in, the individual peculiarities of the phone, and where you're calling, you'll have a few minutes to talk before you begin to hear a series of beeps. This means that within 10 seconds or so you'll be abruptly cut off if you don't put more coins in the slot. The only phones available in many rural areas are at small grocery stores or hotels. These phones may not be coin-operated, so you'll have to let the storekeeper connect you and you'll pay after the call. The country code for calls from outside the country is 506.

Government Agencies in Costa Rica

Several government offices can provide invaluable assistance to backcountry travelers. The **Servicio de Parques Nacionales (SPN)** or National Parks Director-ate has two offices in San José where visitors can obtain information about visiting the parks and preserves. The **Fundación de Parques Nacionales** or National Parks Foundation seems to be a more consistent source of up-to-date information about the parks than the official government offices are; they generally do not have maps, however. The **National Wildlife Directorate** administers the country's wildlife refuges. A group called the **Instituto Nacional de Biodiversidad** or National Institute of Biodiversity offers specialized information on scientific research being conducted in the parks and preserves system. Topographic maps are available at the **Instituto Geographico Nacional (IGN)** or National Geographic Bureau. The **Instituto Costarricense de Tourismo (ICT)** or Costa Rican Tourism Bureau provides information, in English, about bus schedules and private reserves, but its information on national parks is often out of date. The

Dirección Forestal (Forestry Directorate) manages the forest reserve system, but is not very helpful about providing information to visitors. Traffic accidents should be reported to the **Dirección de Transito** (Transit Directorate) by calling 911.

For the addresses and phone numbers of these agencies, see Appendix 1, Recommended Resources.

A Word About Park Entrance Fees

Since the first edition of this book was published in 1993, fees for entering the parks have been on a roller-coaster ride from almost nonexistent to exorbitant to reasonable. The fees for foreign visitors were less than $2 in the early 1990s, but in 1994 they were abruptly raised to $15 per park. The roar of disapproval from tour operators and individual tourists forced entrance fees back to $6 in 1996, and since then different fees are charged for different parks depending on the number of visitors. Higher fees are assigned for parks that attract too many visitors, according to the government, and those with few visitors are less expensive. In practice, many of the less visited areas often don't have the staff or facilities to handle the money collected anyway, and consequently you might not be asked to pay. However, please pay all fees if asked and feel free to ask for a receipt if it is not offered. In 1998, advance purchase of tickets at the two park offices in San José gave visitors a price break of up to 50 percent. If this sounds confusing, that's because it is. The government is still trying to work out how to best capitalize on the popularity of their parks without allowing tourists to love the more popular areas to death. If entrance fees are a concern, it is advisable to call the ICT or parks offices (see Appendix 1, Recommended Resources) for the latest pricing and advance purchase options.

WHAT TO BRING

Remember that everything you bring to Costa Rica is liable to get damp at some time. Books do not do well in tropical climates, so bring only what you really need. Clothes are also vulnerable and, for backcountry travel in particular, 100-percent cotton clothes can rot surprisingly quickly. They also don't dry out after washing, sometimes for days, and then start to mold. Blends of cotton and a synthetic such as nylon work well, and clothes made of all-nylon fabric work even better, though they may be a little less comfortable. Also, though you may not anticipate wearing long-sleeved shirts or long pants because of the heat, you may need them to protect from biting insects or sun exposure.

The Ten Essentials

The Mountaineers recommends ten items that should be taken on every hike, whether a day trip or a multi-day backpack adventure. The Ten Essentials give the backcountry traveler a head start for meeting and surviving the challenges that nature and the unexpected may hold.

1. **Extra clothing**—a complete change of clothes, should the ones you're wearing become soaked or otherwise unwearable.
2. **Extra food**—an extra day's meals, in case your trip is extended for unexpected reasons.
3. **Sunglasses**—look for a pair that screens ultraviolet rays.
4. **Knife**—for first aid and emergency fire building.
5. **Fire starter**—a candle or chemical fuel for starting a fire with wet wood.
6. **First-aid kit**—a detailed list is given below; you should also have basic first-aid knowledge, with CPR skills a plus.
7. **Matches**—in a waterproof container.
8. **Flashlight or headlamp**—with extra bulb and batteries.
9. **Map**—a detailed list is given below.
10. **Compass**—with knowledge of how to use it.

Suggested First-aid Kit

Some of these items are available only by prescription, and you should check with your physician to make sure that you are not allergic to any of them.

- antibiotic cream
- moleskin
- anesthetic ointment
- antihistamine
- cortisone ointment
- "second skin" for burns and blisters
- gauze
- decongestant
- adhesive strips, several sizes
- antibiotic, wide spectrum
- butterfly bandages
- aspirin or other analgesic
- elastic bandage for sprains
- strong painkiller (bring prescription with you)

Clothes

- *Shorts*—light and easily dried; a cotton/synthetic blend is comfortable and rot-proof.
- *Long pants*—light enough to wear even when it's hot and you want to avoid chiggers and mosquitoes.
- *Button-down short-sleeved shirts or tee shirts*—loose and breathable.
- *Long-sleeved shirts*—loose and breathable.
- *Running shoes or lightweight, sturdy boots*—depending upon whether or not you'll be carrying a pack.

Tapantí Wildlife Refuge

- *Socks*—stay away from all-cotton socks. Once wet, they never dry out. A good combination is a nylon sock liner and a synthetic or synthetic-blend outer sock.
- *Hat*—should shade all of your head, face, and ears.
- *Lightweight sweater*—for those chilly nights in San José.
- *Rain gear*—a good combination is a rain jacket and pants for when it's cool, and an umbrella for when it's hot.
- *Jacket, polypropylene long underwear, and warm hat*—for warmth if you plan to spend time in the high *paramo* of Chirripó.

Other Necessities

- *Daypack*—large enough to carry lots of water, field guides, binoculars, etc.
- *Water bottles*—at least three quarts total capacity.
- *Water purification*—tablets or, better yet, a good quality filter.
- *Sunscreen*—with a high sun protection factor, such as SPF 29 to 40.
- *Insect repellent*—at least 75 percent DEET (*diethylmetatoluamide*).
- *Plastic bags*—for keeping books, binoculars, and other items dry.
- *Spanish dictionary and phrase book*—unless you are fluent in Spanish.

For Backpacking

- *Pack*—internal frame packs tend to be more comfortable, with fewer hard, chafing protrusions, and more easily taken on and off buses and taxis.
- *Pack cover*—waterproof nylon.
- *Sleeping bag*—very lightweight synthetics only; goose down does very poorly in a humid climate.
- *Tent*—as airy as possible, but still capable of withstanding a tropical downpour.
- *Stove*—should burn kerosene as white gas is not available. Bluet cartridges, the only brand of compressed-gas fuel sold in Costa Rica, can be found in a few sporting goods stores in San José. Ask for them by brand name, as that is how they are identified.
- *Cookware*—and eating utensils.
- *Toilet paper and a plastic trowel*—and any other necessary sanitary items.

Optional

- *Snorkeling gear*—snorkel, mask, and fins, plus a swimsuit.
- *Camera and film*—buy all film in your home country; it's very expensive in Costa Rica. For rain forest photography, you might get some of the super-high-speed Ektachrome that can be shot at upwards of 3600 ASA. A tripod is also useful, as is a strobe or flash.

Maps

The maps provided in this book are for orientation only. Good topographic maps can be purchased in San José at Librería Lehmann at Calle 3, Avenida Central, and from the Instituto Geographico Nacional at Avenida 20, Calles 5/7. You may have to visit both in order to get exactly what you want, as neither is always fully stocked. Popular maps sometimes go out of print for several months.

HEALTH PRECAUTIONS

Compared to other Latin American countries, Costa Rica is remarkably clean, and preventive health care and sanitation are generally good. What follows is a brief guide to some of the potential health problems that a visitor to the backcountry might encounter.

Drinking Water

Bottled water and soft drinks are all safe. Tap water is generally safe to drink in the Central Valley (San José, Heredia, and Alajuela), but you should filter, chemically treat, or boil tap water elsewhere, and particularly on the Atlantic coast. All water along the trail should be treated. Water can be chemically treated with a variety of agents, including commercially available hydroclonozone, halazone, and iodine. You can also use chlorine laundry bleach at a ratio of eight to ten drops per quart of water—but be aware that chlorine is not effective in killing *Giardia*—or tincture of iodine at a ratio of five to seven drops per quart of water. There are some excellent filters on the market that do not impart a chemical taste to the water, but the good ones are quite expensive. If you treat water by boiling it, do so for a minimum of five minutes. Whatever treatment method you use, make sure you drink a lot of water; a consumption rate of a gallon per day per person on long hikes in the tropics is not out of the ordinary.

Wetlands at the end of the Mangrove Trail, Curú National Wildlife Refuge

Diarrhea

The most common cause of *turista* is a rapid change of diet followed by contact with a new strain or two of *E. coli*, a bacteria that everyone has in their gut, but which can cause the trots for those who do not have the local variety already in residence. Of primary importance in preventing *turista* is drinking only safe or treated water. You can also pick up all sorts of parasites from eating unwashed fruit and vegetables; you need to either stay away from those types that you cannot peel, or wash them well with *treated* water.

The general rule for diarrhea is to let it run its course for 48 hours, making sure that the victim stays well hydrated with clean water or bottled beverages (but no alcohol or caffeine). If the symptoms persist beyond this period, or if they are causing severe dehydration, or if the stools contain blood (a sign of severe infection by amoebas), then you have to do something about it. To stop things up, Lomotil is the best thing; it comes in pill form and is very effective. The problem is that by stopping your body's efforts at getting rid of the pathogen, you allow it to multiply and this can cause even worse problems later on. Lomotil should be looked upon as an emergency drug. A good, wide-spectrum antibiotic such as Bactrim will kill most pathogenic gut bacteria, and if you are planning on doing backpacking or boating trips of several days' duration you might consider also bringing along Flagyl, which kills protozoans such as amoebas and *Giardia lamblia* that antibiotics won't touch. These are all prescription drugs, and you should check with your doctor to make sure that you can tolerate them; some people have allergies to various antibiotics and some drugs are contraindicated for pregnant women. Never drink alcohol while taking Flagyl, as this will make you violently ill. A natural alternative to Lomotil for stopping diarrhea is good old campfire charcoal; use at least a couple of tablespoons mixed with water several times a day. It is not as effective as Lomotil and tastes awful, but it will help in a pinch. Natural antibiotics, which may have some value as preventive treatments, are garlic and papaya seeds. The latter work pretty well to get rid of worms if taken on an empty stomach and well chewed.

Heat

The tropical sun in Costa Rica is much stronger than in temperate zones. Don't make it a goal of your trip to get a terrific suntan in two days; trust me, you will be sorry. Wear sunscreen. Take it easy and acclimatize for the first couple of days before going out even on a long day hike, unless you are extremely fit and have come from a hot, humid climate.

The symptoms of **heat exhaustion**, caused by overexertion at high temperatures, are faintness, rapid and/or fluttery heartbeat, nausea, paleness of the face, and clammy skin. This should be a clear warning to hole up in a shady place for a while and drink a lot of fluids. Eating something sugary also seems to help. This condition is not dangerous in itself, unless it passes on to the next stage, which is **heat stroke**. The symptoms of heat stroke are flushed, hot, dry skin, severe nausea, and severe headache. This is very serious, and brain damage can result.

The treatment is to lower the victim's body temperature as soon as possible, preferably by immersion in a body of water. If this is unavailable, remove the victim's clothing, sponge water over the skin, and fan vigorously. Massage the person's extremities to bring blood to them. Repeat this until the symptoms abate. At this point you need to go for help if possible, because when the person becomes active again, there may be a recurrence.

You may consider bringing along some sort of electrolyte replacement powder for severe cases of dehydration and heat distress, or you can make your own (it's cheaper, but tastes pretty horrible):

$3/4$ teaspoon salt
$1/2$ teaspoon baking soda
$1/4$ teaspoon potassium chloride
4 teaspoons glucose or dextrose
(This amount of powder is for one quart of water.)

Altitude Sickness and Hypothermia

If you are planning to go to Chirripó, the summit of which is at 3,820 meters, you need to concern yourself with **altitude sickness**. You should acclimatize yourself in a mid-elevation area such as Monteverde or Rincón de la Vieja for a few days before making the arduous climb to the highest point in Costa Rica. The symptoms of altitude sickness are headache, nausea, lack of appetite, and breathlessness. The only cures are to tough it out for several days or descend to a lower elevation.

Believe it or not, **hypothermia**, or a lowering of the body's optimal temperature, is a possibility at middle and high elevations in the tropics. Usually this occurs when people don't make provisions for protection from rain and then are exposed to wind. If you are going to travel outside the lowlands, you should

Park ranger taking a sample from mud pots in Rincón de la Vieja National Park. Inexperienced people should never get this close to these volcanic features.

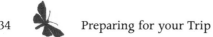

bring along some waterproof rain gear such as a poncho or jacket (see What to Bring, in this chapter), some lightweight long underwear, a lightweight sweater, and perhaps a lightweight warm hat, particularly if you're a cold sleeper and have only a lightweight sleeping bag. Treat hypothermia victims by getting them into dry clothes and warming them with hot fluids. In more severe cases, the victim may have to get into a sleeping bag with one or more people, as the victim may have lost the ability to generate enough heat without help.

Malaria

This disease was almost eradicated from Costa Rica in the 1950s and 1960s, but lately has made a comeback in a few areas because of health-care cutbacks, combined with refugees from Nicaragua bringing the disease in with them. If you plan to spend a lot of time on the border region in the north (Tortuguero, Barra del Colorado, and Caño Negro) or in the Talamanca range near the Indian reservations, you should strongly consider taking antimalarial medication. Luckily, the type of malaria that is cropping up is not chloroquine-resistant, and this is the most benign of the antimalarial drugs. Keep in mind that you need to start treatment two weeks before you are potentially exposed. *Note:* You might want to call the Centers for Disease Control and Prevention (404-639-3311) in Atlanta, Georgia, to make sure that chloroquine-resistant forms have not been reported by the time you go. You should also simply avoid being bitten by malaria-carrying mosquitoes, and this means keeping yourself covered as much as possible when mosquitoes are present, using repellent, and sleeping under a mosquito net if you're not in a tent.

Fungus Infections

The warm, humid climate of most of Costa Rica provides excellent conditions for the growth of fungus, particularly on your feet. Bring along some antifungal foot powder, keep your feet as dry as possible, and change your socks often. You may want to include some sort of antifungal ointment in your medicine kit for more severe cases. The best place to pick up a fungus infection is in cheap hotels where sanitation is lax; you may want to wear flip-flops in the shower.

NOXIOUS FAUNA

The threat of snakes, insects, and big cats in the tropics has been greatly exaggerated by movies and the popular imagination. There are some creatures that you should be cautious of that you won't find farther north, so here's a discussion of the fauna to avoid.

Wasps, Ants, and, Yes, Africanized or "Killer" Bees

If you are allergic to the stings of hymenopterid insects (those listed above), bring along a bee sting kit that includes oral antihistamines and injectable epinephrine, and be well acquainted with how to use it before setting out on your trip. Bees and ants come in all sizes, colors, and shapes and inhabit every imaginable niche; you should be watchful not to sit on nests or disturb those ensconced in thick vegetation. Army ants are fascinating creatures and are well worth stopping to watch when they're in the process of moving from one bivouac site to another, but watch that some of the soldiers don't stray up your pants leg.

Africanized or "killer" bees arrived in Costa Rica some time in the mid-1980s and are a considerable threat in a few areas, mostly in Guanacaste Province. They are noticeably present in Palo Verde National Park and at Barra Honda. These aggressive creatures, which look almost exactly like regular European honeybees, are the products of a misguided experiment by researchers in Brazil, who wanted to find a way to boost honey production. They imported bees from Africa that proved to be poor honey producers, were highly aggressive, and swarmed readily, abandoning commercial-style hives for a free-ranging life in the wild. The bees appear to prefer nesting on rocky, steep hillsides, under large rocks, or in crevices in cliff faces. Should you come into contact with a nest and be attacked, cover your face as much as possible and run in a zigzag pattern until out of the bees' protective range. Please turn to chapters 5 through 8 for more specific details on how to avoid coming into contact with these obnoxious creatures in each locality. Take the precautions about areas to be avoided and the need for guides in other areas very seriously. Africanized bees are aggressive and dangerous.

No-see-ums or Biting Midges

These annoying little insects, known as "flying teeth" in the southeastern United States and as *parrujas* in Costa Rica, are a problem in some areas near both coasts and particularly near mangrove forests and salt marshes. They are small enough to get through conventional mosquito netting, and DEET-containing repellent does not faze them. What they don't like is Avon's Skin-So-Soft bath oil, which can be used straight or diluted 50 percent with water and applied with a spray bottle. A little goes a long way with the latter method.

Scorpions

These distant cousins of spiders are a lot scarier looking than they are dangerous. Most species in Costa Rica possess a sting that is not much worse than your average bee sting. Watch where you put your fingers, particularly when moving rocks or logs, and shake out all clothes and boots before putting them on. Treat stings with an anesthetic cream and cold compress if available, or with analgesics or painkillers.

Chiggers

These tiny mites are usually contacted by walking in grass that has been previously inhabited by cattle or other livestock. Chiggers are the immature form of a common mite that attaches itself to your skin. Contrary to popular belief, it doesn't burrow into you, but inserts its mouthparts into your skin and liquefies a small portion of tissue with its saliva. To facilitate this, it sets up an immune response in your skin that results in the creation of a stylosome, a sort of drinking straw. The incredible itching that the victim experiences is also a part of this

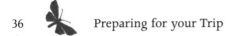

immune response. After four days, the chigger drops off to begin a new life as an adult, and feeds on decomposing plant and animal matter.

You, however, are not happy, and are probably scratching yourself to distraction. Prevention is the best cure for chiggers. Try to stay out of pastures or grassy areas, and if you can't, wear long pants tucked into your socks, and put some insect repellent around the area where the pants and socks meet. Also, chiggers hate sulfur, and if you are planning to go to some of the more seriously chigger-ridden places such as Corcovado (the "lawn" outside the ranger station is loaded with them) you might want to bring some to dust on your pants legs and waist area. If you get a bad case, some anesthetic and/or cortisone ointment will help quell the itching, at least temporarily, and antihistamines help some people. It is also a very good idea to wipe yourself down with alcohol after traveling through potentially chigger-ridden territory, paying particular attention to areas where your clothing binds tightly to your body. The cheap ethyl alcohol sold in just about any countryside *tienda* or drugstore works well for this purpose.

Ticks

Ticks, like chiggers, are fond of pasture areas and tall grass. Fortunately, there are no serious tick-borne diseases (such as Lyme disease) in Costa Rica, but these little arachnids can still be an annoyance. They like to ensconce themselves in the dark crevices of your body and where clothing is tight against the body, such as at your waist. If you are traveling in open, grassy areas, give yourself and your traveling companions the once-over at the end of the day. Ticks are a lot harder to remove the longer they've had their mouthparts in your skin (that's all they have in you, as ticks don't really have a "head"). Very small ones, about the size of a pinhead, called "seed ticks," can be removed with a piece of tape. Larger ones need to be killed with kerosene, gasoline, or alcohol (contrary to popular belief, once a tick has its mouthparts in its victim and begins to feed, it cannot back out) and carefully pulled out with a pair of tweezers, as close to the mouthparts as possible. You don't want to leave the mouthparts in, as the site can become infected. Wash the site well and put some sort of antibiotic ointment on it.

Chigoes or Jiggers

These are small insects related to fleas that grow up to the size of a pea, and that burrow into the bottoms of the feet, usually a toe, of people who walk around barefoot in the villages of the Atlantic side of Costa Rica. You can also pick up hookworms in this way, so it is unwise not to wear sandals or flip-flops. In the unlikely event that you pick up one of these creatures, pick it out with a sterile needle and then put some antibiotic ointment in the hole.

Torsalo Fly Larvae

This is another parasite that is rarely encountered by visitors to the parks, but just in case, here's a description of the beast and how to deal with it. *Torsalos* are the larvae of a fly (*Dermatobia hominis*) that is totally harmless in its adult form; they don't even have mouthparts and live only to reproduce. The process begins when an adult fly finds a mosquito and then forcibly lays her eggs on the underside of the mosquito's abdomen. When the mosquito finds a mammal to feed on, the animal's body heat signals the eggs to hatch and the tiny (at this point) larvae drop down onto the host's skin and burrow in through the mosquito bite or a hair follicle. The larva lives a fat and happy life for between two and three months before dropping out of its burrow to pupate on the ground, by which time it measures up to 2 centimeters.

Human hosts usually discover the presence of this unwanted guest long before that, having felt a persistent itch and then discovering the larva's burrow surrounded by a hardened cyst and an opening from which it extends its breathing tube, located on its rear end. To get rid of them, the best method is to cover the breathing hole with some sort of glue, rubber cement being ideal, and a piece of tape. Then cover this with more glue to completely seal it. In 24 hours you can take the tape off and gently remove the suffocated larva with a pair of tweezers and treat the wound with antibiotic salve. Under no circumstances should you try to pull or squeeze out a *torsalo* without performing the above procedure, as the larva possesses a series of hooks at its mouth with which it will firmly anchor itself in its burrow. If you rupture the larva, an allergic reaction and possibly a serious infection can result. For a humorous description of one man's decision to keep a *torsalo* through to maturity, see the chapter in Adrian Forsyth and Ken Miyata's *Tropical Nature* entitled "Jerry's Maggot."

Snakes

It might surprise you, but visitors to Costa Rica's wild areas seldom see venomous snakes. Most venomous species are nocturnal and sedentary and spend the day in a semitorpor. There are two main groups of seriously venomous snakes in Costa Rica: **pit vipers** and **coral snakes**. Pit vipers such as the fer de lance, neotropical rattlesnake, and bushmaster are relatively heavy-bodied, have a triangular head that is noticeably differentiated from the body, and have a heat-sensing pit between the nostril and the eye. The venom of this group breaks down tissue near the location of the bite, and in some species can affect the central nervous system. Coral snakes are brightly colored, secretive members of the cobra family that are active primarily at night. They have short fangs that are fixed in position at the front of the mouth (versus pit viper's fangs, which are large and fold back) and their venom is primarily toxic to the central nervous system.

Though these reptiles are seldom encountered, you should still be aware that they are around, and always watch where you put your hands and feet, particularly in tall vegetation, and don't go anywhere at night without a flashlight. Should you encounter a snake, do not attempt to kill it unless someone has already been bitten and you need it for identification purposes. These reptiles are an interesting and important part of the biotic community, and many bites occur when someone is attempting to capture or kill one. Give any snake that you see plenty of room to move out of your way, or walk a good distance

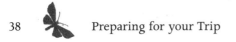

Godman's pit viper, a species of venomous snake found in the Costa Rican uplands

around it. If a snake bites you or a member of your party, the first thing is not to panic. Attempt to identify the snake.

After attempting to identify the type of snake that caused the bite, it is important to keep the victim calm. If you are by yourself, under no circumstances should you take off running for help; if it was indeed a venomous bite, you will only be speeding the spread of venom. Many bites, even from dangerously venomous species, are "dry," that is, they did not include the injection of venom. Keep an eye on the bite for any marked swelling, discoloration, or numbness around the area of the bite, or a tingling or metallic taste in the mouth. If it is an envenomed bite, evacuate the victim as soon as possible. It is generally considered unsafe and not particularly effective to make the traditional crossed razor cuts over the fang marks, but the Cutter company makes something called the Extractor that works well at drawing out venom from snake, bee, and wasp injuries. If you don't have one, you can try sucking some of the venom out as long as you don't have open lesions in your mouth. Carrying antivenin is *not* a good idea, as the potential for an anaphylactic reaction to the serum is a strong possibility. This can be as bad or worse than the snakebite, and the kind of supportive therapy necessary for pulling somebody through this type of reaction is only available in hospitals.

All of this sounds scary, but remember that the chances of seeing a venomous snake in Costa Rica are rare, and of the 500 bite cases reported per year (almost all *campesino* field workers), there are less than fifteen fatalities.

Jaguars and Pumas

More nonsense has been written about these two animals than practically all others. Seeing a jaguar in Costa Rica is a once-in-a-lifetime occurrence, and it will probably consist of a fleeting view of the cat's rear end as it disappears into the forest. Both species are shy and avoid humans completely, even as food items.

SAFETY PRECAUTIONS

Theft

While the vast majority of Costa Ricans are honest, gracious people, you should guard against theft in a few of the most popular parks. Manuel Antonio and Cahuita are very popular and crowded at certain times of the year, and their small size and easy access make them easy hunting grounds for thieves. Never leave your valuables, including your sunglasses and snorkeling equipment, alone while you are swimming. Don't leave valuables in your car, even in the trunk, if you can help it. Women traveling alone in these two places should also exercise caution. The only other "hot spot" within the parks is along the Siquirres Highway through Braulio Carillo National Park. There have been instances of robbery on the scenic turnoffs, and park authorities suggest that you not leave your car at the turnoff to the short trails near the road. Leave it at a ranger station and walk to the trailheads.

This information is not given to make you paranoid and hypervigilant. Exercise caution at these few places. Elsewhere, anyone you meet on trails in the backcountry will be as surprised to see you as you are to see them.

Riptides

Riptides probably injure or kill more people than all other hazards to tourists combined and account for 80 percent of all drownings in Costa Rica. These strong currents run perpendicular to the shoreline. Sadly, most people caught in a riptide would survive if they did not panic and conserved their energy by swimming parallel to the shore, and toward where waves are breaking if possible. The best thing to do is to not swim at dangerous beaches, and to not swim in water over the depth of your thighs. Beaches known for their riptides that are close to the parks are the beach north of Manuel Antonio National Park, Espadilla Sur inside the same park, and the beaches that border both sides of Cahuita National Park. Many others are dangerous, so exercise caution and inquire first whether the beach is safe.

A Note About Safety

Safety is an important concern for all outdoor activities. No guidebook can alert you to every hazard or anticipate the limitations of every reader. Therefore, the descriptions of roads, trails, routes, and natural features in this book are not representations that a particular place or excursion will be safe for your party. When you follow any of the routes described in this book, you assume responsibility for your own safety. Under normal conditions, such excursions require the usual attention to traffic, road and trail conditions, weather, terrain, the capabilities of your party, and other factors. Keeping informed on current conditions and exercising common sense are the keys to a safe, enjoyable outing.

Political conditions may add to the risks of travel in Central America in ways that this book cannot predict. When you travel, you assume this risk, and should keep informed of political developments that may make safe travel difficult or impossible.

The Mountaineers

2
THE TROPICAL FOREST

Welcome to the rain forest! The words "rain forest" have become a generic term used to describe a wide variety of tropical forests that occur (at least historically) in a four-million-square-mile band close to the equator, between the tropics of Cancer and Capricorn. Rain forests cover 7 percent of the earth's land surface, but contain more than half of its living species of plants and animals.

Volumes have been written about tropical forests, but there isn't a tropical ecologist in the world who won't tell you that we've barely scratched the surface on what there is to be known. Still, it's possible to describe what is known. Below is a description of the natural phenomena of some of the different types of forest found in Costa Rica. Following this are some of the species of flora and fauna that you are likely to encounter on your visit to a tropical forest in Costa Rica.

HOW A TROPICAL FOREST WORKS

The Quick Change
Tropical soils tend to be much poorer than soils in temperate zones. One reason for this is that organic matter has little time to build up in the soil; it tends to be reabsorbed by living plants almost as soon as it hits the forest floor. This is accomplished by a host of bacteria and fungi and the generally wet, warm climate. Peel back the thin layer of dead leaves in a tropical forest and you will find a lacy network of fungi. The roots of the trees are aided by other species of fungi, called **mycorrhizae**, which absorb minerals and pass most of them on to the tree.

From the Floor to the Canopy: The Layered Look
Undisturbed tropical forest is usually separated into layers, each of which has its own plant species. At the top are occasional emergent trees, giants that can tower 60 meters above the forest floor. The next layer is the canopy, a dense, interlocking mass of greenery formed by the treetops. It might surprise you to learn that the canopy is the layer that supports the most number of animal species of any part of the forest. The reason is that this is the part of the forest that receives the most energy from the sun, and where the trees flower, which draws birds and insects of almost unimaginable variety. Many species of plants and animals carry out their entire lives in the canopy without ever touching the ground. Under this are one or more layers of understory, smaller trees and shrubs. At the bottom is the ground layer, which is usually surprisingly sparse due to the lack of light reaching the forest floor.

High-elevation forest on the way to the summit of Rincón de la Vieja

Light Gaps

There comes a time in the life of every emergent giant (a tree that rises above the rest of the canopy) when life at the top becomes too rough and it falls to earth, creating a gap where the energy of the sun can penetrate to the forest floor. There then ensues an almost immediate battle for a place in the sun amongst the products of seeds that have been lying dormant in the soil. It may take many years for the fallen giant to decompose, providing nutrients for the victors of the struggle to continue the whole process anew. Light gaps are also places where many species of insects and birds congregate, and they are the favored haunts of many species of snakes, both venomous and not, which love the access to the sun to warm their bodies. It's a good idea to watch your feet and hands when you're passing through a light gap.

Buttresses and Stilt Roots

You will probably notice a number of differences between the trees that you are used to seeing in temperate regions and those in Costa Rican forests. In wetter regions, tree trunks are often buttressed at the base. These buttresses, called *gombas* in Spanish, are mostly for support in thin soils, but may have other functions such as gas exchange. Some types of trees, particularly palms, produce stilt roots for support, but again, these may have other functions.

41

Buttress roots, or "gombas," on forest giants, Corcovado National Park

FLORA

Life Zones: It Isn't Just "Jungle" Anymore

Tropical forests are divided into three broad categories: tropical dry forests, tropical moist forests, and true rain forests. Each of these is further divided into subcategories, based on factors such as elevation, climatic conditions, and soil type. At first glance, a tropical forest may look like one solid wall of greenery, but on closer examination, the variation in plant life is striking, to say the least.

Even though Costa Rica is only the size of the state of West Virginia, there are twelve distinct subdivisions of plant community types, called "life zones," found there. They range from the tropical wet forests of the Caribbean lowlands to the subalpine *paramo*, a high, cold grassland that is most typical of the Andes Mountains much farther south. Identifying what life zone you are passing through often takes a lot of work. There are a number of variables, including elevation, rainfall, the heights of vegetation layers, and species composition.

If you started a trip from west to east and coast to coast starting in the northwestern region, say, in Santa Rosa National Park, you would pass through quite a few of these life zones. Coming in from the beach, you would pass through an area of **tropical moist forest**. This is the most extensive life zone in Costa Rica. Tropical moist forest is characterized by tall evergreen forest (meaning that most of its trees do not lose their leaves, not that these are conifers) with multiple layers. Canopy trees are 40 to 50 meters tall. Most canopy trees have straight trunks that are relatively slender and are unbranched until 25 to 35 meters. Subcanopy trees are about 30 meters tall, and understory trees are 8 to 20 meters tall. Palms are common in the understory. Epiphytes, vines, and woody lianas ("Tarzan vines") are abundant.

Traveling a little farther inland, but still in Santa Rosa, we pass through a transition zone (a mixture of two life zones) before entering true **tropical dry forest**. This forest has a distinctive, seasonal change of appearance. In the dry season, most of the trees are leafless (to save water) and the land is in shades of gray and brown. When the rains come, all is green. The forest is fairly short in stature, with canopy trees being between 20 and 30 meters in height. The understory layer is usually 10 to 20 meters tall, and members of the coffee family (*Rubiaceae*) are common. Woody vines are common, but herbaceous vines are uncommon. There are some epiphytes (plants that live on trees—see the section to follow), consisting mostly of **bromeliads**. This has been one of the most heavily used and abused life zones in the country, being easy to clear and burn because of the distinct dry season.

After traveling across a human-made landscape of pasture and grassland, you come to the volcanoes of Guanacaste National Park. These rise precipitously, and the vegetation change is dramatic. After passing another band of tropical moist forest, the transition is made to **premontane wet forest**. The forest is semi-evergreen (a few canopy species shed their leaves in the dry season) and reaches a height of 30 to 40 meters. The buttresses on trees are smaller than are those of lower-elevation forests. Understory trees are 10 to 20 meters tall with smooth, often dark bark. Stilt roots and long strap-shaped leaves are common. There are some tree ferns (plants that have been around since before the dinosaurs; these will be discussed later). The shrub layer is 2 to 3 meters tall and often dense. The ground layer is usually bare except for ferns.

Around the very tops of the volcanoes are examples of **lower montane rain forest**, one of the life zones that is commonly referred to as "cloud forest." The forest has shrunk in stature, with the canopy at 35 to 30 meters tall, but with occasional oaks reaching upwards of 50 meters at the lower altitudes. Buttresses on trees are uncommon, and the understory is dense. The ground is covered with moss and herbaceous plants. The higher you go, the colder and mistier it gets, eventually stunting the plant growth enough to create "elfin forest."

Moving back down the other side of the mountains, you pass through variations of the same life zones that you encountered coming up, with the exception of tropical dry forest. You travel across the Tortuguero Plains, which were once covered with dense tropical moist forest, and pass remnants of this life zone in Tortuguero National Park. Also contained in the park are examples of **tropical wet forest**, which is the most species-rich life zone in Costa Rica. The forest is tall, evergreen, and has distinct vegetation layers. Canopy trees are 45 to 55 meters tall, with some emergents even larger. Trees tend to have high, well-developed buttresses. Subcanopy trees are 30 to 40 meters tall, and have narrow conical crowns and slender boles that are often twisted or crooked. Stilt-rooted palms are often abundant. There are lots of dwarf palms in the shrub layer. The ground layer is sparse, with a few ferns.

There are lots of variations on this scenario. For a complete breakdown of all of the life zones, please see one of the sources in Appendix 3, Suggested Reading.

Epiphytes

Look up into the trees of any of Costa Rica's forests, and you will see that almost all trees have at least some form of epiphytes growing on them. *Epiphyte* is a Greek word for "upon plants" and refers to any type of flora that uses another plant for support. These include **orchids** (more than 1,200 species), **bromeliads** (pineapple family), and many other species of seed-bearing plants. Bromeliads are interesting in that the larger varieties hold up to a gallon of water in their centers, creating an aquarium of sorts that contains an amazing variety of plant and animal life. Also present in wetter forests are many species of **ferns, mosses, liverworts,** and **algae**. In the dry forests of the northwest there is even a cactus, called the **night-blooming cerus,** that grows in trees. It blooms only at night with large, spectacular white blossoms that smell like jasmine.

Trees

To the average temperate-zone naturalist, tropical trees come in a bewildering variety. They are difficult to identify because of the huge number of species present, the often-similar appearance of their barks, and the thickness of the canopy, which makes it difficult to pick out individual leaves. Some of the easiest distinguishing characteristics are their seeds, found around their bases.

The **balsa** is a "pioneer species" that is often one of the first on the scene after a light gap is created by the fall of a forest giant. It has a 0.5-meter-long seedpod that is covered with golden "hair," giving it the appearance of a huge woolly caterpillar. The **monkey pod** is a relative of the Brazil nut and has a woody fruit about 4 centimeters in diameter containing twenty to fifty large seeds. The **stinking toe** or *guapinol* has a distinctive 3-centimeter-long, sausage-shaped seedpod that contains seeds that are a favorite food of rodents.

When you examine seeds on the forest floor, it's interesting to speculate how they are dispersed. Some, like **wild nutmeg,** have a brightly colored, fleshy "aril" that surrounds the seed. Many species of birds are attracted to the fruit, swallowing it whole to digest the aril and depositing the seed elsewhere. Other seeds are wind dispersed, such as those of the **mahoganies,** and have dispersal mechanisms similar to the maples of temperate regions.

Other interesting trees include the so-called **"naked Indian."** This tree sheds its reddish outer bark (hence the insulting name) to reveal a layer of photosynthesizing cells underneath. This allows the tree to carry on producing food even though it loses its leaves during the dry season to conserve water. A more politically correct and descriptive name has been proposed: "sunburned gringo."

Strangler figs start life when a monkey or bird leaves a seed, usually contained in feces, somewhere in the crown of a tree. The seed germinates and sends tendrils to the ground. The tendrils fuse together, eventually creating a crude mesh, and the fig develops a crown of leaves that eventually shade out those of its host. The strangler is left standing long after its host has decomposed, and can become a large tree itself.

Most people know that maples and birches are tapped for their sap in the

Northern Hemisphere, but few know that there are tropical trees that are utilized in a similar way. The **cow tree** (*Brosimum utile*) is recognizable by its large size and distinctive reddish gray bark. This species was tapped for centuries for its drinkable white latex. It is thought that the large homogeneous stand of this tree on Isla del Caño south of Manuel Antonio National Park represents an "orchard" planted by pre-Columbian people for this use. The sap is supposedly quite nourishing, and Alexander von Humboldt, who was the first to scientifically describe this species in Venezuela, reported that slaves there grew "visibly fatter" during the season when the trees give the most "milk."

FAUNA

Below is an overview of some of the animals that you are likely to encounter in Costa Rica's parks.

Insects

Butterflies. Costa Rica is home to more than 1,239 species of butterflies of every imaginable color. Most spectacular are the bright blue, iridescent members of the genus *Morpho,* called *celeste común* in Spanish. Six species are found in Costa Rica, and they seem to be most commonly observed on the Atlantic side. Males, which are more brightly colored than females, can often be seen patrolling along streams during the morning hours. Males are quite aggressive toward each other, and perhaps have territories that they defend with swooping aerial attacks on potential rivals.

Another interesting species is the **owl butterfly**, so called because of the two large eyelike spots on the bottom of its wings. It's thought that the butterfly uses this as a defense, flashing the eye spots at a predator to make the attacker think that it has taken on something larger and more formidable than it expected.

Moths are also in great abundance, as a visit to a lamp at night will attest. **Sphinx moths** are a varied family, but all have a distinctive resting position with swept-back wings like those of a jet fighter. One species has a caterpillar that seems to mimic the venomous coral snake. It has a bright yellow body and an orange head, and thrashes about vigorously when molested.

Ants. One of the most noticeable and interesting types of ants is the **leafcutter ant** of the genus *Atta.* These are commonly seen on the forest floor, carrying cut-up leaves back to their nests, which can be more than 3 meters across. The workers chew up leaves and plant a species of fungus on the plant material. This is all that they eat, and the fungus is found nowhere else.

Bull's horn acacia shrubs have a mutualistic relationship with **acacia ants** of the genus *Pseudomyrmex.* The ants live in the hollow thorns of the acacia and protect it from any and all attackers, from caterpillars to deer (or the hapless hiker), by biting and stinging vigorously. They even prune back vines or branches that intrude on the acacia's growing space. The acacia not only shelters the ants, but also feeds them nectar from special glands and with lipid-rich "Beltian bodies" located at the leaf tips.

Army ants have an undeservedly fearsome reputation. They are almost blind and have no fixed address. They bivouac for a night to several weeks in hollow logs or underground. Each morning, raiding columns fan out from the bivouac in search of prey up to the size of baby birds, bringing back the spoils to be shared by the entire group. Contrary to popular belief, they don't attack and eat people, but if you stand in the way of a column, they will bite, hard!

Termites. The brown lumps up to the size of a bushel basket, but usually smaller, that you see adhered to trees and fence posts are termite nests. The nests are made of a substance called "carton," a mixture of regurgitated wood pulp and feces. The larger nests are home to up to 100,000 termites. In addition to the nest builders, some small parrots nest nowhere else, and there are a number of insect specialists who make a living off the termites. Included in this bunch of ingrates is a type of **assassin bug** that camouflages itself with bits of carton and preys on hapless workers at the entrance to the nest.

Amphibians

Poison dart frogs (*Dentrobatidae*) are brilliantly colored amphibians that are commonly encountered in the humid lowlands on both sides of the country. The reason that they hop around the forest floor so brazenly is that their bright coloration is meant to warn any potential predator of the poison contained within the frog's skin. Indigenous peoples from several parts of the American tropics discovered this, and used the poison to tip their blowgun darts. Usually, the poison was extracted by impaling the unfortunate frog on a stick and subjecting it to the heat of a campfire; this drives the poison to the surface. One species in this family (*Phylobates terribilis*), found in the Colombian Amazon, is so toxic that one merely needs to rub the dart on the frog's back to equip it with a lethal dose of poison. There is no record of indigenous people in Costa Rica utilizing the poison dart frogs for this purpose, perhaps because the species found here are not as toxic as those farther south. Nevertheless, they have enough toxins in their skins to protect them from predation.

These frogs are also interesting in that for an amphibian they display a great degree of parental care. The eggs are laid in moist humus on the forest floor, and when they hatch each tadpole is individually carried on the back of an adult up into the canopy and deposited in a bromeliad containing water, one tadpole to a plant. As if this were not task enough for so small an animal, the females of some species return to each tadpole several times to lay an infertile egg for it to eat.

Other interesting amphibians include the **glass frog**. There are several species, but they are all small, translucent green tree frogs with round pads on the ends of their toes to help them cling to leaves. Put one belly down on a piece of glass and a startling sight will confront you as you can see many of the animal's internal organs, including its busily beating heart!

Another common amphibian that is often seen congregating around lights in search of insects is the **marine** or **cane toad**. These large brown and tan toads eat anything they can stuff into their mouths, but are not particularly palatable themselves. They have two large poison glands on the top and toward the back of their heads. When squeezed, these release a toxic substance that can kill any hapless dog or cat that grabs one. When picked up by humans, they tend to defend themselves by urinating copiously.

One of the most famous residents of the Monteverde Preserve is (or was) the **golden toad** (*Bufo periglenes*). This amphibian was never common and was extremely secretive, coming out of cover to breed only for a few days out of the year. It has not been sighted in several years, and it's widely feared that this species is extinct. This could be true, despite the protected status of the toad's tiny range (it is only known from the Monteverde area), because of the same mysterious cause or causes that are behind a worldwide reduction of all types of amphibians. The golden toad's fate may be an example of how the ecological health of a protected area can be affected by causal factors outside its borders.

A tree frog from the Pacific lowlands

Reptiles

Sea turtles. These are perhaps Costa Rica's most famous reptiles. Four species are found here: the **green, hawksbill, olive ridley,** and **leatherback.** The **green turtle** averages about 80 centimeters in length and weighs between 65 and 120 kilograms. It is found on both coasts, but nests mostly from October to March on the Pacific side and July to October on the Atlantic (Tortuguero National Park). The **hawksbill** is the species that is the source of "tortoiseshell," which has led to its slaughter over the entirety of its range. It feeds largely on sponges and seaweed, and adults range from 65 to 90 centimeters and 35 to 75 kilograms. Hawksbills rarely nest in Costa Rica, but young individuals are commonly encountered by divers on the Pacific coast near Santa Rosa.

Sea turtle and friend, Curú Wildlife Refuge

Large adult green iguana, Palo Verde National Park

The **olive ridley** is the species that is responsible for the famous *arribadas* or *barricadas*, mass nestings of tens of thousands of individuals, that take place at unpredictable intervals (but usually between September and October) on the Pacific coast. Most famous of these nesting sites is Nancite Beach in Santa Rosa National Park. Olive ridleys are the smallest of all turtle species here, with adults having a shell length between 55 and 75 centimeters and weighing 35 to 45 kilograms.

The **leatherback** is the largest species, and has the most bizarre life history of the lot. They are huge, having a length of up to 250 centimeters and weighing in at 1,000 kilograms. Instead of a shell, they are covered with a leathery skin in which small bones are imbedded. Leatherbacks dine almost exclusively on jellyfish and Portuguese man-of-war, and this has created a real problem for them in that they sometimes mistake floating plastic garbage for their normal prey and die as a result. These giants come ashore to nest from October to March, with peaks from November to December. One of their most important nesting beaches has been protected as a park, Las Baulas National Park on the Nicoya Peninsula. All species of sea turtles that nest here are threatened or outright endangered due to overhunting, beachside development, and accidental death in trawls. Costa Rican parks and preserves contain areas that are a very important part of worldwide efforts toward sea turtle preservation.

One lizard that is hard to miss while hiking in any of the lowlands is the **basilisk** or **Jesus Christ lizard**. Basilisks are large brown or green (depending on the species) lizards that get their common name from their ability to run on the surface of the water for short distances. **Common** or **green iguanas** are considered a delicacy, particularly on the Atlantic side, and there are projects to breed them in captivity to replenish wild stocks. There is some hope that iguanas will help in rain-forest conservation by giving people an incentive to save forest if they can draw protein from it in the form of iguana meat. The *gorrobo* or **ctenosaur** is a tan-to-black cousin of the iguana that lives most of its life on the ground. They are proficient burrowers, and roads have collapsed in a few instances where the roadway was undermined by the burrows of the female's

egg-nesting sites. They will eat practically anything that is or once was living, including young ctenosaurs. Consequently, the little ones are a bright green color and stay hidden in foliage until old enough to protect themselves.

Snakes. Snakes are not as commonly encountered in the tropics as the old Tarzan movies would have you believe. This is particularly true in deep forest, where there are lots of places to hide, and at higher elevations, where it's hard to keep warm enough to be active. There are 162 species of snakes found here, only 22 of which are venomous. Bites from venomous snakes are a greatly over-rated hazard; remember that you have a higher statistical probability of being struck by lightning than being bitten by a snake (see Noxious Fauna in Chapter 1, Preparing for your Trip). Commonly encountered nonvenomous species include the **boa constrictor**, which reaches a maximum length of about 3 meters and eats everything from birds and reptiles to the occasional dog. The **tropical indigo snake** is a large, active, tan snake that is fairly common, particularly in Guanacaste. They are very opportunistic about what they eat, taking everything from fish to rodents and even venomous snakes.

Venomous species include twelve species of pit vipers. Among this group is the arboreal (dwelling in trees or bushes) **eyelash viper**, called *bocoracá* or *oropel* in Spanish. They come in a variety of colors, from camouflage tan and green to bright lemon yellow. The English common name comes from raised scales above their eyes.

Also included in this family is a species that is roundly feared by agricultural field workers, the **fer de lance** or *terciopelo*. This is a large, heavy-bodied species that is quick to strike, and is responsible for the majority of bites in the country. Visitors to the parks have little to be concerned about with this species, as it prefers cleared areas with tall grass. **Vine snakes** are a tan-colored, pencil-thin arboreal species whose fangs are located at the back of the mouth; they feed on small lizards and, though mildly venomous, are no threat to people.

Eyelash viper, Arenal National Park

Birds

Costa Rica is justifiably famous for its birding. Studies are still being done, but the list has topped more than 850 species. Of these, 225 are migrants that fly north or south during different seasons, but depend on Costa Rica's forests for at least part of the year. This number includes many of the warblers and birds of prey commonly seen in North America from spring through fall. Certainly, this is one of many arguments for the preservation of tropical forests.

Quetzals, magnificent iridescent denizens of the cloud forest, derive their name from the ancient Aztec word for "beautiful" or "precious." Only the males grow the long emerald-colored tail feathers that were once the adornment of Mesoamerican royalty. Quetzals are most easily viewed during the mating season from March to June and into July and early August, when trees of the avocado (*Lauraceae*) family come into fruit, drawing the birds into feeding congregations in remnant trees left in places such as the cleared pasture around the Monteverde Preserve. During the rest of the year, when they're not preoccupied with the business of mating or stuffing themselves, they're a lot more difficult to see. While quetzals are usually thought of as a high-elevation species, recent radiotelemetry studies show that they migrate altitudinally in search of seasonal food, showing the importance of conserving tracts of land at all elevations.

There are two species of **macaws** (large birds related to parrots), the **scarlet** and the **great green**. Both are becoming rare, but the **scarlet macaw** is commonly seen in Carara Biological Reserve, Palo Verde National Park, and most notably at the Sirena Field Station in Corcovado National Park. The **great green macaw** is a shy species that is dependent upon intact forest on the Atlantic slope, a habitat that is becoming increasingly restricted. Both birds also command a high price on the illegal market, and nest raiding is a common cause of their disappearance from areas that still have forest.

There are many species of **hummingbirds** present in Costa Rica, and some of them are very difficult to tell apart, particularly the females. They feed on nectar and occasionally small insects throughout the day to keep up with their metabolisms, which are among the highest per weight of any animal. Recently, it was found that many species, particularly those that dwell at high elevations, "hibernate" through the night to conserve energy.

Mammals

Monkeys. Four species of monkeys are found here; **howler monkeys** are the largest of the four. They travel in groups averaging eleven to eighteen animals, led by the young adult males. The bulk of their diet consists of leaves, with the remainder being fruit and flowers. The deep rumbling growls that the males produce are primarily territorial calls, but may also function to communicate within the group. The male vocalizations carry for several kilometers, and the uninitiated often mistake the sound for the calls of jaguars.

Spider monkeys get their name from their long, spidery limbs and tail. They live in groups of up to twenty individuals, but usually split into smaller

White-faced monkeys, Corcovado National Park

groups to forage during the day. They are elegantly graceful while swinging through the treetops. Spider monkeys' tails are totally prehensile, almost like a fifth hand, and can support their entire body weight.

The **white-faced** or **capuchin monkey** is not a picky eater, and will take fruit, flowers, insects, and bird eggs. The name capuchin comes from the animal's white face and chest, which has a vague resemblance to a monk's hood.

The **squirrel monkey** is the smallest of the four, and resides only in the southwest corner of the country. Manuel Antonio National Park is the northern limit of its range. They are easily recognized by their small size and distinctive black muzzle surrounded by a white face. Squirrel monkeys are an endangered species in Costa Rica due to their dependence on the much-reduced lowland forest on the Pacific side.

Cats. It is a once-in-a-lifetime experience to see a **jaguar** or *tigre*. Jaguars are the largest of the five species of cats found in Costa Rica, reaching a length of more than 2 meters and standing a little over a meter high at the shoulder. They eat anything they can tackle, from sea turtles to tapirs, but seem uninterested in eating people. They are shy, secretive animals, and have become extinct in most of the country. This was not always the case: there is a record of a cattle ranch on Volcán Irazú that closed down in the mid-1800s because of jaguar predation.

Jaguars need very large home ranges, and this consigns them to the larger of Costa Rica's protected areas, such as Corcovado and La Amistad National Parks.

The second-largest cat is the **puma**, often called a mountain lion in North America. They are distinguished from the jaguar by their unspotted, tan-to-brown fur. The **margay** or *tigrillo* is somewhat larger than a housecat, but with a spotted coat. They are nocturnal and spend most of their time in trees in primary forest. They seem to be very sensitive to human disturbance and are becoming increasingly rare throughout their range.

The **ocelot** is usually larger than the margay, and is similar in appearance. Its tail is shorter, and it spends most of its time on the ground. Ocelots are active both day and night, and often use man-made paths to hunt on. The fifth cat is the odd-looking **jaguarundi**. They are the most variably colored of all the cats, ranging from reddish to black. At first glance, they look like a cross between a cat and a weasel with their short ears, low-slung body, and short legs.

Bats. There are more than 100 species of bats in Costa Rica, and they come in every possible size and shape. The **vampire bat** is found here but presents little hazard to humans, unless you are in the habit of sleeping outside without a mosquito net in the lowlands. Vampire bats have a complex social life, and spend a lot of time grooming each other. The discovery of this has led to a popular way of getting rid of them. This involves capturing a vampire bat and coating it with a poisonous sticky substance; when the others clean it, all are poisoned.

Fishing bats have long, curved talons that they use to hook their prey, which they find by echolocation, even under the water's surface. The **false vampire** is a huge species with a wingspan of 90 centimeters that hunts sleeping birds at night. **Tent-making bats** bivouac together under tents of helaconia leaves that they produce by carefully biting holes on the spine of the leaf. Other species of bats occupy niches from fruit specialists to insect eaters.

Sloths. Almost everyone who comes to Costa Rica expects to see a sloth. There are two species here, the **three-toed** and the **two-toed**. The **three-toed sloth** is the more commonly seen of the two because it is active during the day, while the **two-toed sloth** is nocturnal. While they are one of the most common large mammals in tropical forests, they are difficult to see because of their slow movements and natural camouflage, which makes them hard to distinguish from termite nests. They have extremely slow metabolisms, and often go to the top of the canopy to bask in the sun long enough to get up to operating temperature. They feed exclusively on leaves, and have a highly specialized gut, much like that of a cow, to deal with this hard-to-digest fare. One of the weirdest things about sloths is their toilet habits; they store up urine and feces for a week, descend to the ground, and dig a hole at the base of the tree with their stubby tails. They then defecate, urinate over it, and cover it all with leaves, using their hind feet, before reascending. Why they go through this laborious process that exposes them to predation on the ground is unknown. One theory is that they are fertilizing their favorite food trees, but no one really knows.

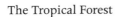

Anteaters. These come in two species in Costa Rica. The **northern tamandua** is commonly seen, most often at night, as it forages for ants, termites, and occasionally bees, ripping into the insects' nests with their stout claws. In fact, the claws are so well developed that they have to walk on the outside edge of their feet with the claws curved inward. They have no teeth, and trap their prey with their long, sticky tongues. The second species of anteater found here is the rarely seen **silky** or **pygmy anteater**. They are a striking golden color and are totally arboreal, spending all of their life off the ground.

Tapirs. Other interesting mammalian oddballs include the **Baird's tapir**, a distant relative of the rhinoceros. It is the largest native terrestrial mammal in Costa Rica, and adults weigh up to 300 kilograms. These lumbering vegetarians have very poor eyesight, and like to live in thick vegetation near water. Baird's tapir is an endangered species, due to overhunting and habitat loss. Tapirs, along with their only natural enemy, the jaguar, need large areas of undisturbed forest within which to live.

Peccaries. The closest relatives of these mammals are pigs, but they don't belong to the same family. Peccaries give birth to one or two young, which are precocial and can follow along with their mothers shortly after birth. In contrast, pigs have large litters of altricial young that are helpless at birth. There are also differences in their dentition and skeletons. One characteristic they share with pigs is that **peccaries** are not picky eaters; they take fruit, seeds, tubers, small animals, and carrion. There are two species, the **collared** and the **white-lipped**. The **collared peccary** is the smaller of the two and is found in a variety of habitats, including dry scrub, while the **white-lipped peccary** prefers humid lowland forests. Peccaries' aggressiveness has been greatly exaggerated, but the white-lipped, in particular, has very bad eyesight and will sometimes blunder right past you if you're downwind. You should avoid surprising them, as their "tusks" are large and sharp and even a passing nip could do some damage.

Raccoons. The raccoon family is a diverse group in Costa Rica. The **common raccoon's** range overlaps that of the **crab-eating raccoon**. They don't normally encounter each other, as the crab-eating raccoon prefers mangrove swamps. The **kinkajou** and the **olingo** share the same niche, both being nocturnal and feeding on fruit and invertebrates high in the treetops. The kinkajou is about twice as large as the olingo, and has a prehensile tail. The **coati** is one of Costa Rica's most frequently seen mammals; wait by a lodge's garbage facility, and you are sure to see one eventually. They look like a raccoon with an elongated snout. Females and young adults travel in groups of up to thirty, but older males frequently leave the group to travel alone.

3
A BRIEF HISTORY OF CONSERVATION IN COSTA RICA

The conservation movement in Costa Rica is a rich tableau of influences from both within the country and elsewhere. Costa Ricans have more interest and pride in their environment than many other Latin Americans because the Spaniards who settled permanently in Costa Rica tended to be educated, middle-class, small landowners with a long-term stake in their holdings. Large land-holding families like those who control most of the land in Guatemala are the exception rather than the rule. The lack of a military and the expenditure associated with supporting one has allowed Costa Ricans the opportunity to educate and feed most of their population, leaving some room for them to be concerned about saving some of their natural heritage. The country also has been blessed with a string of visionary conservationists, from the late President José Figueres Ferrer to Mario Boza, former director of the national parks. It's a good thing that people like these are around, because as we'll see later, the forces of ecological destruction for profit are present as well.

When the Spanish conquistadors arrived in what is now Costa Rica, they found tropical forests stretching from coast to coast. The form of agriculture practiced by the estimated 60,000 indigenous people was of a sustainable, shifting type that allowed for a long period of regeneration of secondary forest between plantings, giving the land a rest. The Spaniards decimated the native tribes partly through enslavement and outright murder, but primarily with introduced diseases to which the natives had no resistance. The conquistadors eventually grew frustrated with the lack of gold and a concentrated population from which to draw slaves, and left. Spain showed little interest in what was considered an isolated backwater, and it wasn't until the early nineteenth century that the territory's population again reached 50,000 via a slow trickle of immigration and increases in the indigenous and mixed-race populations. By the 1850s, however, a wave of immigration from Spain started the agricultural expansion out of the Central Valley and into the surrounding mountains and lowlands. Deforestation began to cause some concern, at least from a cosmetic standpoint, and in 1863 a law was passed stating that 2,800 feet on either side of the Northern Highway was government property and was not to be cut. This was the first of many laws to be ignored by both the populace and those in charge of enforcement.

For many years conservation laws came and went, most rendered unenforceable

Due to the rapid rate of deforestation outside of protected areas, old forest giants such as this one are becoming increasingly rare in Costa Rica.

because of lack of funds and political will. In 1958, the government body in charge of tourism appointed a commission to study places that should be protected as national parks. In 1966, a law was passed that granted the commission the power to establish and maintain the first park, Santa Rosa. The national parks office existed under the aegis of the Ministry of Mines, Agriculture, and Livestock until 1976, when it was given ministry status comparable in political weight to its former parent.

Today, administration of the parks and preserves is in a state of flux. Ways of cutting costs and providing better administration and management at the same time are being sought. A major development in these efforts was the creation of nine regional "conservation units" meant to integrate national parks and preserves, reservations for indigenous peoples, and forest reserves into a cooperative management system. As of 1998, a few conservation areas, including Arenal and Guanacaste, are well solidified and are partially supported by foreign funds. Others, such as Osa, are in total disarray. If a national system becomes functional, a director and a management committee made up of officials from each type of protected area will govern each unit and ostensibly will seek counsel from local scientists and conservation organizations. There are some pros and cons to this plan. While it would give each area greater freedom to develop for its particular needs without as much centralized inefficiency and control, pressure might be placed on each unit to go out and find its own operational funds. Another big question is whether or not the committees would be replaced every time there is a change in government. This would lead to the same lack of long-term management vision that many conservationists claim has plagued conservation efforts in recent years. In short, the situation is fluid and complex, and the future of Costa Rica's protected areas will be interesting to watch.

The fate of the forest on the borders of Chirripó National Park

Outside the parks and reserves, there is the second half of a paradox. Many people are shocked to learn that the country has one of the highest deforestation rates in the world. In 1989, between 30,000 and 40,000 hectares were cut. This represents a decrease since the 1970s, when the disappearance rate was 60,000 hectares a year. Recent satellite studies put Costa Rica's forest cover at around 17 percent. Costa Rica is now facing a wood shortage that will make the country a net importer of timber products in the near future, a situation that will cost the country an estimated $290 million a year and put increased pressure on the forests of neighboring countries. Lack of enforcement of existing regulations—because of lack of money, as well as changes in government policy with almost every election and some corruption—seem to have gotten in the way of a sustainable forest products industry.

Obviously, the parks and reserves cannot continue to exist without proper management of the rest of the country's resources. If the country's soils are depleted and water cycles disrupted, if there is no reasonably priced wood available, then there will be pressure to open some areas to exploitation. Unfortunately, the political scene in the 1990s has been extremely unkind to Costa Rica's environment. The Calderón and Figueres administrations weakened forestry laws, allowed construction of an illegal and environmentally destructive mega-tourism project on the Nicoya Peninsula called Papagayo, and blocked the creation of an integrated preserve system in the Golfo Dulce area that would have secured wildlife habitat from Corcovado National Park all the way to Mangrove Forest Reserve. On a hopeful note, there are a great variety of environmental organizations operating in Costa Rica that are concerned with finding solutions to the country's problems. Groups with focuses on reforestation, volunteer forest regulation enforcement, and other concerns are very active. (See Appendix 2, Conservation Organizations, for a list of groups and how they can be contacted.) Foreign organizations, from the government of Sweden to the Agency for International Development to groups of schoolchildren, have been major instigators and supporters of conservation projects here, particularly in the last twenty years.

TYPES OF PROTECTED AREAS

Protected areas described in this book include parks, reserves, refuges, and other designations. The designations dictate the level of environmental protection and recreational use allowed in a given area.

National Parks

Managed by the National Parks Directorate, national parks are areas of outstanding interest. They consist of more than one million hectares of untouched wilderness and encompass at least a sample of a significant ecosystem. They are established to conserve outstanding natural zones and scenery by perpetuating representative examples of physiographic regions, species, and communities, genetic resources, and species in danger of extinction. Scientific studies and

Hiker en route to Barva Lake, Braulio Carrillo National Park

environmental research are encouraged. Introduction of exotic species is prohibited. Visitors are allowed; controlled fishing is permitted; hunting is prohibited. Recreational and educational facilities are permitted, but hotels are not.

Biological Reserves

The National Parks Directorate also manages biological reserves. Biological reserves differ from national parks chiefly in having lower scenic and recreational values. They are untouched areas containing ecosystems with a marked diversity of plant and animal life, and are established to protect, conserve, and maintain natural processes in an unaltered state for study and scientific research. Reserve management prohibits activities that modify the biological equilibrium. Introduction of exotic species and development are prohibited. Fishing, hunting, and collection are prohibited except for investigative purposes approved by the directorate.

Resource Reserves (Forest Reserves)

Forest reserves are a transitory management category administered by the Forestry Directorate. They are generally large, difficult to reach, and sparsely populated. Theoretically, they are established to protect natural resources for future use. Development activities are limited until a plan for the use of the area is completed. Hunting is prohibited and recreational use is strictly regulated. Unfortunately, changes in land-use law instituted by the Calderón administration made it easier for private timber firms to log some of these areas, and these changes had yet to be rectified in 1998. As forest reserves provide a dubious level of protection for the resources contained within them, and because recreational use is discouraged, only one such area is featured in this book. The Mangrove Forest Reserve, located in the southwestern part of the country, has been left largely undisturbed because of its importance as a breeding ground for commercially valuable fish, crustaceans, and mollusks, and has relatively easy access. See Chapter 6 for more details.

Wildlife Refuges

Managed by the Wildlife Directorate, wildlife refuges are areas where protection is essential to perpetuate defined species populations and habitats. The size of a refuge depends on the habitat needs of the species. Many wildlife refuges have little recreational or scenic value and can include private land. Scientific and recreational uses are permitted when they don't endanger protected species. Introduction of exotic species and any activity that may harm protected species is prohibited. However, it is permitted to increase or decrease population numbers of the protected species if necessary. If this sounds vague, that's because it is. Wildlife refuges traditionally have been one of the weakest designations for protected areas, as there are a lot of loopholes for development to slip through.

Biosphere Reserves

UNESCO, the United Nations environmental wing, bestows the biosphere reserve designation. La Amistad National Park is included in one, as are several reservations for indigenous peoples.

Other Categories

Monteverde Forest Preserve (also known as Monteverde Cloud Forest Reserve) and the Children's Eternal Rain Forest Preserve are managed by the Tropical Science Center, a nongovernmental organization. They are included in this book because of their importance to conservation in Costa Rica and because they possess significant trail systems.

4
ETHICS AND THE SOCIALLY RESPONSIBLE ECOTOURIST

The term "ecotourism" has been so bandied about and abused in recent years that Costa Rican conservationists have felt it necessary to amend the term to "socially responsible ecotourism." This new term is being used to make a distinction between those facilities and services that benefit the environment and local people and seek to broaden the visitor's understanding, as opposed to those that seek to make large profits at the environment's expense while doing business with tourists interested in Costa Rica's natural history. Costa Rica is far from being environmentally spoiled, but there is growing concern that a lot of damage is being done under the guise of a poorly defined catch phrase.

The Talamanca Association for Ecotourism and Conservation (ATEC) has come up with a good working definition of the socially responsible ecotourism experience. It reads:

1. Enjoy, appreciate, and learn about aspects of tropical ecology.
2. Meet local people and learn from them their traditional knowledge, cultures, and lifestyles.
3. Contribute to sustainable economic development and the expansion of social and educational opportunities for local residents.
4. Become more knowledgeable about the social causes of environmental degradation and more committed to living in environmentally responsible ways in both host and home countries.

What follows are some thoughts about how to put these principles into practical use during your trip.

In Appendix 1, Recommended Resources, I list services such as guides, boats, planes, and other transport, emphasizing locally based operations. The reasons for this are simple. All too often, big companies with big profits in mind hang out their shingles as "ecotourism" operators, building large businesses that ignore the knowledge and talents of local people and are inappropriate in scale for the health of the biotic community. By utilizing the services of local people, you contribute to the value of rain forest and coral reefs in the eyes of those who may ultimately control the fate of these ecosystems. You also gain firsthand knowledge from the people who know the most about the natural and human histories of an area, being the recipients of the fruits of generations of observation and experimentation.

Well-maintained trail through "elfin" forest, Poás National Park

If you suspect that the hotel where you're staying is piping its sewage out onto a reef, politely inquire. If the answer is yes, suggest to them that they install a cesspool. If you're eating in a restaurant frequented by tourists and you see turtle (*tortuga*) or agouti (*tepisquintle*) on the menu, *don't* order it, and suggest to the owners that, although you like their establishment and love their food, they should take wild game off the menu if they want to keep and expand their business with the (one would hope) increasingly enlightened tourist market. Likewise, you should tell the other restaurant owners in town that you appreciate the fact that they don't serve items such as turtle eggs, turtle meat, or game, and that they might consider advertising this fact openly. Wild game can be a sustainable resource for local use, but the influx of large numbers of tourists wanting to taste sea turtle steak could create unacceptably high demands on the turtle population. Overharvesting of lobsters for the tourist trade is occurring on the Caribbean coast. The catch has been declining since the influx of tourists from San José and abroad in the 1970s. The price is going up and fishermen are having to go farther and farther out every year to get a profitable catch. It's a matter of controversy, but it has been suggested that tourists avoid eating lobster until the government takes steps to better regulate the industry.

If your experiences in Costa Rica move you to action, there's a list of conservation organizations along with descriptions of their concerns in Appendix 2, Conservation Organizations. Avoid being a "recreational imperialist." Contact the Instituto Costarricense de Tourismo (ICT) or Costa Rican Tourism Bureau (its address is in Appendix 1) and tell them what you liked and didn't like about what you saw in the backcountry. Remember, tourism is Costa Rica's third-largest industry (after coffee and bananas) and your suggestions will not go unheard.

TRAIL ETHICS

Just as in the United States or Europe, a visitor to Costa Rica's backcountry should remember to follow the "no-trace ethic." Although these recommendations come from the United States Forest Service, they still apply in Costa Rica. This might seem like a lot to think about and may even seem unnecessarily restrictive. Please remember that it's important that foreign visitors treat the land well, not only for ecological reasons but also to assure that we'll continue to be welcome visitors.

Plan Ahead to Avoid Impact
- Travel and camp in small, family-size groups.
- Buy gear in subdued forest colors.
- Prepackage foods to reduce the use of containers.
- Take a litterbag and carry out all refuse.
- Carry a stove and foods requiring little cooking.

Travel to Avoid Impact
- Walk single file in the center of the trail.
- Stay on the main trail even when it's wet.
- Never shortcut switchbacks.
- Look and photograph, never pick or collect.

Make No-trace Camps
- Choose well-drained, rocky, or sandy sites if possible.
- Never cut standing trees.
- Avoid leveling or digging hip holes and trenches.
- Campfires are, in general, to be avoided, but if one is necessary for some reason, keep it small and in safe areas.
- Make camp at least 60 meters away from shorelines of lakes or streams.
- Use lightweight, soft shoes in camp; avoid trampling vegetation.
- Wash at least 30 meters from water sources.
- Use biodegradable soap.
- Bury human waste at least 6 inches deep. Carefully burn toilet paper.
- Stay as quiet as possible. Leave radios and tape players at home.

Leave a No-trace Campsite
- Pick up every piece of litter, including litter left by other people.
- Erase all signs of fire.
- Replace logs and rocks where they were.
- Report all significant information to park authorities.
- Look for signs of disturbance. Did you leave any traces?

HUMAN RELATIONS

While exploring a remote corner of the Gandoca–Manzanillo Wildlife Refuge in the southeastern part of the country, I unexpectedly came upon the evidence of an incursion by squatters: felled, burned trees with young corn sprouting from the ashes. My first reaction was sadness and then anger toward the people responsible. Coming up over a hill, I saw their houses, hastily constructed of rough-cut planks. As I passed their doorways, the occupants eyed me suspiciously. A man and one of his small, barefoot children came out to investigate the intentions of this stranger. I ended up spending the better part of an afternoon with this man and his family, in the course of which I learned a great deal about the plight of the landless, even in a relatively prosperous country such as Costa Rica. It was brought home to me that social justice and conservation must be mutually inclusive for either to be successful.

Should you come upon a similar situation, remain courteous and report the activity to the park authorities, either locally or in San José. Express your concern without coming across as a self-righteous rich gringo. The government has made great strides in protecting the parks from further incursion by squatters.

Orosi Volcano, Guanacaste National Park

Most of the squatter activity is now situated on the properties of absentee land-lords who sometimes even encourage it in order to force the government to buy the land from them for inclusion in land reform schemes.

Of greater concern right now are the sometimes legal but often illegal timber-ing and mining operations in the buffer zones around the parks and occasionally within their boundaries. At the same time that Costa Rica has almost 28 percent of its area under some sort of protection (at least on paper), it also has the highest rate of deforestation in Latin America and one of the highest in the world. This seeming contradiction is possible because most of the timbering occurs on pri-vate land. While the government is taking steps to ameliorate these and other environmental problems, much work needs to be done.

When visiting the more remote parks such as Hitoy-Cerere, it's nice to bring along some extra supplies, cigarettes, cocoa, etc., to give to the rangers and other people working there. These people live in isolated conditions on little pay, and are often hungry for conversation and news from the outside world. Newspa-pers, magazines, and other reading material are always welcome. Don't worry if your Spanish isn't the greatest; they will appreciate your interest in wanting to converse. Often, park personnel are willing to take time out from their other duties to guide you around or take you to something that you've expressed a particular interest in seeing. It's good to be able to offer something in return, even if it's as simple as a pound of coffee or this week's *La Nación*.

Raccoon in oil palm tree, Curú Wildlife Refuge

Part II

5
NORTHWESTERN REGION

Isla Bolaños Wildlife Sanctuary
Santa Rosa National Park
Guanacaste National Park
Rincón de la Vieja National Park
Lomas Barbudal Biological Reserve
Palo Verde National Park
Barra Honda National Park
Guayabo, Negritos, and los Pájaros Islands Biological Reserves
Curú Wildlife Refuge
Cabo Blanco Biological Reserve
Ostional Wildlife Refuge
Las Baulas National Park and Tamarindo Wildlife Refuge
Monteverde and the Children's Eternal Rain Forest Preserves
Arenal National Park
Tenorio National Park
Peñas Blancas Wildlife Refuge
Caño Negro Wildlife Refuge
Diriá National Park

Imagine hiking through a cloud forest in the morning, exploring a limestone cavern in the afternoon, and watching nesting sea turtles in the evening. All these are possible in Costa Rica's northwestern region, due to the area's vast ecological diversity.

Guanacaste Province, in which all but one of the parks in this chapter are located, is considered Costa Rica's "Wild West." A large part of the region's lowlands is taken up with cattle ranching, and cowboys working cattle are a common sight. There are some magnificent beaches here, and surfers and fishermen from the world over come here to partake of the ocean's recreational resources. However, it's the hiker and naturalist who stand to get the most out of the region's unique treasures. The park system in the northwestern region contains pristine coastline where sea turtles nest, misty high-altitude forests where resplendent quetzals are found, and limestone caverns and lowland tropical forests where untold biological secrets hide.

ISLA BOLAÑOS WILDLIFE SANCTUARY

Size: 25 hectares
Distance from San José: 281 kilometers
Camping: Not permitted
Trails: Around the island on the shoreline at low tide only; on beaches covered at high tide, incoming tide surge is rapid and dangerous
Map: 1:50,000 Bahia de Salinas
Dry season: January through March
Transportation: No public transportation available

Isla Bolaños is 2 kilometers from the northern border of Santa Rosa National Park, and 1.5 kilometers by boat from the mainland. It was established to protect nesting areas for **brown pelicans** and **oystercatchers** and is the only known nesting site for **frigate birds** in Costa Rica. Vegetation consists of low shrubs such as **paira** (*Melanthera nivea*), **frangipani** (*Plumeria rubra*), and **crown fig** (*Ficus ovalis*) trees. There is a white sand beach on the island's eastern tip, and the crystal-clear water around it teems with mollusks, fish, and other marine life.

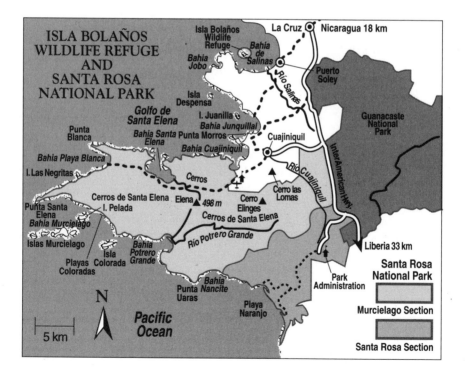

LOCATION AND ACCESS

Isla Bolaños is located 1.5 kilometers off the Pacific coast in Bahia de Salinas near Punta Descartes. A boat and someone who knows how to handle waves and strong tidal currents are necessary to reach it. Ask at the Santa Rosa park office about current status regarding access for visitors and about hiring a boat.

VISITOR FACILITIES

There are no facilities on this island.

TRAILS

There are no trails per se on Isla Bolaños. It is possible to walk around the island at low tide along the shore.

SANTA ROSA NATIONAL PARK

Size: 49,515 hectares
Distance from San José: 260 kilometers
Camping: Permitted
Trails: Yes, from 1 to 20 kilometers
Map: 1:50,000 Santa Rosa
Dry season: January through March
Transportation: Express bus from San José to Peñas Blancas departs every day at 5:00 A.M., 7:45 A.M., and 4:15 P.M. from Calle 14, Avenidas 3/5; returns at 7:15 A.M., 10:30 A.M., and 4:15 P.M. from Peñas Blancas; call Transportes Vargas Gonzales (224-1968).

Santa Rosa National Park was created in 1971 to preserve the site of the battle of Santa Rosa, one of Costa Rica's most important historical events. On March 20, 1856, the battle of Santa Rosa occurred in the area surrounding an old farmhouse or *hacienda* located near park headquarters. Here, Costa Rican expeditionary forces engaged the mercenary "filibusters" led by an American named William Walker. Walker had a grandiose scheme to take over the five nations of Central America to form his own republic, or to annex them to the slave-owning southern states of the United States. He got as far as to proclaim himself the commander of the armed forces of Nicaragua, and invaded Costa Rica from the north. After a bloody battle, the filibusters were routed from the *hacienda* and those that were not killed were pursued back into Nicaragua, Walker among them.

Another *hacienda* battle occurred in Nicaragua. This second battle produced Costa Rica's national hero and martyr, sixteen-year-old Juan Santamaria, who volunteered for the suicide mission of setting the *hacienda* aflame. He managed to accomplish this despite being mortally wounded, and his act of bravery resulted in the capture of Walker, who was sent to Honduras to be tried and subsequently hanged.

Unfortunately, the battle of 1856 was not the last time that the Santa Rosa

Naked Indian (or Sunburned Gringo) tree, Santa Rosa National Park

Hacienda was to be the site of war. In January 1955, several groups of invaders crossed into Costa Rica from Nicaragua. This time, they were an army of mercenaries put together by a combination of Costa Rican politicians and the Nicaraguan dictator Anastasio Somoza, both parties being interested in the overthrow of the popularly elected government of José Figueres Ferrer. One of the most decisive battles occurred in and around the *hacienda*, in which Costa Rican militia (the country had formally abolished the army in 1948) battled mercenaries backed by Somoza's air force for 2 hours, 45 minutes before the invading army was forced to retreat. Twenty-four people were killed and many wounded on both sides.

Much has changed since then, and it is unlikely that such violence will ever recur here. But the Costa Rican people's passion for independence and democracy remains constant, and this is exemplified by the fact that the Santa Rosa Hacienda is one of the most visited sites in all of the park system.

Santa Rosa National Park also protects one of the last remaining fragments of tropical dry forest and several other plant communities. Excellent opportunities for wildlife observation and photography exist during the dry season, due to concentrations of animals such as **peccaries, coatimundis,** and **tapirs** at water holes. The beaches of Nancite and Naranjo are among the most pristine in Costa Rica, and are famous for their mass nestings of **sea turtles.** An excellent trail system offers hikes ranging from 1 kilometer to 22 kilometers that allow access to all of the park's varied habitats.

The first feature of the park that will attract your attention is the extensive, thinly wooded savanna on both sides of the entrance road. These grasslands are not a natural occurrence, but the result of extensive clearing and burning for cattle pasture. They are slowly reverting back to forest. During the dry season, this area is in shades of gold and brown, but when the rains begin an amazing change takes place in the landscape. Almost overnight it turns into a sea of green, the trees leaf out, and frogs call from temporary ponds by the side of the road. No matter what the season, keep an eye out along the road for some of Santa Rosa's abundant wildlife. **Coyotes,** peccaries, and many of the park's other mammals are frequently seen here.

The Murcielago Section is the newest addition to Santa Rosa National Park. Located southeast of the town of Cuajiniquil on the Santa Elena Peninsula, this rugged, spectacular area of rocky peaks and valleys is rarely visited. It is largely deforested, and is a center of ecological restoration efforts. The area contains several secluded beaches. Camping is permitted on any of the beaches. Hiking is limited to cross-country hikes with map and compass.

LOCATION AND ACCESS

Santa Rosa National Park is located 37 kilometers north of the city of Liberia on the west side of the InterAmerican Highway. If you're traveling by car, look for an obvious sign and paved road off the highway. If you're traveling by bus, ask the driver to let you off at the park entrance road. From here it's an 8-kilometer walk to the campground and administrative center.

To get to the Murcielago Section, proceed on the InterAmerican Highway 10 kilometers past the Santa Rosa turnoff to the paved road to Cuajiniquil. There are usually a couple of rural guard officers tending a checkpoint on the turnoff; just tell them that you are going to Murcielago and they will let you pass. The road passes down into a spectacular valley and after 8 kilometers takes you into the town of Cuajiniquil. You will probably need to ask directions for the correct road out of town. Make sure that you do not end up on the paved road heading northwest to Punta Morros; you want the dirt road heading southwest. The road is best done with a four-wheel-drive vehicle, particularly in the wet season.

In 5 kilometers you come to the park station. The Nicaraguan dictator

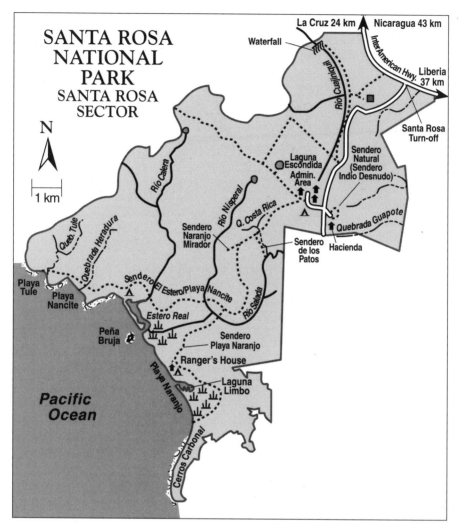

SANTA ROSA
NATIONAL
PARK
SANTA ROSA
SECTOR

N

1 km

Pacific
Ocean

La Cruz 24 km — Nicaragua 43 km
Waterfall
Río Cuajiniquil
InterAmerican Hwy.
Liberia 37 km
Santa Rosa Turn-off
Río Calera
Laguna Escondida
Sendero Natural (Sendero Indio Desnudo)
Admin. Area
Río Nispera
Q. Costa Rica
Quebrada Guapote
Sendero Naranjo Mirador
Sendero de los Patos
Hacienda
Queb. Tule
Quebrada Heradura
Sendero El Estero/Playa Nancite
Playa Tule
Playa Nancite
Río Salada
Estero Real
Peña Bruja
Sendero Playa Naranjo
Ranger's House
Playa Naranjo
Laguna Limbo
Cerros Carbonal

Anastasio Somoza used to own the ranch that was expropriated to make this section of the park, and the locals are happy to regale you with stories from this period. From the station, continue on the road 11 kilometers to Bahia Santa Elena and another 10 kilometers to Playa Blanca. Check with the park people about the latest regulations regarding camping at these sites.

VISITOR FACILITIES

Sixteen kilometers from the beginning of the park access road you come to the *hacienda*, the historic focal point of the park. It contains some fascinating interpretive displays and even a small bat colony. A few hundred meters farther is the campground, pleasantly shaded by a grove of ancient fig trees. Facilities include picnic areas, restrooms, showers, and potable water. There are picnic

tables and grills here, but you can camp anywhere on that side of the road. A hundred meters beyond the campground is the administrative headquarters, where you can inquire about trail and water conditions.

If you don't want to camp in the park, there are a number of hotels in Liberia that run the gamut price-wise. Liberia is also the place to buy food and fuel if you didn't do so in San José.

TRAILS

Sendero Natural (Nature Trail)
Distance: 1-kilometer loop
Hiking time: 2 to 3 hours
Elevation gain: Almost none
Map: Not necessary

This trail is a must for every visitor to the park. Despite its short length, it's a perfect introduction to the dry tropical forest community. The best times of day to take this hike are before 8:00 A.M. and after 4:00 P.M.

Coming from the campground, the trail starts off the road just before you reach the hacienda. You'll crest a small rise in the road and see an old stone corral. At the far side of the corral is a sign reading SENDERO NATURAL. All of the interpretive signs are in Spanish, but concentrated translations of them are given in the description below. The first sign calls this the Sendero Indio Desnudo (Naked Indian Trail). If you look at the trees around you, you'll notice a medium-size tree with red, peeling bark that exposes a green layer underneath. This is the **Indio desnudo** or naked Indian (*Bursera simaruba*) tree. It's thought that though the tree sheds its leaves in the dry season to conserve water, it is able to continue the photosynthesis process with the green underlayer on its trunk. A hundred meters later you come to the second sign, which explains that the forest community you're walking through is typical of the dry tropical forest, and that it is called a community because of the interrelatedness of its organisms.

Continue on until you come to a small decline leading down to a creek bed that is usually without water during the dry season. Opposite the third sign, the trail passes over a natural bridge formed by the action of water eroding the soft bedrock. Approach it quietly; there is a sizable colony of bats living under the bridge. There are three species present, all fruit, nectar, and pollen feeders important in the dispersal of the seeds of many of the plants around you. Take a look at the rock face next to the bridge to see petroglyphs, designs chipped into the stone, made by people who came in search of water hundreds or even thousands of years ago.

The waterholes that these people came for are still important to the area's wildlife, and provide excellent opportunities to view and photograph otherwise shy species. Walk down the river course, keeping to the right side. In 50 meters you come upon a large, conveniently placed rock that provides partial cover on a raised area just out of the riverbed. Potential visitors include **collared peccaries** (*Dicotyles* *tajacu*), animals that look like a long-legged welterweight pig, and **coatimundis** (*Nasua narica*), members of the raccoon family whose tails indicate their owners' inquisitive nature by looking like question marks. If you're really lucky (and patient) you might see a **Baird's tapir** (*Tapirus bairdii*), a pony-size, prehensile-snouted mammal rarely seen by visitors.

Back on the trail, you come up out of the depression formed by the creek and find the fourth sign, which explains the special relationship between the

The bat roosting site, Sendero Natural, Santa Rosa National Park

bull's horn acacia tree (*Acacia cornigera*) and **ants** (*Pseudomyrmex sp.*). The acacia, which is common along this stretch of trail, is a shrub that possesses 3- to 4-centimeter-long thorns paired along its stems. These are hollow, and within them live ants that rush out to defend the plant against anything intent on feeding on it, and even clip back encroaching vegetation. They bite and sting ferociously, so watch your fingers! In exchange for guard duties, the acacia feeds the ants with nectar secreted by special glands found at the base of the leaf stems, and with protein and lipid-rich structures found at some of the leaf tips.

Continuing on down the trail, you come to the fifth sign, and a grove of large **guapinol trees** (*Hypenia courbaril*). These are easy to distinguish from most other tree species in this forest, because they are one of the few that keep their leaves throughout the dry season, and because they drop large, dark brown seedpods that litter the ground here. The smell of the rotting pods gives the tree its other common name: stinking toe.

Approximately 100 meters farther you come to a second riverbed, which runs in the rainy season and then gradually dries to a series of small pools. As the sixth sign points out, these pools are not only important sources of water for land-dwelling wildlife, but also reservoirs of aquatic life such as fish, insects, and turtles.

The trail continues to the seventh sign, and into a patch of secondary forest and thicket created by clearing before the creation of the park. This is a good area to see **long-nosed armadillos** (*Dasypus novemcinctus*) foraging for invertebrates in the underbrush. This is the end of the loop. The hacienda is after your next turn to the right.

Naranjo and Nancite Beach Trails

Distance: 22 kilometers one way
Hiking time: 2 or 3 days
Elevation gain: 319 meters on the return
Map: 1:50,000 Santa Rosa

This is the premier trip in the park. Highlights include sea turtle watching, beachcombing, and a chance to see a variety of plant communities, including tropical moist forest and a mangrove estuary. There are several good camping areas near the beaches, and the one near Playa Naranjo has piped-in well water. Please note that no more than 20 people at a time are allowed to camp at Nancite, and you must check in at the "ecotourism" office near the *casona* for a permit. During the dry season, check with the people at the administrative office to make sure that creeks are running, and have at least three quarts per person per day carrying capacity. Some of the route is out in the open and hot, so get an early start both going and returning.

The trail is an old four-wheel-drive track (park service vehicles only) that begins in front of the administrative office. Here there is a sign reading PLAYA NARANJO, 11 KILOMETERS. The track leads you in a southwesterly direction through open *juaragua* grassland that is slowly returning to forest. After 2 kilometers, you ford a small stream, the Quebrada Costa Rica. On your right you should see the entrance of the Valle del Tigre overlook trail, marked SENDERO DE LOS PATOS on the map. (This trail takes you on a pleasant 1-kilometer side trip through remnant gallery (streamside) forest to two overlooks where there is excellent birding in cool, shady surroundings.)

The main trail passes through a flat area of secondary forest until, at about 3.5 kilometers from the trailhead, it comes to a sign for the 0.75-kilometer Naranjo Mirador Trail. (This is a worthwhile side trip, since the overlook affords you a great view of where you're headed.) Shortly after the side trail entrance, you should see a sign reading ALTOS DE LA CUESTA (top of the hill), which marks the beginning of a 2.5-kilometer descent to near sea level.

About 1 kilometer after the sign, watch for large trees on the sides of the road that bear a series of diagonal scars on their trunks. These are **chicle trees** (*Manilkara zapota*). Until about 25 years ago, these trees were tapped on a regular basis for their sap, which contains the raw material for chewing gum, and constituted a source of side income for local people. The industry died out with the advent of butyl rubber gum base, a synthetic replacement for chicle.

At the end of your descent, you come to a Y intersection at about 6.5 kilometers from the trailhead. The left-hand trail, marked LA PLAYA (The Beach), takes you 3 kilometers to a campsite with water near Playa Naranjo. The right-hand path, marked EL ESTERO (The Estuary), leads to a picnic area and campsite 4 kilometers away, and then onward to Playa Nancite 2.5 kilometers farther.

If you decide to take the left-hand trail and head for Playa Naranjo, you cross the Río Salada in about 250 meters. This is the last water until you reach camp. After 3 kilometers, you'll find a somewhat rundown house (locked) that is used as a temporary residence for park rangers. Close by is a windmill-driven water pump, and toilet facilities complete with a sink and shower. There are picnic tables, and you can camp anywhere in this area.

From the house it's about 200 meters to the beach. Playa Naranjo is 6 kilometers long from end to end, and is one of the least crowded and most beautiful on the Pacific coast. Please be cautious of the occasional rip currents that occur here. Try not to swim out beyond waist depth. Walking south on the beach you come to Laguna Limbo, an excellent birding spot.

Back on the main trail, you skirt the marshes around Laguna Limbo, and come out onto the southern end of Playa Naranjo. Fifty meters from where you come out onto it, the beach ends, gradually turning into the rocky headlands (the ocean-facing side of the Cerros Carbonal) that extend to the park boundary.

Heading north on the beach from camp, it's a 4-kilometer hike to Estero Real, the estuary of the Río Calera. The influx of fresh water has created the habitat needed by an interesting plant and animal community not found elsewhere in the park. If you are really lucky, you might see a **crocodile** (*Crocodylus acutus*) amongst the mangroves. Individuals up to 2 meters in length have been spotted here, usually at night. Another nocturnal visitor to the estuary is the **fishing bat** (*Noctilio lepornius*). This highly specialized bat can sometimes be seen skimming the surface of the water with its claws poised to snag any small fish it detects with its sensitive sonar.

If you are planning to camp at the Estero Real campground, fill up your water bottles here. Go a little upriver beyond the influx of the sea to reach fresh water. After wading the mouth of the estuary, you come abruptly to a headland. Turn right and travel along the bottom of the cliff until the trail passes into the forest behind the estuary. Here, you will find the Estero Real campground. A trail leads east from here for 4 kilometers back to the Y intersection with the Naranjo Beach Trail described earlier.

To get to Playa Nancite, go back to the beach and continue following the cliff for another 300 meters, where you will see a thin but obvious trail leading up onto the headland. From here, it's 4 kilometers to Nancite Beach over some hot, open terrain. The botanically minded will find this part of the hike interesting, because the vegetation on the headlands is uniquely adapted to dry, windy conditions. Species found here include a relative of the **naked Indian tree**, *Bursera permolis*, plus several kinds of cactus. Please note: The headlands and Playa Nancite, along with Tule Beach, may be designated a restricted area. Secure permission from the park administration before going there.

Playa Nancite is smaller (slightly more than 1 kilometer in length) and less visited than Naranjo. There is a nice camping area near the Quebrada Heradura, which serves as a fairly reliable source of water. Perhaps its isolation is one of the reasons that sea turtles prefer Nancite to the more open Naranjo for nesting.

The **olive ridley turtle** (*Lepidochelys olivacea*) is the most common of the three species that come here, and is responsible for the world-famous *arribadas* or mass nestings that sometimes occur between August and December. During one season in 1971, it was calculated that 288,000 turtles laid a total of 11,500,000 eggs here in three *arribadas* that lasted three to four days each! Even if you are not fortunate enough to witness an *arribada*, you stand a good chance of seeing at least some turtles coming out of the ocean at night to nest.

Please be a conscientious turtle watcher. All sea turtles are extremely wary about coming out onto dry land, and if they see anything resembling artificial light before they have dug their nesting holes and begun laying, they will turn around and go back into the ocean. Even though they would probably return on another night, this places an unacceptable level of strain on the animals. Wait until the turtle has started laying before turning on your flashlight, or turtle watch on moonlit nights without the aid of artificial light.

Laguna Escondida and Cuajiniquil River Trail

Distance: 14 kilometers round trip
Hiking time: 5 to 7 hours
Elevation gain: Almost none
Map: 1:50,000 Santa Rosa

This hike takes you to a freshwater pond that acts as a magnet for thirsty wildlife during the dry season. The trail then follows the course of a river to a waterfall. The best time of day to set out is before 8:00 A.M.

This hike begins behind the administrative headquarters. Follow the same dirt road (park vehicles only) that goes to Playa Naranjo for about 50 meters until you come to a Y intersection with a sign for LAGUNA ESCONDIDA to the right. The road passes through old pasture that is returning to forest. The palm trees that are common here are **coyol palms** (*Acrocomia vinifera*). This fire-resistant species is thought to have been introduced here by pre-Columbian people from Mexico for its edible seeds.

After continuing for about 2 kilometers you come to another Y intersection, with a sign for the LAGUNA on the right. The lagoon persists through the dry season, and is filled with a species of moisture-loving **sensitive mimosa**. If you touch the plant's leaves, water is released from vacuoles from near the leaf stems, causing them to fold inward. During the dry season, the lagoon is an important source of water for wildlife. Early morning and early evening are best for wildlife viewing and photography.

The road continues for 0.5 kilometer to yet another Y intersection. The left-hand fork continues through old pastureland for nearly 5 kilometers to the park boundary. The right fork is the one to take for the Cuajiniquil River section. The abandoned dirt road passes through secondary forest for about 4.5 kilometers and comes out onto the main entrance road to the park. From here, follow the paved road north for about 50 meters until you see another dirt road leading off to the left. This side road follows the Cuajiniquil River for about 2 kilometers, then turns to the right. It leads to one of the sites of the battle of 1955, mentioned at the beginning of this park description. There are the remains of a couple of armored vehicles and a monument for the men who died on the site.

Returning to the Cuajiniquil Trail, continue to follow the road along the river for another 2 kilometers to a waterfall. It runs throughout the wet season, but sometimes stops in the dry season. There are short trails that lead to both the top and bottom of it. The road continues past the waterfall for another 2 kilometers through mixed secondary forest and recovering pasture to the park boundary. From here, you must retrace your steps to the asphalt entrance road.

GUANACASTE NATIONAL PARK

Size: 700 square kilometers
Distance from San José: 280 kilometers
Camping: Not permitted
Trails: Yes
Map: 1:50,000 Cacao
Dry season: January to March
Transportation: For bus schedule to Peñas Blancas, see Santa Rosa National Park.

Guanacaste National Park was created in 1989 to protect the volcano slope evergreen forests and cloud forests of Orosi and Cacao Volcanoes, and to increase the restored dry tropical forest and other lowland forest habitats. Dr. Daniel Janzen

Orosi Volcano, as seen from Maritza Biological Station, Guanacaste National Park

and his associates at Santa Rosa National Park had long recognized the need for protective status for the area, not only to conserve its unique forests for their own sake but to provide migrational corridors for animals that move into the highlands during the dry season. Many species of birds, butterflies, and moths have been found to migrate from the Guanacaste lowlands over the *cordillera* and into the moist rain forests of the Atlantic side.

The park contains an interesting if undeveloped trail system and four research stations, at least one of which will remain open to nature tourists, hikers, and photographers. The verdant forests that swathe the volcanoes are a pleasant contrast to the ecological monotony of the human-created grasslands that surround them. This park is as yet little visited, but it is well worth the trouble of getting to it.

LOCATION AND ACCESS

Guanacaste National Park is located east of the InterAmerican Highway, across from Santa Rosa National Park. Maritza Biological Station (the hub of research and tourism in Guanacaste National Park) is located 17 kilometers from the InterAmerican Highway on a dirt road that is best traveled by four-wheel-drive vehicle. The road begins on the opposite side of the InterAmerican Highway from the turnoff to the town of Cuajiniquil, 42 kilometers from Liberia. If you don't want to take the bus to the turnoff for Cuajiniquil and walk the 17 kilometers, taxi service can be arranged in Liberia.

VISITOR FACILITIES

Located at the foot of Volcán Orosi, Maritza Biological Station is beautifully situated and, at 600 meters elevation, it's somewhat cooler than the lowlands. Sleeping areas are dormitory style, but airy and comfortable. Blankets and sheets are provided, but towels are not. It may be possible to arrange for the wife of one of the rangers to cook for groups; otherwise, bring your own food. Arrangements to stay at Maritza should be made well in advance by calling the Santa Rosa National Park office at 695-5588. All communication with the station is by radio.

TRAILS

Llano de los Indios

Distance: 3 kilometers round trip
Hiking time: 2 hours, 30 minutes
Elevation gain: 40 meters
Map: 1:50,000 Cacao

This trail travels through a mixture of patchy forest and pasture to a boulder field that contains petroglyphs left by pre-Columbian peoples. It has good views down into the Guanacaste lowlands, and good bird watching.

The trail starts at the opposite side of the field across from the dormitories at

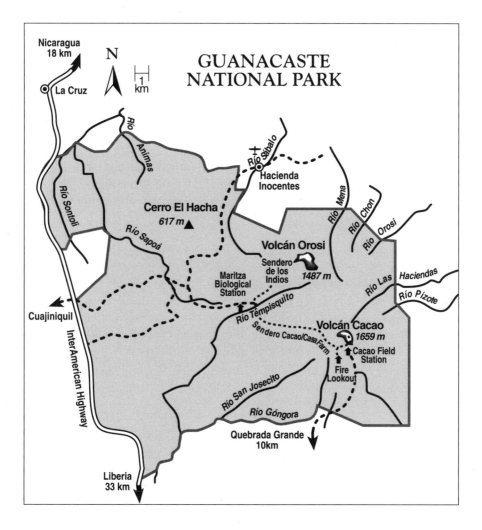

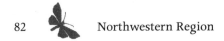

Maritza Biological Station. Continue through the field until you get to a fence. Turn right and follow along it until you come to a gate. Go through it, and be sure to close it after you. The trail enters a remnant patch of forest and descends to a stream at about 0.5 kilometer from the fence. Cross the stream and head to your left. The trail climbs out to another gate and, after passing through it, traverses a section of old pasture before coming to the boulder field on the flanks of Volcán Orosi. The petroglyphs are scattered amongst the boulders.

Volcán Cacao

Distance: 18 kilometers round trip from Maritza
Hiking time: 9 hours
Elevation gain: 1,100 meters to the summit of Cacao
Map: 1:50,000 Cacao

This strenuous hike takes you from Maritza Biological Station to Cacao (sometimes referred to as Mengo) Field Station, and on to the summit of Volcán Cacao. It passes through volcano slope rain forest and into cloud forest near the summit of Cacao. Cacao Field Station can also be reached by taking the very rough four-wheel-drive track from the town of Quebrada Grande 14 kilometers away.

The trail begins in an abandoned roadbed behind the ranger's house. Follow it down to a gate at the Río Tempisquito, less than 100 meters from the house. After crossing it, the trail passes through a section of old pasture that is returning to forest. Continue until you come to a sign reading SENDERO CASA FARM, a little more than 2 kilometers from the beginning of the trail. Take the trail that leads slightly uphill to the left (the other trails are horseback routes out of the park) and pass into the forest.

In about 200 meters the trail goes steeply downhill and then back up to a fence. Go through and close it. There are several interesting examples of **matapalo** or **strangler fig** trees along this section of trail. These trees begin their lives when a bird deposits feces containing matapalo seeds in the crotch of a tree containing some organic matter. The seed germinates and sends roots down the tree's trunk, begins to draw nourishment from the soil, and begins to encircle and coalesce around the trunk. Meanwhile, the strangler develops a crown that eventually shades out that of the host tree. Usually the host tree dies, and after it rots away a hollow shell created by the strangler's roots remains. Stranglers are amongst the largest trees in the lowland and mid-elevation forest; be sure to watch for some particularly impressive examples later on.

The trail continues to a short downhill section that is so steep and slippery a rope has been attached to trees to use as a rail. The trail crosses a river and then passes into a clearing. You should see another sign for the Casa Farm Trail about 4 kilometers from the beginning of the trail. Stay right at this fork, and reenter the forest. Continue on to a short, steep downhill section along a rock face, and continue on to a river crossing. The forest here is heavy and lush, with some trees reaching a height of 40 meters. Notice that their branches and crowns are almost completely free of **bromeliads**, **orchids**, and other epiphytes. This indicates that although the soil is damp, the air is relatively dry, coming up from the Guanacaste lowlands.

From here, the trail climbs steeply for 2 kilometers. Near the top of a false summit, a branch of the trail leads to a fence on your left. Go beneath the fence and out onto a saddle that has been cleared for pasture. If you take the poorly cleared right-hand fork of the trail for a short side trip, you will come to a fire lookout shelter in 1.5 kilometers. This is occupied off and on during the dry season to watch for fires in the Guanacaste lowlands. It affords a sweeping view of the lowlands, ocean, and, on a clear day, Lake Nicaragua.

The main trail, from the Y intersection with the lookout side trail, continues across the saddle and uphill to the Cacao Field Station. The station is usually in use by researchers, and conditions are primitive: no electricity, only cold water, and only the food that is brought with you. Although this station will probably be closed to tourists, you can still ask at the conservation unit office about the possibility of staying there.

From the Cacao Field Station (located at 1,100 meters elevation), it's another 2.5 kilometers and 559 meters elevation gain to the summit of Volcán Cacao. The trail begins at the back of the station, and passes steeply up the ridge through increasingly misty, dripping cloud forest to the summit. The top of the volcano is shrouded in trees, but there is a lookout that gives you views of the surrounding forest and deep valleys on the volcano's flank.

Another poorly maintained trail leads from Cacao Field Station to Pitilla Field Station. If you can finagle permission to visit it, the staff at the Santa Rosa National Park office can give you the particulars.

Strangler fig tree, Guanacaste National Park

RINCÓN DE LA VIEJA NATIONAL PARK

Size: 14,083 hectares
Distance from San José: 264 kilometers
Camping: Permitted
Trails: Yes
Map: 1:200,000 Liberia
Dry season: January to March
Transportation: Express bus from San José to Liberia departs every two hours from the Pulmitan station at Avenidas 1/3, Calle 14. Telephone: 222-1650. Bus from Liberia to Curubandé departs Liberia at 2 P.M. Monday, Wednesday, and Friday, returning the same days at 5:30 A.M.

Rincón de la Vieja (Old Woman's Corner) contains an active volcano (the last major eruption occurred in 1991), mud pots, steam vents, and hot springs, and has excellent wildlife viewing and birding opportunities. More than 200 species of birds have been observed here.

The park protects examples of four types of forests: riparian forest, premontane rain forest, lower montane wet forest, and, in the higher elevations, montane wet forest. There are several nice camping areas, some of which are accessible by road, and it is possible to stay in dormitory-style accommodations that are part of the historic Santa Maria Hacienda. Horseback trips are possible to various points in the park, including close to the summit of the volcano.

LOCATION AND ACCESS

Rincón de la Vieja is located northeast of Liberia. The park is usually reached by taking a 21-kilometer dirt road that is best traveled by four-wheel-drive vehicle from the city of Liberia to the *hacienda*. You can also get a taxi in Liberia, and arrange for it to come and pick you up. There is another route that begins in the town of Cereceda, 5 kilometers north of Liberia. It passes north to the town of Curubandé and on to the Las Espuelas ranger station. It's slightly longer than the Liberia route, but the road has been covered by gravel in the worst spots and is quite passable. There are regular buses to Curubandé from Liberia.

Las hornillas, *volcanic features of Rincón de la Vieja National Park*

VISITOR FACILITIES

It is possible to stay at Santa Maria Hacienda, which now contains the park offices and living quarters for park guards, visiting scientists, and travelers. (Before it was acquired by the park service, this building was once owned by U.S. President Lyndon Johnson.) It's inexpensive to stay in the dormitory-style accommodations—100 colones a night—but the mattresses are extremely musty and mildewed. Bring your own blankets or sleeping bag. Otherwise, you can camp near the hacienda or at the campsite on the Río Colorado near Las Espuelas ranger station. The nearest hotels are in Liberia.

TRAILS

All of the trails described here begin at the hacienda. Distances are given from both the hacienda and the Las Espuelas Ranger Station, which is situated at the end of what will be the paved route into the park that passes through the town of Curubandé.

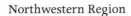

Summit of Rincón de la Vieja

From the Santa Maria hacienda:

     Distance: 18 kilometers one way

     Hiking time: 2 days

     Elevation gain: 1,095 meters

     Maps: 1:200,000 Liberia; 1:50,000 Curubandé

From Las Espuelas Ranger Station:

     Distance: 7 kilometers one way

     Hiking time: 9 hours

     Elevation gain: 895 meters

     Map: 1:200,000 Liberia

Note: Check on trail conditions near the summit before setting out; volcanic eruptions can play havoc with the trails near the summit.

The trail starts in front of Santa Maria Hacienda, and starts out as an old road. In 0.75 kilometer a trail signed BOSQUE ENCANTADO (Enchanted Forest) leads off to your left. A short side trip leads to a small area of old forest, replete with springs, a small waterfall, and a healthy population of Costa Rica's national flower, the **guaria morada orchid** (*Cattleya skinneri*). Back on the main trail, in another kilometer you come to a turnoff to your left and a sign reading AGUAS THERMALES (hot springs).

To get to the springs, take the side trail for about 2.5 kilometers, passing out of the park for a short time and then back into it near the springs. It passes through some pretty boring, overgrazed territory, but the hot bath is worth it, particularly if you visit the springs after making the hard climb to the summit. Follow the path until you come to a forested area next to a creek. The springs are on the far bank; there is an obvious soaking pool that you can roll out of and then into the creek to cool off.

The trail to the summit continues from the junction with the hot springs side trail for 4 kilometers farther before coming to another trail junction. Take the right-hand trail, heading uphill. You crest a hill and come to a grassy, open area. Shortly you'll come to a sign reading PILAS DE BARRO (mud pots), with a short side trail leading to them.

If you take this side trip, you will hear the mud pots before you get there. There are three "pots" filled with smooth gray mud. Every second or so, steam under the mud raises a big bubble, which bursts with a characteristic "blup" and sends mud as high as 2 meters into the air. Please exercise caution around the mud pots and around any of the geothermal features in the park. The sides are often overhanging, so don't get right up to the edge. In the largest mud pot, a pool of water has collected, and here lives a species of **blue-green algae**. These primitive single-celled organisms live in water that is close to boiling and filled with sulfites and other compounds that are toxic to almost everything else. They harken back to a time early in the history of life on the planet, and played a very important role in our evolution. They were the first organisms to produce their own fuel by photosynthesis and thus the first to produce oxygen.

Back on the main trail, continue through an area that was cleared before the creation of the park, but is only slowly returning to forest due to the poor soils here. On a wooded, low ravine, you will notice clouds of steam rising from the trees. This signals that you are close to the *hornillas* (kitchen stoves), a series of steam vents and boiling pools. Shortly, you come to a sign pointing to a side trail off to the right that leads to them. They are caused by water coming into contact with hot, volcanically active areas not far below the earth's surface. Again, be careful while exploring this eerie, mysterious landscape. Try to stay away from the edges of the pools and vents, and stay on the rocks whenever you can. The crust can be thin in places.

From this last junction, the main trail begins to climb. About 0.75 kilometer after the *hornillas*, you come to a nice campsite and picnic area on the banks of the Río Colorado. This might be a good site to stay the night, and then day-hike to the summit very early the next day. The Las Espuelas Ranger Station comes shortly after the river crossing. This is the last place to get water before the summit, so tank up here.

From Las Espuelas, it's 5.5 kilometers uphill to the tree line. Ignore any side trails leading off to the left. Wildlife is particularly abundant on this section of trail. **Black guan** (*Chamaepetes unicolor*), large turkeylike birds, are frequently seen in the canopy, noisily hopping from branch to branch. As you go up the hill, notice the gradual change in the character of the forest as it makes the transition from premontane rain forest to lower montane rain forest. The trees start decreasing in size, and eventually the understory becomes bamboo and small palms.

One of Rincón de la Vieja National Park's hornillas, *or kitchen stoves*

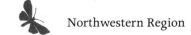

As you get close to the tree line, the forest becomes an almost homogeneous stand of **copey** (*Clusia rosea*), trees with round, waxy leaves that have been stunted by the thin soil and cold winds. If you have sufficient water, this campsite, about 5 kilometers from Las Espuelas, is a good place to wait out bad weather. From here, it's 0.5 kilometer and about one hour through grassland and up steep pumice scree slopes to get to the ridge. You should see rock cairns marking your route to the summit of Von Seebach, about two hours and a little over 1 kilometer away. From Von Seebach to the crater of Rincón de la Vieja proper, there was a 3-kilometer trail that was destroyed in the 1990 eruptions, but it may have been reconstructed by the time you get there. Remember that the weather here can turn bad fast, with thick mist and driving rain. So if it really starts to look ugly, turn around or be prepared to use a compass to find your way back.

LOMAS BARBUDAL BIOLOGICAL RESERVE

Size: 2,279 hectares
Distance from San José: 219 kilometers
Camping: Permitted
Trails: Yes
Map: 1:50,000 Tempisque
Dry season: January through March
Transportation: Express bus from San José to Liberia departs every two hours from the Pulmitan station at Avenidas 1/3, Calle 14. Telephone: 222-1650.

Lomas Barbudal is often referred to as the "insect park," because of the immense variety of insects present here. Some 240 species of bees alone have been recorded, along with 60 species of moths. The reserve protects interesting examples of dry tropical forest, with patches of evergreen and riparian (riverside) forests. Several endangered tree species are protected here, including **Panama redwood** (*Platymiscium pleiostachyum*), **mahogany** (*Swietenia macrophylla*), and **gonzalo alves** (*Astronium graveolens*). There is a great swimming hole on the Río Cabuyo, which also serves as an important watering place for birds and other wildlife during the dry season. This reserve is best visited during the dryer part of the year, when there are fewer biting insects.

The *poza*, as the swimming hole is called, contains a number of interesting fish species, and if you have a mask and snorkel it is well worth taking a look around it. It's located about 300 meters upstream from the visitor center. Many of the fish in it will be familiar to people who have aquariums at home, including the **green molly** (*Poecilia gilii*) and the **convict cichlid** (*Cichlasoma nigro-fasciatum*).

For more information about the reserve, or to make a donation, contact the Friends of Lomas Barbudal, 691 Colusa Avenue, Berkeley, CA 94707-1517. Don't expect much out of them unless you are making a donation; for up-to-date information about changes in trails and visitor facilities, it is better to talk to the Costa Ricans working at the reserve.

LOCATION AND ACCESS

The reserve is located southwest of the town of Bagaces and north of the town of Liberia in Guanacaste Province. There are two ways to reach two different parts of the reserve. The route that takes you directly to the park office, swimming holes, and trails starts at the 221-kilometer marker on the InterAmerican Highway, near the town of Pijijes, 12 kilometers northwest of Bagaces. Look for a sign on the west side of the highway at the turnoff. From here, it is 7 kilometers to the reserve headquarters. You can't actually drive into the reserve from this side; you have to park your car at the visitor's center at the end of the road along the shallow Cabuyo River and wade or walk (depending on the time of year) into the reserve proper. The reserve can also be reached from the south from Palo Verde National Park (see Palo Verde National Park, Location and Access). Taxis can be arranged in Bagaces.

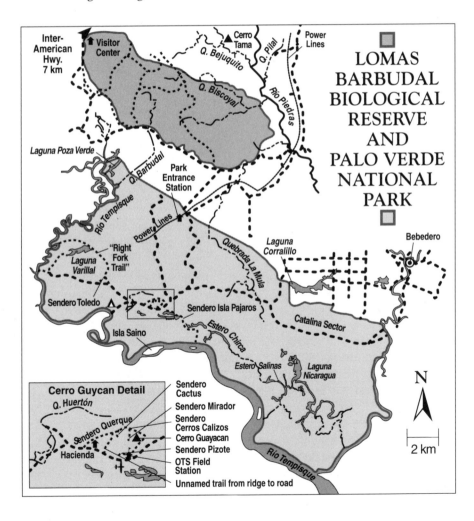

VISITOR FACILITIES

There is a visitor center with a refreshment stand, and interpretive displays are being developed. The visitor center is open on a rather bizarre, ten-days on, four-days off schedule. The staff is helpful, but most do not speak English. Camping is permitted near the visitor center; check with the staff before setting up your tent. The closest lodgings are in Bagaces (very basic) and in Liberia, or at the Organization for Tropical Studies (OTS) Field Station in Palo Verde National Park (see Palo Verde National Park).

TRAILS

Trails oriented to nature-tourist use are still in the process of development. A 0.75-kilometer nature trail has been developed, which will eventually be lengthened to 9 kilometers. An amusing and informative guide to the nature trail, entitled *A White-Faced Monkey's Guide to Lomas Barbudal*, is available at the visitor's center. For the mountain biker, there is a maze of potential routes on the old roads that bisect the reserve. Before setting out, please check at the visitor center to make sure that the reserve's policy about biking has not changed and to learn what routes are open.

PALO VERDE NATIONAL PARK

Size: 13,058 hectares
Distance from San José: 240 kilometers
Camping: Permitted
Trails: Yes
Map: 1:50,000 Tempisque
Dry season: January through March
Transportation: Express bus from San José to Liberia departs every two hours from the Pulmitan station at Avenidas 1/3, Calle 14. Telephone: 222-1650

Palo Verde National Park protects a portion of what is called the Río Tempisque lowlands, an amazingly diverse patchwork of habitats, including fresh and saltwater marshes; deciduous, riparian, and evergreen forests; and mangrove swamps. The marshes are extremely important stopover points for migrating waterfowl and wading birds, and during the peak season in January and February, the largest concentrations of these birds in Central America occur here.

The Catalina sector of the park, in the northeast area, contains some interesting primary forest, but no trails per se. A four-wheel-drive vehicle is necessary to travel it, or you can walk. **Peccaries** are frequently seen crossing the road, and some of the largest trees in the park grow along it.

Important safety note: Unfortunately, **Africanized honeybees** have set up permanent residence in the park. Before setting out on any of the trails listed below, you must check with the Organization for Tropical Studies (OTS) Field Station manager about the location of any bee nests on your intended route. If

View downriver on the Río Tempisque, Palo Verde National Park

you want to go anywhere there is an active nest, the station manager will most likely insist upon going with you, and there are some places that will be off-limits because of the bee danger. If you come upon a nest unexpectedly and are attacked, try to cover your head and run in a zigzag pattern away from the nest. I say "run" with some reservation, because it's easy to trip and fall on the sharp protruding limestone found along many of the trails here, and this could do you as much damage as the bees. The main thing is not to panic. Report all bee sightings and incidents to the OTS Field Station manager. Park personnel will destroy the nests. If you have a sensitivity to bee stings, always carry your bee sting kit with you.

LOCATION AND ACCESS

The easiest and most common route into the park starts at the town of Bagaces in Guanacaste Province north of Liberia. Look for a road that turns off to the west, marked by a sign for PARQUE NACIONAL PALO VERDE. The pavement ends soon after the turnoff, but the road should be passable to all vehicles, even during the wet season. Signs should guide you most of the way, but the route can be a bit confusing once you come to an area of rice paddies with a number of service roads for them. Follow the power line, passing the turnoff for Lomas Barbudal. The power line makes a sharp turn to your right; continue for about 1 kilometer until you come to a new park entrance station, where you pay your entrance fee. At the station, make a left. From here, ignore any roads leading off to your left and down toward the rice fields. Pass a turnoff for the Catalina sector of the park, discussed above. The OTS Field Station is 7.5 kilometers from the park entrance station, and the park headquarters is 2 kilometers farther. Travel time on this route is usually about 1 hour, 30 minutes.

The alternate route is to take the Río Tempisque ferry to Puerto Moreno, and head north on a meandering route bound for the bankside town of Puerto Humo. You need a good map and a lot of patience for this route, and be prepared to ask for directions anyway. Once in Puerto Humo, it is possible to hire a skiff to take you upstream 6 hot, slow kilometers to the park dock. From here you have to walk 2 kilometers to the park headquarters, or 4 kilometers to the OTS Field Station. This rather involved route might be worth it if you don't plan on spending any more time on the river during your visit. It's a fascinating and integral part of the reserve that is discussed at length later.

VISITOR FACILITIES

If you want to camp in the park, you have two options: you can camp either at the park headquarters or near the park's Río Tempisque dock. The latter site is more aesthetically pleasing, but the biting insects are very bad during the wet season. You can also make arrangements to stay at the OTS Field Station by calling the San José office (240-6696). It may be possible to arrange for food, but otherwise, you'll have to bring what you need. The OTS Field Station manager is a tremendously knowledgeable and helpful person. It may be possible (and in some cases necessary) for him to guide you along some of the park's trails. If you don't want to stay in the park, there are hotels in Bagaces and Liberia, and food and supplies can be purchased in either location.

TRAILS

Pizote, Querque, Cerros Calizos, and Cactus Trails

Distance: 4 kilometers round trip
Hiking time: 3 hours, 30 minutes
Elevation gain: 200 meters
Map: 1:50,000 Tempisque

This hike is a series of short loop trails off the main road. Start behind the OTS Field Station, near the water cisterns. Find the entrance to Sendero Pizote, which slopes down into the forest westward. There are several examples of a species of **spiny palm** (*Bactris guinensis*) here. The nasty-looking spines are meant to keep rodents and other predators away from the palm's seeds, but also afford protection to the nests of several bird species, including **streaked-backed orioles** and several species of **wrens**.

The trail joins the main road in 120 meters, in front of the field station. Turn right and walk on the road 1 kilometer to the hacienda. En route, the marsh on your left and the mature forest on your right are excellent bird-watching areas. Keep your eyes open for the wildlife that is attracted to the mango grove near the road. **Collared peccaries, coatis, white-tailed deer,** and **white-faced monkeys** are frequently seen here. It will also be worth your time to come back at night, when a different round of visitors arrive, including **spotted**

skunks and **agoutis**, large, big-eyed rodents related to guinea pigs.

Continue on the road until you come to a spring and a water cistern, which is an excellent spot for insect watching. Soon you come to the hacienda, center of cattle operations and living quarters for the park guards. If you stop in to see the guards, they can direct you to a huge **kapok tree** (*Ceiba pentandra*) down toward the marsh. The fluff from the fruit pod of this species was widely used as stuffing for sleeping bags and flotation devices during World War II.

The Sendero Querque can be found at the right (east) side of the hacienda. This beautiful trail goes past the springhead that fills the cistern you passed on the road. There are concentrations of wildlife at the spring in the dry season, and there are many magnificent old trees. One interesting phenomenon that frequently occurs here is concentrations of the "cracker" butterfly (*Hamadryas februa*). They perch on the larger tree trunks, head down, and "snap" their wings as an aggressive display to others of their species.

Continue on the trail through old-growth forest up the ridge face. It turns east and goes past two huge rocks that provide a good view of the marsh below. The trail soon comes to a junction; one is a short but very steep trail that leads back to the main road near the mango grove. The other trail becomes the west end of the Sendero Cerros Calizos. Interesting trees along this route include the **huevos del caballos tree** (*Stemmadenia obovata*), so called because its paired green fruits look like a horse's testicles, and the **lignum vitae** (*Guiacum san ctum*).

The lignum vitae is interesting for a number of reasons. It possesses the heaviest wood in the world—it even sinks in water. Its name comes from the fact that it was used to cure syphilis before the use of modern antibiotics. This tree is now so rare that its wood is sold by the pound. A magnificent specimen, probably the largest in the world, can be seen about 200 meters up the hill from the OTS Field Station, around the corner from a huge limestone boulder. Lignum vitae has a distinctive bluish cast to its bark and fine, acacialike leaves. Ask one of the field station managers to point it out to you if you get a chance to walk with them.

Shortly after joining up with the west end of Sendero Cerros Calizos, you come to the Sendero Cactus. This short side trail goes up to the ridge top and cuts west to a spectacular overlook on the western edge of the bluff.

Continuing on the Sendero Cerros Calizos, you come to a fork in the trail at the top of the ridge. The right-hand trail is the Sendero Mirador leading up to a lookout, which unfortunately has a large, active **Africanized bee** colony on it. The left fork, still the Sendero Cerros Calizos, traverses the back of Cerro Guayacan and takes you back to the OTS Field Station.

Other trails in the vicinity of the OTS Field Station that are potentially interesting, but have bee problems, are the Sendero Cueva del Tigre, which goes to a bat (and now bee) cave, and the Sendero Guayacancito, which heads up the ridge to a lookout over the marsh. Check with the OTS people before venturing out on these trails. They are not on the map for safety considerations.

El Bosque Primario

Distance: 7 kilometers without car, 4 kilometers with car
Hiking time: 3 hours without car, 2 hours with car
Elevation gain: 233 meters
Map: 1:50,000 Tempisque

This route takes you through some of the oldest forest in the park. Follow the main road west past the hacienda, making sure to shut all gates that you pass through. In 1.5 kilometers, at a prominent fork in the road, the left fork should be signed for El Colmenar (apiary, or beekeeping area). If you drove, park your car at this fork.

Take the left fork. First you cross one small, intermittent streambed, and then a second called the Quebrada Almenda. Shortly before coming to the Almenda, a sign on the right points to a short (less than 100 meters) side trail, the Sendero Ojo de Almenda. This goes to a spring, lorded over by a magnificent **brosimum tree**.

Back on the left fork of the main road, continue until you come to an abandoned shack and some leftover beehive boxes. This area was once an important commercial apiary, but it was invaded by **Africanized bees**. It's best to stay away from the dilapidated hives.

About 50 meters past the *colmenar* there is a 0.75-kilometer side trail that cuts off toward the left and goes directly to the Río Tempisque. This is a worthwhile short side trip, because you have an excellent chance of seeing **crocodiles** (*Crocodilus acutus*) in the river and along its bank. There are four species of **mangrove trees** present here. Mangroves are interesting not only because they are essential elements of the river's ecosystem, providing growing space for "pastures" of algae for fish and other organisms to feed on and breed amongst, but also because they plant their own seeds. The seeds sprout while still on the tree and then drop off, driving the spear-shaped sprouts into the mud.

Walking back on the main road toward the fork where you left your car, there is a trail off to your left about 600 meters before the fork. This is the Sendero Toledo. It cuts across the forest and meets up with the other side of the fork of the road in about 0.75 kilometer. Sendero Toledo takes you through some pretty impressive forest on the way. One huge fig tree growing in the center of the trail harbors a large bat colony.

When you reach the right fork of the road, you'll find it's really more of a trail since it's just the remnants of a road. It climbs to a saddle between Cerro Alto Viejo and Cuesta del Tigre, and descends the northern side. This is an interesting area of savanna, an extension of the native grasslands that make up much of Lomas Barbudal Biological Reserve to the north. From the bottom of the hill it is possible to walk 4.5 kilometers through the seasonal wetlands of the Laguna Varillal to the Río Tempisque, at least in the dry season. Retrace your route to return to your car or to OTS.

Isla Pájaros (Bird Island)
Distance: 6 kilometers
Hiking time: 3 hours
Elevation gain: Almost none
Map: 1:50,000 Tempisque

This hike takes you directly through a freshwater marsh to a lookout point for a famous wading-bird rookery. To get to the trail, cross the landing strip in front of the OTS Field Station and head for its left (east) end. You should be able to see a well-beaten trail leading off into the marsh, heading southeast. It can be an arduous, soggy hike, particularly in the wet season. The island is covered with four species of **mangroves**, and is an important nesting area for **herons, ibises,** and **egrets.** Also present are truly astounding numbers of **boa constrictors**, making an easy living by feasting on young birds. You should resist the temptation to cross the Río Tempisque to the island. Not only is the island off-limits to foot traffic to protect the birds, but the river contains plenty of **crocodiles**, remember? You'll have to content yourself by watching the action through binoculars.

The alternative to hiking to the island is to make arrangements with the park guards to take you close to the island by motorboat. This will depend on how busy they are and if there is fuel available, which you will have to pay for. You can also see the island by taking one of the kayak trips offered by several outfitters, listed in Appendix 1, Recommended Resources.

BARRA HONDA NATIONAL PARK
Size: 2,295 hectares
Distance from San José: 335 kilometers
Camping: Permitted
Trails: Yes
Map: 1:200,000 Nicoya
Dry season: January through March
Transportation: Bus from San José to Nicoya departs every two hours from Calle 14, Avenida 5: call the Alfaro Company (222-2750). Bus from Nicoya to Santa Ana departs 12 noon daily.

Barra Honda National Park was created in 1971 primarily to protect its famous cave system. Although most of the park has been cut over in the past, wildlife is fairly abundant and increasing with protection. A good trail system takes the visitor to the caves, unusual limestone formations, and a spectacular lookout.

LOCATION AND ACCESS
Barra Honda National Park is located east of the town of Nicoya, on the northern part of the Nicoya Peninsula. There are two routes to this park. If you have your own vehicle, take the InterAmerican Highway from San José to the

BARRA HONDA NATIONAL PARK

N

1 km

Corralillo

Cerro Caballito

Puerto Moreno Ferry 6 km

Millal

Cerro Corralilla

Las Cascadas

Cerro Quebrada Honda

Quebrada Honda

Loma Zacate
Cerros Barra Honda

Cerro Cacao
Cerro Taburate

Cerro Minisango

Sendero Cieba

Sendero Caverna

Sendero Ventiador

Los Mesones

Finca San Diego

Santa Ana

Tres Quebradas

Tres Esquinas

Río Chiquita

Nacaome (Barra Honda)

Río Nacaome

1 Nicoa   2 La Terciopelo   3 La Trampa   4 Santa Ana   5 Pozo Hediondo

Río Tempisque ferry; the turnoff is 20 kilometers south of the town of Cañas. After getting off the ferry at the town of Puerto Moreno, head west 6 kilometers to the town of Quebrada Honda. From here, take the road heading southeast out of town for about 5.5 kilometers before coming to a dirt road heading toward Nacaome (also known as Barra Honda). Continue on toward the village of Santa Ana (the headquarters for the park are here). Shortly before you get to the village, take the rough-looking dirt road off to your right with a sign for the park. It's about 7 kilometers farther to the ranger station and campgrounds.

The second route is from Liberia via Highway 21, passing through the towns of Filadelfia and Mansion. You can also reach Santa Ana by taking a bus from San José to Nicoya, and a second bus from Nicoya to Santa Ana. You can walk or take a taxi for the 7 kilometers to the park.

VISITOR FACILITIES

There is a pleasant, shady campground near the ranger station. The charge for using it is 40 colones in addition to the 100-colón entrance fee. There are showers that are usually dirty and sometimes not running; if this is important to you, call about them in advance to see what shape they're in. Hopefully, the park service will upgrade this a little. If you don't want to camp and are planning to stay in the area for more than a day, there are *pensiónes* in Nicoya, and there might be rooms for rent in Santa Ana if you ask around in town.

CAVES AND CAVING

Barra Honda's caverns are renowned for their pristine condition. The reason they have managed to retain all their geological and biological features is that they all have vertical entrance shafts requiring special equipment to get into them. One cave, La Trampa, has a vertical drop of 52 meters from the entrance to the first ramp. One might think that the technical nature of gaining entrance to the caves makes them inaccessible to those not in possession of the necessary equipment and knowledge, but it's not the case. The park service personnel can take you into La Terciopelo cave, which contains some of the most impressive formations of all in the system. The descent is by cable ladder, and the rangers tie a rope around you and set up a two-person belay around a tree in case of a slip. They then come down after you and will guide you around the cavern. You need to set this up well in advance with the parks people, by a week at least. Call the San José National Parks office to make arrangements (257-0922); they have contact with the park by radio.

To explore other caves in the park on your own, get permission from the park supervisor through the radio number above, or by writing him in care of Parque Nacional Barra Honda, Quebrada Honda, Costa Rica. You need to be well experienced in the use of rappelling and ascending devices, and have at least one experienced caver in your party.

Like all limestone caves, these were (and are being) formed by the action of water mixed with small amounts of atmospheric carbon dioxide, forming carbolic acid, on the limestone. This dissolves the calcium carbonate out of the limestone, which is redeposited as cave formations with the evaporation of the water that holds it in suspension. There is some evidence that this process has been accelerated since the introduction of cattle into the area, which destroyed much of the native vegetation, increasing the rate of runoff.

Some of the commonly encountered formations are stalactites—hollow, more or less cone-shaped formations that hang down from the ceiling—and stalagmites, which are the same except they grow from the floor up. Columns are formed when stalagmites and stalactites meet and join. "Soda straws" are thin, hollow tubes that form when the water that runs through their centers leaves rings of precipitated calcium carbonate. "Curtains" form when drops of water slide over an inclined surface, forming sheets of calcium carbonate; these are often translucent and can cover a large area. "Pearls" of up to 2.5 centimeters in diameter form around a grain of sand in the lagoons where the water is constantly moving. One of the weirdest formations found here is "fried eggs," formed when a stalagmite dissolves because of changes in the water chemistry; exactly why and how this happens is still a mystery.

A considerable amount of wildlife is found inside the caves. Besides several species of bats, there are blind salamanders and fish, and many species of arthropods, some of which are probably yet to be discovered and described by zoologists.

Here are some of the highlights of the explored caves in the park. Directions to get to them follow in the trail section.

La Terciopelo

This is the best-explored cave in the park. It got its name from a **fer de lance**, or *terciopelo*, viper that was found dead in the bottom of the cave during the first exploration. It contains some of the most unusual formations of any cave in the park, including fried eggs, "popcorn," and shark's teeth. There is an initial drop of 15 meters and then a smooth ramp covered with massive formations of stalagmites and stalactites that ends in a large, fantastically beautiful chamber. One of the formations in this chamber is called the "organ" because it produces various tones when tapped at different points.

The entrance to Terciopelo Cave, Barra Honda National Park

La Trampa (The Trap)

This cave has the largest single drop of any in the park: 52 meters from the entrance to the first ramp. Remember that this is more than 170 feet, so you will need two joined ropes for the rappel in. La Trampa has the largest rooms, with one chamber made of pure, white calcite.

Santa Ana

This is the deepest cave yet explored in the park, reaching at least 170 meters, and it probably goes deeper yet. It contains magnificent examples of some of the smaller, more fragile formations. Miguel Salguero of the Speleological Society, who made the first extensive surveys of this cave in 1971, wrote this description of it for the Costa Rican newspaper *La Nación*:

The first drop is 30 meters deep, at which point there is a ramp with a little chamber and two pits. The explorers climbed down one of the pits with a free fall of 45 meters, which brought them to a depth of 75 meters. From the second ramp they went down to a depth of 110 meters, where several pits opened up and where there were two enormous chambers with remarkable formations of stalagmites and stalactites. From 140 meters the descent continued slowly until the bottom was touched at 170 meters.

Pozo Hediondo (Stinkpot Hole)

This cave got its name due to the odor of the *guano* (dung) of thousands of **bats**. For some reason, there is a large concentration of these mammals here and almost none in the other caves of the region. No serious attempt has been made to figure out exactly how many bats roost here, but an early explorer likened the noise created by them flying around inside the cave to that of a steam engine. Strangely, the smell of the *guano* decreases the deeper you descend, becoming almost imperceptible at 60 meters. The initial drop is 35 meters to a ramp, and then 25 meters to the floor. The cave has three main rooms.

Nicoa

This cave has two entrances, with drops of 25 and 30 meters. It's an interesting cavern, not only because it contains some huge collapsed stalactites, but also because it is the only cave in the system that contains human remains. It is generally believed that bodies were tossed down into the cave, evidenced by the scattered placement of the remains. The mystery is that they are found in all five rooms of the cavern. They seem to represent a wide span of time, with some of the bones covered with calcium carbonate; one skull was found with a stalagmite growing from it. Another skull had intentionally-induced frontal deformities such as those typical of some South American cultures; this is intriguing evidence of ancient cultural exchange. There is much work to be done here. If you get permission to enter this cave, do not disturb any remains or artifacts that you come across.

TRAILS

Sendero Cavernas and Sendero Ceiba

Sendero Cavernas
> Distance: 8 kilometers
> Hiking time: 5 hours
> Elevation gain: 300 meters
> Map: 1:200,000 Nicoya

Sendero Ceiba
> Distance: 7 kilometers
> Hiking time: 5 hours
> Elevation gain: 300 meters
> Map: 1:200,000 Nicoya

This two-trail loop takes you to many of the park's caves and to a spectacular lookout. Much of this trail is exposed and hot, so bring plenty of water. Please note that the lookout may have a nest of **Africanized honeybees** nearby; ask at the ranger station as to whether or not it's been located and destroyed. (For information about these obnoxious creatures, see Palo Verde National Park.)

The trail starts as a continuation of the dirt road leading to the ranger station. It heads straight up Cerros Barra Honda for about 1.5 kilometers before coming to a fork and a sign for the Sendero Cavernas to the right and the Sendero Ceiba to the left. Taking the right fork, continue up the hill for 1 kilometer before coming to a sign for the short side trail to Nicoa cave.

Continue for 0.75 kilometer and to the sign on your right for the 0.5-kilometer side trail to the *ventador*, or lookout. Along the trail to the *ventador* are severely eroded limestone formations that look like scalloped knife blades sticking out of the ground. The *ventador*'s expansive view includes the ancient uplifted reef encompassed by the park, and the Gulf of Nicoya, including Isla Chira.

Back on the main trail, you soon come to a sign and short side trail to La Terciopelo cave. **Howler monkeys** (*Alouetta palliata*) are common and easy to observe here. Continue for 0.75 kilometer until you come to a T intersection in the trail. Take a right here and in 1 kilometer you will see a side trail leading off to your left into an area of limestone outcroppings and heavier forest than what you've been passing through. This is where La Trampa and a series of smaller caverns are located.

In 1 kilometer more you come to a large **ceiba tree** in the middle of the trail; why it was left by the people who logged this area before it was included in the park is a mystery. From here, it's another 1.5 kilometers to the junction with the Sendero Cavernas and another 1.5 kilometers back down the hill to the ranger station.

There is also another trail that starts at the T junction and goes on for about 6 kilometers before passing out of the park. It follows the ridge for 1 kilometer before descending, losing about 300 meters, before ascending the southeastern

Howler monkeys taking a siesta, Barra Honda National Park

flank of Cerro Corralillo. It then follows along the top of the ridge for about 1 kilometer before descending out of the park to an old dirt track. If you take a left here you will end up in the village of Corralillo in 3.5 kilometers, and if you take a right you will come to a junction with a dirt road, where, if you take a right, you will end up in the village of Millal in 1.5 kilometers.

Los Mesones and Las Cascadas

Other destinations in the park include Los Mesones and Las Cascadas, both cross-country routes with nearly nonexistent trails. These are trips to be taken with someone who knows how to get there. Los Mesones is a 4-kilometer hike through a grove of old-growth, evergreen forest trees. Las Cascadas is an 8-kilometer hike to a travertine deposit where calcium carbonate from the caves has precipitated out onto the surface into a series of small waterfalls. Both hikes travel through large areas of pasture, and the many intertwining cow trails make the route almost impossible to describe. Get a ranger to take you.

GUAYABO, NEGRITOS, AND LOS PÁJAROS ISLANDS BIOLOGICAL RESERVES

Sizes: 6.8, 80, and 3.8 hectares, respectively
Distance from San José: 118 kilometers via road and boat
Camping: Not permitted
Trails: On Guayabo Island, on the beach around the high-tide line
Map: 1:200,000 San José
Dry season: January through March
Transportation: No public transportation available

These three islands, located in the Gulf of Nicoya, are important nesting areas for seabirds such as **frigate birds**, **brown pelicans**, and **brown boobies**. Guayabo is an important wintering area for **peregrine falcons**. Marine life is abundant in the waters around all of the islands.

Isla Guayabo from the passenger ferry to Paquera; the island is a favorite wintering site for peregrine falcons.

LOCATION AND ACCESS

These islands are located off the southeastern side of the Nicoya Peninsula in the Gulf of Nicoya. Access to these reserves is very restricted and requires chartering a boat. Check with the National Parks Directorate (257-0922) for information. If you take the *lancha* (foot-passenger ferry) from Puntarenas to the town of Paquera, you pass fairly close to Isla Guayabo (see Curú Wildlife Refuge). Look for an island with a large, flat area on the top that slopes down on the side facing you.

VISITOR FACILITIES

There are no visitor facilities.

TRAILS

There are no trails per se; hiking can be done on the beach around the high-tide line on Guayabo Island.

CURÚ WILDLIFE REFUGE

Size: 84 hectares
Distance from San José: 151 kilometers via road and boat
Camping: Not permitted
Trails: Yes
Map: 1:50,000 Tambor
Dry season: January through March
Transportation: *Lancha* from Puntarenas to Paquera departs daily at 6:00 A.M. and 3:00 P.M.; returns at 8:00 A.M. and 5:00 P.M. Ferry from Puntarenas to Playa Naranjo departs daily at 7:00 A.M. and 4:00 P.M., plus 11:00 A.M. on Thursdays and weekends; returns at 9:00 A.M. and 6:00 P.M., plus 1:00 P.M. on Thursdays and weekends. Bus from Paquera to Montezuma departs at 7:30 A.M. and 4:30 P.M.; returns at 5:30 A.M. and 1:30 P.M.; bus is timed to meet the *lancha*.

Despite its small size, Curú is an ecological gem. Located on the largely deforested Nicoya Peninsula, it is an important repository for plants and animals that have been largely extirpated from their former ranges in this part of the country. There is excellent birding and wildlife watching here, and a good network of trails. Plant communities found here include mangrove swamp, littoral woodland, and semideciduous and deciduous forest. The beach is an important nesting area for **leatherback, ridley,** and **hawksbill turtles.**

The Shutz family, who own the *finca* (farm) surrounding the reserve, are responsible for its preservation. In Costa Rica, 50 meters from the low-tide line is considered public property, no matter what is behind it. As marine resources were being used up elsewhere, people from the area and elsewhere began overfishing Curú's waters, and overharvesting oysters and other shellfish. The family's concern for the ecological integrity of the area reached its peak when they got wind of a plan by some businesspeople from Paquera to develop the waterfront into a deepwater dock. In desperation, they contacted the Wildlife Directorate about giving the 50-meter beachfront zone protected status, and thus Curú Wildlife Refuge was born.

The Shutzes consider the reserve to be an integral part of the overall ecological scheme of their 1,214-hectare cattle ranch, mango plantation, and selective timbering operation, with most of the cut timber going for their own needs. Close to 1,000 hectares remain in forest. They try to use natural methods of pest control as much as possible, and the late Señor Shutz was an early innovator in the use of plantings of **oil palm, plantains,** and other food crops strategically placed to keep animals such as **white-faced monkeys, coatis,** and **raccoons** out of the mango plantations. The wildlife of the area has responded to this nonhostile approach by becoming amazingly easy to approach, making this a great place for birding and wildlife photography.

Common boa, Curú Wildlife Refuge

LOCATION AND ACCESS

Curú is located south of the town of Paquera, in the southeastern corner of the Nicoya Peninsula. Because access to the reserve is strictly controlled, you need to get directions from the Shutzes when you call to make arrangements for your visit. If you are not driving, you can take the *lancha* from Puntarenas to the Paquera boat dock. From here take a bus or taxi to the locked gate on the road to the farm. The Shutz family has a microwave telephone (661-2392) that works intermittently, and this is a good reason to arrange your visit at least a week in advance.

VISITOR FACILITIES

First priority for staying overnight at the reserve is given to researchers, and then to tourists. The facilities are primitive; bring a mosquito net and be prepared to share your sleeping quarters with other visitors and some of the reserve's abundant wildlife. The cost of room and board is $30 per night. There is a strict rule against camping, so don't bother asking. The reserve and surrounding forest can be visited as a day trip, but you still need to call in advance, or go on a tour with one of the local ecotourism outfits listed in Appendix 1, Recommended Resources.

TRAILS

Curú's trails are short and some have unmarked entrances. Other trails are in the planning stage, so check with a member of the Shutz family about what's been completed.

Mangrove Trail

> **Distance:** 0.5 kilometer
> **Hiking time:** 30 minutes
> **Elevation gain:** None
> **Map:** 1:50,000 Tambor

Two trails come directly off the main road and have signs directing you to their entrances. The first is the Mangrove Trail, which takes you 0.5 kilometer through a section of pasture to a mangrove slough. **Roseate spoonbills, wood storks,** and other wading birds are commonly seen here.

Sendero Finca de los Monos

> **Distance:** 1.5 kilometers
> **Hiking time:** 1 hour
> **Elevation gain:** 30 meters
> **Map:** 1:50,000 Tambor

A little farther on and on the other side of the road, you will see a sign for the Sendero Finca de los Monos. The trail crosses a river and passes for 1.5 kilometers

Curú Wildlife Refuge

through semideciduous forest and mangrove swamp. It is possible to cross the river mouth at the end of the trail and go on to the beach at low tide, but there are numerous stingrays hiding in the mud on the bottom, so it probably isn't worth the risk.

"Killer" Trail
Distance: 2.5 kilometers
Hiking time: 3 hours
Elevation gain: 300 meters
Map: 1:50,000 Tambor

The "Killer" Trail is a strenuous 2.5-kilometer hike that goes up and over a ridge covered with tropical moist forest. It is poorly marked and you should probably try to do this trail with Adelina Shutz or another person who knows it well.

Quesera Trail
Distance: 3 kilometers
Hiking time: 4 hours
Elevation gain: 300 meters
Map: 1:50,000 Tambor

The Quesera Trail travels a strenuous 3 kilometers up and out onto the Punta Curú Peninsula and to a lovely, secluded, white-sand beach. This trail is also difficult to find, so get a member of the Shutz family to show you the entrance.

CABO BLANCO BIOLOGICAL RESERVE

Size: 1,172 hectares
Distance from San José: 300 kilometers
Camping: Not permitted
Trails: Yes
Maps: 1:200,000 Nicoya; 1:50,000 Cabo Blanco
Dry season: November to April
Transportation: *Lancha* from Puntarenas to Paquera departs daily at 6:00 A.M. and 3:00 P.M.; returns daily at 8:00 A.M. and 5:00 P.M. Ferry from Puntarenas to Playa Naranjo departs daily at 7:00 A.M. and 4:00 P.M., plus 11:00 A.M. on Thursdays and weekends; returns daily at 9:00 A.M. and 6:00 P.M., plus 1:00 P.M. on Thursdays and weekends. Bus from Paquera to Montezuma departs at 7:30 A.M. and 4:30 P.M.; returns at 5:30 A.M. and 1:30 P.M.

Cabo Blanco Biological Reserve occupies the southern tip of the Nicoya Peninsula. It protects an extremely important example of mixed evergreen and deciduous moist tropical forest, the last large tract in the area. It is home to many rare and threatened species, including **curassow, crested guan, brocket deer,** and **jaguarundi**, along with more common species such as **white-faced** and **howler monkeys, raccoons,** and **kinkajous**. There are excellent tide pools along the coast, and Isla Cabo Blanco is an important seabird breeding site.

The reserve was established by executive decree in 1963. It is the only government-protected area created before the inception of the park service in

Balsitas Beach, Cabo Blanco Biological Reserve

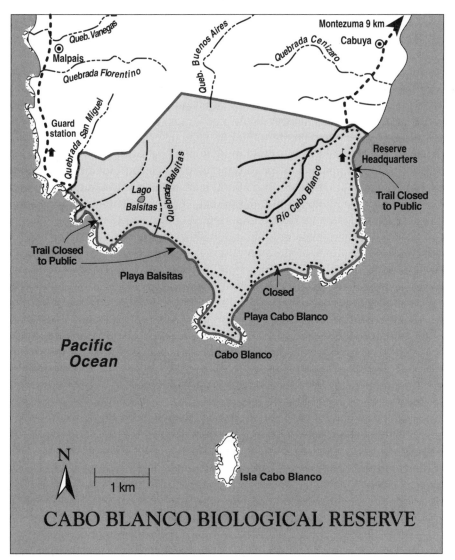

CABO BLANCO BIOLOGICAL RESERVE

1970 that has survived to this day. Cabo Blanco owes its existence as a protected area to Olaf and Karen Wessberg, who moved from their native Sweden to a small ranch on the peninsula in 1955. Not long after arriving, the Wessbergs discovered that the last of Nicoya's once-magnificent forests were in danger of destruction from rapidly expanding agricultural settlement and lumbering. They set about collecting the funds necessary to purchase the last large stand of forest, and in 1963 they bought the land that now comprises the reserve. Mr. Wessberg was killed while in the process of trying to gain protection for what was to become Corcovado National Park; Mrs. Wessberg still lives in the town of Montezuma and can tell you much about the early days of the reserve.

LOCATION AND ACCESS

The reserve is located 11 kilometers south of the town of Montezuma, near the southeast tip of the Nicoya Peninsula. You can get as far as Montezuma by bus. There is a sign at the south end of town for the road to the reserve. A four-wheel-drive vehicle is necessary to make the trip, even during the dry season, because of a river crossing about 4 kilometers from the park. Please take this crossing seriously, particularly after a heavy rain.

VISITOR FACILITIES

No camping is permitted in the reserve, but it is possible to camp near the village of Cabuya, 2 kilometers north of the park boundary. Ask at the *pulperia* in the middle of town. The closest hotels are in Montezuma. Guides and transportation to the reserve can be hired in Montezuma at Chico's Bar.

TRAILS

Balsitas and Cabo Blanco Beach Trail

Distance: 7 kilometers
Hiking time: 5 hours
Elevation gain: 250 meters
Map: 1:50,000 Cabo Blanco

This is the only trail in the reserve that is presently open to nonresearchers. It passes through a nice example of mixed deciduous and evergreen moist forest containing abundant wildlife and takes you to the park's two beaches.

After paying your entrance fee at the headquarters, have a look at the stretch of rocky headland in front of the building. At low tide, pools form among the rocks, and these contain an amazing variety of sealife. The **tusk shell** (*Siponaria gigas*) is a predatory mollusk with a tubular shell that hunts other mollusks and small fish in the pools. **Keyhole limpets** (*Tetraclita stalactiera*) are common here. They look like miniature gray volcanoes. Recently, it was discovered that they cling to the rocks not only with their powerful muscular "foot," but also with a kind of glue they manufacture, which is being investigated for use as a denture adhesive, among other things. Several species of **starfish** and **sea cucumbers** (*Holothuria sp.*) are also common, along with several species of colorful **gobies** and other fish.

The trail starts off the entrance road; you probably saw the sign for it on the way in. The forest is remarkably moist and verdant, reflecting the fact that this area receives the highest rainfall on the Nicoya Peninsula, 2,300 millimeters annually. The most abundant tree species along the trail is the **pochote**, recognizable by the conical bumps that cover its trunk. This is an important timber species, and some of the largest specimens left in Costa Rica are found here.

After an initial climb, the trail descends steeply along the course of a small stream, the Río Cabo Blanco. Keep an eye out for wildlife on this downhill stretch, particularly for **white-tailed** and **brocket deer**. The **brocket deer** is smaller than the white-tailed, with antlers that don't grow larger than spikes. About three-quarters of the way down the hill, you pass a large **balsa tree** (*Ochroma lagopus*) marked with a sign. This fast-growing "pioneer species" is often the first tree to colonize disturbed areas, and is interesting in that it produces the lightest commercially used wood in the world, and weird, hairy fruits that look like half-meter-long mutant caterpillars.

Another common resident of the forest here is the **land crab** (*Gecasinus quadratus*). They are usually encountered as they feed on detritus close to their tunnels, but in March the females troop en masse to the ocean to lay their eggs, which have been previously fertilized on land. Once their eggs are liberated into the ocean, the crabs make the long trip back up into the forest, repeating the process the following year.

At the bottom of the hill, at about 2.75 kilometers from the trailhead, you come to a trail junction. The right fork takes you 0.5 kilometer to Balsitas Beach (the trail going northwest up the beach is closed) and the left fork takes you a short distance to Cabo Blanco Beach (this trail going northeast up the beach is also closed). Visible from parts of both beaches is Cabo Blanco Island, so called because of the white bird guano that covers it. It is an important nesting site for a variety of seabirds, including **pelicans** and **brown boobies**. The abandoned lighthouse on the island ceased functioning in 1976. It is possible, although difficult, to visit the island by boat, and special permission is required from the manager of the reserve.

There is an alternative route to get from Cabo Blanco Beach to Balsitas Beach, and that is to follow the thin 2.5-kilometer trail that goes around the point at beach level. Several parts of the trail are obscured at high tide, so timing is critical. Check with the people at the headquarters for permission to take this route; you will have to convince them that you know how to time your walk with the tides. The route is interesting because of some fossil beds of Middle Miocene age (about 20 million years old) that are located at the very southern tip of the cape. An extinct species of giant oyster is the most common fossil here. Remember that this is a biological reserve and nothing can be removed from it, so look and admire the residents (including fossils), but please leave them in place.

OSTIONAL WILDLIFE REFUGE

Size: 162 hectares of land; 587 hectares of sea
Distance from San José: 371 kilometers via Liberia
Camping: Permitted
Trails: Along beach
Map: 1:200,000 Nicoya
Dry season: January through March; turtles nest during wet season, July to November
Transportation: Buses from San José to Santa Cruz leave from Calle 20, Avenidas 1/3 daily at 7:30 A.M., 10:30 A.M., 2 P.M., 4 P.M., and 6 P.M., returning 4:30 A.M., 6:30 A.M., 8:30 A.M., 11:30 A.M., and 1 P.M. Call Tralapa Co. 221-7202. Most Nicoya buses pass through Santa Cruz, departing every two hours from Calle 14, Avenida 5. Call the Alfaro Company at 222-2750. Bus leaves Santa Cruz for Ostional 12:00 P.M. every day during dry season, returning 5:00 A.M.

This refuge contains the second most important nesting site for the **olive ridley sea turtle** (*Lepidochelys olivacea*) in Costa Rica, the first being Nancite Beach in Santa Rosa National Park. The turtles sometimes come ashore in huge numbers, called *arribadas*, during the months of July to November. This is the wettest time of the year in the Nicoya, when the roads are often in horrific shape, but if you want to view sea turtles on the Pacific side, this is the time and place. **Leatherback turtles** (*Dermochelys coriacea*) and **Pacific green turtles** (*Chelonia mydas*) also nest here.

Ostional is the site of an innovative but controversial program in which people from the village of Ostional, who once plundered nests for the commercial *boca* (bar snack) trade and slaughtered adult turtles for meat, now have the right to collect 200 eggs per family per season. These are sold for about 3 colones each to a middleman, who then distributes them locally and in San José. Although this gives local people a stake in protecting the turtle population from the illegal, uncontrolled collection of eggs by poachers, it's argued that this just encourages poaching elsewhere in the country by opening a loophole for illegal street vendors, who simply say that their eggs come from Ostional.

Many observers think that Costa Rica needs either a coordinated, countrywide, sustainable harvest program that would make eggs so cheap as to make poaching unprofitable, or to cure Costa Ricans of their taste for turtle eggs by rigid enforcement of existing laws. Both options require funding that is presently unavailable, unfortunately. During the nesting season, there is almost always someone from the egg cooperative at a guardhouse near Punta India, and they are usually glad to take you to see the turtles at night or to discuss with you their thoughts about the egg business and turtle conservation. If you speak Spanish, a good way to find out if turtles are nesting and for assistance with finding basic lodgings in the area is to call the village *pulperia* at 680-0467.

The vegetation of the reserve is sparse, consisting of the white-flowered, sweet-smelling **frangipani tree** (*Plumeria rubra*), **cacti**, and other succulent, drought-resistant vegetation.

Most of the coastline in the reserve is sandy beach, but Punta India at the north end of the reserve is an interesting area of rocky headland containing some great tide pools. At low tide, it's possible to examine a wide variety of sea life, including **sea urchins**, **starfish**, **anemones**, and many species of fish. **Sally lightfoot crabs** (*Graspus graspus*) hold tightly to rocks in the crashing surf, and **hermit crabs** (*Coenobita sp.*) forage at the tide line. Near the middle of the reserve at the mouth of the Nosara River is a mangrove swamp where more than 100 species of birds have been seen. You can either walk to it along the beach, or drive to the town of Santa Marta and try to rent a dugout or hire someone with a small fishing boat to take you.

LOCATION AND ACCESS

Officially, the reserve stretches between Punta India and the village of Rayo to the north and Punta Guiones to the southeastern part of the country. The reserve can be reached by car by going to the town of Filadelfia, then southwest to Santa Cruz. From here, take the main road out toward the coast and south to the small town of San Juanillo. You can take the bus from San José direct to Santa Cruz, and most Nicoya buses pass through Santa Cruz. A bus leaves Santa Cruz for Ostional at 12:00 P.M. every day during the dry season, returning at 5 A.M.

VISITOR FACILITIES
Camping is allowed on the beach in the reserve, but this could change, so you might want to talk to the National Wildlife Directorate (233-8112 or 222-9533) before relying on it. There are cheap beach *cabinas* in Ostional village, and more upscale accommodations in Nosara.

TRAILS
There are no trails per se, but you can walk the entire length of the refuge along the beach.

LAS BAULAS NATIONAL PARK AND TAMARINDO WILDLIFE REFUGE
Size: 552 hectares
Distance from San José: 321 kilometers via Liberia
Camping: Not permitted
Trails: Along beach
Map: 1:250,000 Nicoya
Dry season: January through March
Transportation: Express bus from San José to Tamarindo departs daily at 3:30 P.M. from Calle 14, Avenidas 2/5; returns at 5:45 A.M. Call the Alfaro Company at 222-2750. Daily SANSA flights from San José to Tamarindo depart at 9:30 A.M. and return at 10:10 A.M. Call 220-3054 for latest times.

Tamarindo is an important nesting beach for the **leatherback turtle** (*Dermochelys coriacea*). This species, called *baula* in Spanish, is the world's largest sea turtle; adults average 360 kilograms in weight and 160 centimeters in length. They get their English name from their lack of a true shell, the carapace being composed of small bones contained within the leathery skin that covers them. They feed almost exclusively on jellyfish and their kin, and even consume the infamous **Portuguese man-of-war**. They're the world's most wide-ranging sea turtle, with nesting beaches as far away as Surinam and Malaysia, and individuals have been found as far north as Iceland and Scandinavia. How they maintain a workable body temperature in those freezing climes is a mystery, one of the many unknown facets of their natural history.

Leatherbacks arrive at Tamarindo in early October and nest until March, with the peak activity occurring during November and December. Other important nesting beaches for leatherbacks in Costa Rica are Naranjo Beach in Santa Rosa National Park and Matina on the Caribbean coast. Tamarindo's status as an important nesting area for leatherbacks and other turtles was recently imperiled

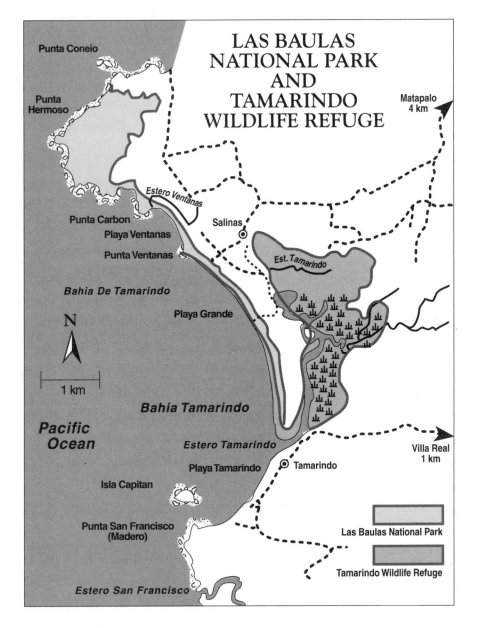

LAS BAULAS NATIONAL PARK AND TAMARINDO WILDLIFE REFUGE

Punta Coneio

Punta Hermoso

Matapalo 4 km

Estero Ventanas

Punta Carbon
Playa Ventanas

Salinas

Punta Ventanas

Est. Tamarindo

Bahia De Tamarindo

Playa Grande

N

1 km

Bahia Tamarindo

Pacific Ocean

Estero Tamarindo

Villa Real 1 km

Playa Tamarindo

Tamarindo

Isla Capitan

Punta San Francisco (Madero)

Las Baulas National Park

Tamarindo Wildlife Refuge

Estero San Francisco

by an American investor's scheme to put a large hotel just above the high-tide mark on the beach. Construction of this potentially disastrous project (the electric lights would have scared off the turtles) had already begun when the desperate staff of the Wildlife Directorate intervened by hastily having the reserve status of the beach section upgraded to that of national park. Hopefully, this will hold any future plans of hotel development at bay.

LOCATION AND ACCESS

The park is located on the northern Nicoya Peninsula, near the town of Salinas. From Liberia, head southwest on Highway 21 for 26 kilometers until you reach the town of Filadelfia. From here, it's 25 kilometers by paved road to Huacas, and another 8 kilometers to Salinas via Matapalo on a gravel road. There are express buses from San José to Tamarindo departing daily at 3:30 P.M. from Calle 14, Avenidas 2/5; returning at 5:45 A.M. For more information contact the Alfaro Company at 222-2750. SANSA flies from San José to Tamarindo daily at 9:30 A.M., returning at 10:10 A.M. Call 220-3054 for latest times.

VISITOR FACILITIES

No camping is allowed in the park. There are several hotels in the town of Tamarindo, with more to come. Boats into the mangrove swamp can be arranged at the Hotel Tamarindo.

TRAILS

South of the beach at the mouth of the Río Matapalo is an extensive mangrove estuary. Unfortunately, most of it is accessible only by boat, but it's well worth trying to arrange this. There is a short trail that leads past Salinas's central plaza southward and skirts the edge of the swamp for about 1.5 kilometers before coming out to the beach. The swamp contains all five of Costa Rica's mangrove species, as well as almost 200 species of birds. Do not attempt to cross the river mouth by foot; the currents are notoriously treacherous here.

MONTEVERDE AND THE CHILDREN'S ETERNAL RAIN FOREST PRESERVES

Size: Monteverde, 22,000 hectares; Children's Eternal Rain Forest, 18,652 hectares
Distance from San José: 184 kilometers
Camping: Permitted at shelters
Trails: Yes
Map: Tropical Science Center map, available at visitor center
Dry season: December to May, relatively dry but windy; June to November are the rainiest months
Transportation: Express bus from San José to Monteverde departs Monday through Friday from the Tilaran Terminal at Calle 12, Avenidas 9/11 at 2:30 P.M. and 6:30 A.M. and Saturday at 6:30 A.M. Returns Tuesday to Thursday at 6:30 A.M. and Friday and Sunday at 3:00 P.M.; call Tilaran Transportation (222-3854). Bus from Puntarenas to Santa Elena departs daily at 2:15 P.M.; returns daily at 6:00 A.M. Call for latest schedule, as times are subject to change.
Daily buses from San José to Fortuna depart from the Coca-Cola bus terminal at 6:15, 8:40, and 11:30 A.M. Call the ICT at 222-1090 for the latest schedule. Travelair (232-7883) may be operating daily flights from San José to Fortuna by the time you read this.

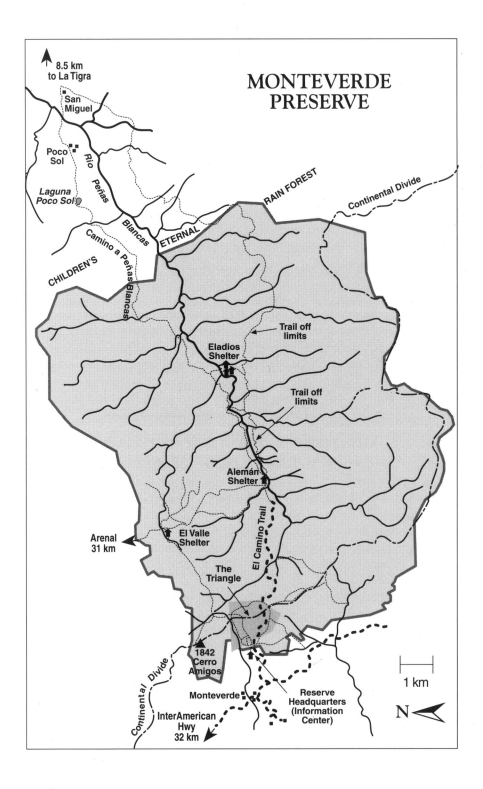

MONTEVERDE PRESERVE

8.5 km to La Tigra

San Miguel

Poco Sol

Laguna Poco Sol

Rio Peñas Blancas

Camino a Peñas Blancas

CHILDREN'S

ETERNAL

RAIN FOREST

Continental Divide

Trail off limits

Eladios Shelter

Trail off limits

Alemán Shelter

El Camino Trail

Arenal 31 km

El Valle Shelter

The Triangle

1842 Cerro Amigos

Continental Divide

Monteverde

InterAmerican Hwy 32 km

Reserve Headquarters (Information Center)

1 km

N

Monteverde Preserve (also known as the Monteverde Cloud Forest Reserve) ranks as one of the best-known protected areas in the tropics. Its creation can be traced to 1951, when a group of Quakers from Alabama arrived in the area. The land they occupied had been mostly cleared of forest by the previous owners, but it wasn't long before they realized the importance of keeping the surrounding forest intact for the continued health of the watershed. In 1972, when a wave of settlement threatened the area's remaining forest, visiting scientists George and Harriet Powell and Monteverde resident Wilford Guindon teamed together to work for the purchase of land and the creation of a forest reserve. They then convinced the Tropical Science Center, a research and education organization based in San José, to take over ownership and management of the preserve. The initial tract amounted to only 328 hectares, but through the efforts of the Monteverde Conservation League, the preserve's protected area now amounts to 22,000 hectares and continues to expand.

The Children's Rain Forest Preserve, which borders Monteverde Preserve's eastern side, is an example of how important conservation ideas often start small but can have far-reaching effects. It all began when a primary school teacher from Sweden came to do biological research at Monteverde, and became concerned about the destruction of the unprotected forest surrounding the preserve. She brought this concern back to her classroom, and the nine-year-olds responded by starting a drive to save and collect enough money to buy fourteen hectares of endangered forest through the Monteverde Conservation League. The idea spread throughout Sweden and then on to other countries, including Japan, England, Canada, and the United States, and consequently more than 7,000 hectares have been placed under protection. The idea is to save the remaining forest in the area, and then to move on to other parts of the world to establish other Children's Rain Forest preserves.

Both preserves contain a considerable variety of highland biotic communities, including **"elfin" forest** (stunted forest growing on exposed, windy ridges) and several types of montane forests containing large trees heavily festooned with **orchids, bromeliads**, and other epiphytes. All told, more than 2,500 species of plants have been cataloged in the area, along with 100 species of mammals, 400 species of birds, and 120 species of reptiles and amphibians. It's estimated that tens of thousands of insect species also reside here.

The resplendent **quetzal** is probably the most sought-after bird sighting in the country. This brilliantly iridescent, emerald-green bird was revered by the Maya and other Central American cultures, but is now endangered over all of its range due to destruction of its cloud forest habitat. Visitors to the preserve are often disappointed when they don't see at least one quetzal during a short visit to Monteverde. These are shy animals, and viewing them and other birds through the dense understory of the forest can be frustrating. The best times of the year to see quetzals are in the mating and breeding season from March to June (when they are too busy to worry about ecotourists with binoculars) and in July and August when trees left in open pastures come into fruit, bringing the birds out in the open.

Taking a guided tour through the Monteverde Preserve
Photo by David H. Thompson

Other interesting species found in both preserves are the **three-wattled bell-bird**, whose loud, one-note territorial call resounds through the forest, and the rare **bare-necked umbrella bird**. The area's most famous nonbird species is probably the **golden toad** (*Bufo periglenes*). For information about this species, see Chapter 2, The Tropical Forest.

LOCATION AND ACCESS

The Monteverde and Children's Eternal Rain Forest Preserves are located north of Puntarenas in the Tilaran Mountains. The quickest way to Monteverde is to take the InterAmerican Highway north from San José to the 149-kilometer marker at Lagarto, turning right just before crossing the bridge over the Río Lagarto. This dirt road has a lot of protruding rocks and gets progressively rougher and steeper the closer you get to Monteverde, 35 kilometers and two hours later. It can be done by two-wheel-drive vehicle, but you need to take it slow. So many oil pans have been smashed out of rental cars on this road that many rental agencies put a sign in their vehicles warning the driver that they are not to take the car to the preserve.

Another slower and even rougher route starts in Tilaran (near Lake Arenal), passing through the towns of Quebrada Grande and finally through Santa Elena to Monteverde. The last 8 kilometers to Santa Elena are really bad, particularly during the wet season, and four-wheel drive is recommended.

To get to Monteverde by bus, you can take an express from San José. The Children's Eternal Rain Forest Preserve can be reached by taking a bus to Fortuna and hiring a four-wheel-drive taxi to go to the Poco Sol Field Station. Alternately, you can walk through Monteverde to Poco Sol. This option is for experienced backpackers only, and advance permission is required from the Children's Eternal Rain Forest staff, contacted through the Monteverde Conservation League. This option is discussed in the trail section.

VISITOR FACILITIES

There are numerous hotels (probably too many, considering that the reserve imposes limits on the numbers of day-use visitors) in Monteverde, from the inexpensive to the very expensive. It is also possible to camp at some of them, such as the Flor y Mar. Santa Elena has some cheap *pensiónes* if things are full in Monteverde. This is a real possibility, particularly during the high season of December and January. The Monteverde Conservation League maintains three dormitory-style lodges, located near the reserve entrance, at Poco Sol in the Children's Eternal Rain Forest, and at San Gerardo near Santa Elena. They are often in use by field researchers or university groups, but you can call to check (645-5112). There is a hut system along the longer trails, which is discussed later. Gasoline is available in Monteverde, along with supplies at a couple of small grocery stores. The dairy cooperative runs a store selling excellent local cheese and other products. For more information, to make hut reservations, or to arrange for guides, contact:

Monteverde Conservation League
Apartado 10581-1000
San José, Costa Rica
Email: acmmcl@sol.racsa.co.cr
Home page: www.monteverde.or.cr
Telephone: 645-5112 for the information office and reservations; and 645-5003,
645-5200, 645-5305 for other business.
Fax: 645-5104

TRAILS

The network of trails throughout Monteverde has improved in both quality
and access since the writing of the first edition of this book. Most visitors to
Monteverde hike within the so-called "Triangle," the three sides of which are
formed by the Río, Pantanoso, and Bosque Nuboso trails, but it is now possible
for visitors to use a series of three huts along the El Valle Trail, which leads into
the Children's Rain Forest at Poco Sol. The entrance fee for the reserve is $8.50 for
adults and $4.50 for students with a valid student identification card. Guided
tours of the reserve are available for an additional $15. The charge for overnight
stays at the huts along the El Valle Trail is $3.50 per person per night for the
Alemán and El Valle shelters, and $5 per person per night for the shelter at Eladios.

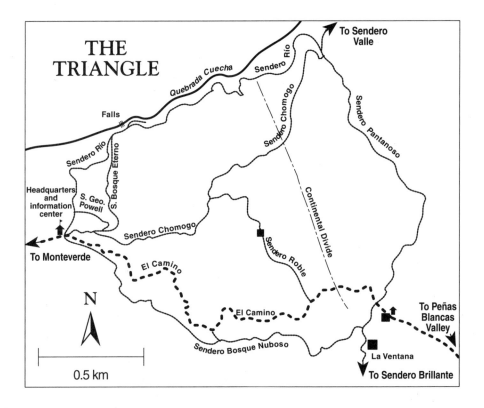

Sendero Río (River Trail)

Distance: 1.9 kilometers
Hiking time: 1.5 hours one way
Elevation gain: 65 meters
Map: Monteverde Reserve map, available at entrance

This trail leads along the Quebrada Cuecha passing a short trail to La Cascada, a triple waterfall, at 0.75 kilometers from the preserve entrance. The beginning of the trail features **avocado trees** (*Lauraceae*) which attract the resplendent **quetzal**; here you will also see patches of second-growth forest. Near the waterfall are good examples of **zapote trees** with buttressed roots. Toward the end of the trail, you might see **tapir** tracks.

Sendero George Powell

Distance: 0.2 kilometers
Hiking time: 10 minutes one way
Elevation Gain: 20 meters
Map: Monteverde Reserve map, available at entrance

This short, gently sloping trail takes its name from one of the preserve's founders. It leads through an area of second-growth forest. This is the easiest trail in the preserve.

Sendero Bosque Eterno (Eternal Forest Trail)

Distance: 0.6 kilometers
Hiking time: 20 minutes one way
Elevation gain: 35 meters
Map: Monteverde Reserve map, available at entrance

Good examples of **strangler figs** can be seen on this short but lovely trail between the Senderos Chomogo and Río.

Sendero Chomogo

Distance: 1.8 kilometers
Hiking time: 1 hour, 30 minutes one way
Elevation gain: 150 meters
Map: Monteverde Reserve map, available at entrance

The Chomogo Trail has existed since the founding of the preserve. It is the highest trail in the Triangle, reaching an elevation of 1,680 meters. **Oak, bamboo,** and **heliconia** (*heliconia monteverdensi*) are common around the higher areas. **Tapir** tracks sometimes are seen toward the end of the trail. There are also many examples of **Stenorrhynchos orchids** and the **hot lips plant**. The trail leads steeply uphill to a wide clearing atop the continental divide where there is a

beautiful vista of the Pacific and Atlantic slopes. The trail falls steeply on the Atlantic slope where it joins Sendero Pantanoso and Sendero Río; here you will also see patches of second-growth forest.

Sendero Roble (Oak Tree Trail)

Distance: 1 kilometer
Hiking time: 30 minutes one way
Elevation gain: 89 meters
Map: Monteverde Reserve map, available at entrance

The Sendero Roble can start 1 kilometer from the reserve headquarters on the Río Chomogo, or 2.7 kilometers from the headquarters on El Camino Trail. It connects Sendero Chomogo with El Camino. It is the newest trail in the preserve. As you descend to El Camino, there are views of the Atlantic and Pacific slopes.

Sendero Bosque Nuboso (Cloud Forest Trail)

Distance: 2 kilometers
Hiking time: 1.5 hours one way
Elevation gain: 65 meters
Map: Monteverde Reserve map, available at entrance

This trail is a good place to see the legendary resplendent **quetzal**, particularly during the mating season in April and May. There are also good examples of **strangler fig trees**. Along one segment of the trail is an area of second-growth forest. At breaks in the canopy layer, look for **bamboo**. As you walk along the trail, you will pass through a moisture gradient. Notice changes in vegetation, humidity, and temperature as you approach the continental divide. This trail has educational stops along the way corresponding to a self-guiding natural history booklet. The booklet can be purchased for a small fee at the reception building.

Sendero Pantanoso (Swamp Trail)

Distance: 1.6 kilometers
Hiking time: 1 hour, 15 minutes one way
Elevation gain: 40 meters
Map: Monteverde Reserve map, available at entrance

This trail passes through a swamp forest, a denser and wetter area than others in the Triangle. Because of its high elevation, strong winds frequently cause trees to fall, creating numerous light gaps. Here you will find **magnolias**, many plants with stilt roots, and *Podcarpus*, the only conifer in the preserve. This trail is covered with a raised wooden walkway.

Footbridge in the Monteverde Preserve
Photo by David H. Thompson

Sendero Valle (Valley Trail)

Distance: 4 kilometers
Hiking time: 2.5 hours one way
Elevation gain: None
Map: Monteverde Reserve map, available at entrance

This trail begins at the end of the Sendero Río and leads to the El Valle shelter in the northern half of the preserve. Along this flat trail, you pass through second-growth forest and you might see **tapir** tracks. A new trail leads northeast from the El Valle shelter to Volcán Arenal (one and a half to two days past the El Valle shelter).

El Camino (The Road)

Distance: 2 kilometers from the headquarters to the junction with Sendero Pantanoso. 35 kilometers from headquarters to Poco Sol in the Children's Eternal Rain Forest
Hiking time: 1 hour one way to the junction, two to three days one way to Poco Sol
Elevation gain: 45 meters. Longer trip is mostly downhill.
Map: Monteverde Reserve map, available at entrance

Please note that if you plan on hiking through to Poco Sol, you must obtain permission from the staff of the Children's Eternal Rain Forest before proceeding. Call 645-5003 or 645-5200, or send e-mail to acmmcl@sol.racsa.co.cr for more information.

This dirt road leads to the beautiful Peñas Blancas Valley. Because it is more open than the other trails, the sunlight on El Camino attracts butterflies and is a good place for bird-watching. This route is actually an old road that used to be a continuation of the main road into Monteverde and extended into the Peñas Blancas Valley. The lands next to it were some of the first purchased by George Powell in the 1950s in order to control access to the valley and slow the rate of deforestation. The road is wide enough for sunlight to penetrate its sides, creating an ideal environment for the non-native **impatiens** plant and many plants of the **aster** (*Asteraceae*) family. The colorful blooms of the impatiens attract many species of insects, including the **glass-winged, postman,** and **morpho butterflies.**

At 1.2 kilometers you will come to a signed trailhead with four options. To the east is the continuation of the Sendero El Camino to Peñas Blancas, to the north is the Sendero Pantanoso, to the west is El Camino, and to the south is a short trail called Sendero Brillante (Bright Trail) that leads 0.3 kilometer to La Ventana, a scenic overlook. Please note that this trail is restricted to research use only beyond La Ventana. Back on El Camino, the trail leads steeply downhill from the junction to the Peñas Blancas Valley and 6.8 kilometers to the Alemán shelter, where the trail splits. You should avoid the trail to your right (south), and stick to the fork that veers to the north side of the Río Peñas Blancas. The south fork is used by reserve staff only, and involves several potentially dangerous river crossings. From the Alemán shelter, the trail continues downhill another 5 kilometers to the Eladios shelter. The elevation change is about 110 meters and the trip takes two hours after leaving the Alemán shelter. The trail continues northeast for approximately 14 kilometers to the Poco Sol Field Station in the Children's Eternal Rain Forest. This section of trail is not well maintained, and is recommended for experienced hikers only. The Poco Sol Field Station is 13 kilometers off the main road from San Ramón to Fortuna, and is surrounded by lush tropical rainforest ranging in altitude from 500 to 1,000 meters. The station offers comfortable accommodations for up to twenty people, a covered front porch for bird watching and relaxing, more than 10 kilometers of hiking trails, and spectacular natural features, including a waterfall, hot mineral springs, and a beautiful 3.8-hectare lake. From Poco Sol, it is approximately another 10 kilometers to the village of La Tigra, and then on the highway it is about 20 kilometers from La Tigra to Fortuna. In Poco Sol, there are a few houses where hikers can ask to use a telephone or pay a small fee for a ride to La Tigra if they find anyone at home. Otherwise, it is necessary to hike to La Tigra on the dirt road and hope to hitch a ride.

Sendero de las Dantas

Distance: 32 kilometers
Hiking time: Two days minimum each way
Elevation gain: 1,400 meters
Map: 1:200,000 San José

Long-time Monteverde resident Wilford (Wolf) Guidon has been developing this trail for several years. It begins in the Monteverde Reserve and leads to Arenal National Park. The trail is still rough and difficult to follow in places, and consequently the Monteverde Conservation League has requested that potential hikers contact them in advance for current information (See Appendix 2 for contact information). A guide is strongly recommended, and the Monteverde Conservation League can help you with these arrangements. The route begins near the Sendero Valle refuge, and it is advisable that people stay the night there before heading out very early the next day. The trail follows an arduous route that necessitates hiking up and down from ridge to ridge. The trail is extremely steep and muddy in places. Once you cross the continental divide to the Atlantic side, there is a good chance of rain, even during the dry season. All but the most athletic hikers will need to camp at least one night in the forest, so a tent is a necessity. The trail ends near the Arenal Observatory Lodge, a rather expensive but extremely comfortable place to stay and rest your weary bones after the hike. You could arrange for a taxi to pick you up at the lodge and take you to Fortuna, about 20 kilometers distant.

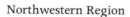

Bajo Tigre Trail

Distance: 1.5-kilometer loop
Hiking time: 2 hours, open daily from 8:00 A.M. to 4:00 P.M.
Elevation gain: Almost none
Map: None available

This is a short trail officially outside of the Monteverde Preserve, but worthwhile nonetheless. The trail is located off the main road near the Pensión Quetzal in the town of Monteverde. The trail is at a lower elevation than the preserve, and the forest here offers a different array of flora and fauna. Administered by the Monteverde Conservation League, there is a small fee to walk the trail.

Cerro Amigos Trail

Distance: 3 kilometers round trip
Hiking time: 2 hours
Elevation gain: 300 meters
Map: Monteverde town tourist map

Another worthwhile walk is the hike to the top of Cerro Amigos, where you can get a view of the steam and ash that issue out of Volcán Arenal when it is active. If you're willing to make the walk at night, and are lucky enough to have clear skies and enough volcanic activity, you'll see some of the mountain's pyrotechnics. To get to the trail, go to the Hotel Belmar and ask where the entrance is. From here, it's a steady uphill trek to the summit.

ARENAL NATIONAL PARK

Size: 12,016 hectares
Distance from San José: 152 kilometers
Camping: Not permitted
Trails: Yes
Map: 1:50,000 Arenal
Dry season: December to May, relatively dry but windy; June to November are the rainiest months
Transportation: Buses leaving San José from the Coca-Cola bus terminal depart to Fortuna at 6:15, 8:40, and 11:30 A.M. Call the ICT at 222-1090 for the latest schedule.

Arenal National Park was created in 1994, primarily to protect the watershed supplying the hydropower facilities at the dam that holds back Lake Arenal. The park is also one of the world's premier volcano-watching areas. Hotels and private nature preserves now ring the base of the rumbling giant, and visitor facilities are being developed in the park. Almost nowhere else in the world is it possible to get so close to one of the most powerful natural forces on the planet in relative safety and comfort.

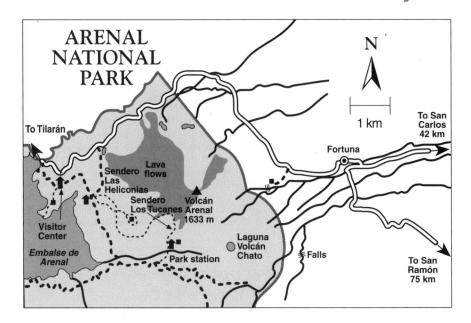

Recent evidence suggests that Arenal was violently active between 1200 and 1500 A.D., but for most of modern history, it was thought that Arenal was inactive and not a direct threat to the non-indigenous people settling in the area. The mountain was relatively quiet when Spanish settlers arrived in the area; largely covered with forest, it emitted nothing more than warm thermal springs to suggest there was anything going on in its interior. All of this changed abruptly and dramatically in 1968 when the west flank of the volcano blew open with an explosive "pyroclastic" type eruption consisting of hot gas, ash, and avalanches of red-hot rocks that killed 78 people. No seismic instruments were housed near the volcano at the time, so there was very little warning that this would occur. However, locals will tell you that people climbing the mountain had noticed heat between large boulders near the summit and an increase in the temperature of the Tabacon River. Since 1968, the volcano has been more or less continually active.

Arenal, which now has an elevation of 1,657 meters, is a classic example of what volcanologists call a "stratovolcano." A stratovolcano is made up of alternating layers of lava flows and chunky, pyroclastic material, and typically has a symmetrical, conical shape. Like all of Costa Rica's active or recently active volcanoes—Miravalles, Tenorio, Rincón de la Vieja, Poás, and Irazú—Arenal sits on a subduction zone. A subduction zone occurs when two of the earth's tectonic plates (in this case the Cocos and North American plates) converge and push together. Eventually, one plate slides beneath the other, and when the descending plate gets deep enough inside the earth's mantle, some of the plate's material melts to form magma (molten rock) that can move upward to erupt at the surface. Mount Saint Helens and the rest of the Cascade Mountains in the northwestern United States are also stratovolcanos, created by the Juan de Fuca plate subducting

Arenal Volcano, seen across Lake Arenal

under the western margin of the North American plate. Other types of volcanoes, not found on the Costa Rican mainland, are created in the regions at the edges of two spreading plates, or when a plate passes over a "hot spot" in the earth's mantle.

Hardcore volcano freaks can access a very detailed record of all of Arenal's activity since 1968 at the Smithsonian Institution's Global Volcanism Program home page: www.volcano.si.edu/gvp/volcano/region14/costaric/arenal/gvnb.htm.

LOCATION AND ACCESS

Arenal National Park is located in the northwestern portion of Alajuela Province, near the border with Guanacaste. The main gateway into the park is the town of Fortuna. Most people come on Route 142 from San José via the outlying town of San Ramón. Buses leaving San José from the Coca-Cola bus terminal depart at 6:15, 8:40, and 11:30 A.M. From Fortuna, it is easy to get a taxi to wherever you want to go within the park. Travelair (232-7883) may be running daily flights from San José to Fortuna by the time you read this. There is also a trail under development that runs from Monteverde to Arenal National Park; see the Monteverde section for details.

VISITOR FACILITIES

Due to the park's newness, Arenal has few facilities for visitors. There are presently two park stations, and what promises to be a full-service visitor center was under construction in 1998.

The two stations up and running at the time of this writing are a small station near the lake, at which one can talk to a ranger to obtain basic park information, and another small shack at the beginning (or end) of the Sendero Los Tucanes (Toucan Trail). The visitor's center will be located at the end of the dirt road on a peninsula jutting out into the lake, a spot known as *Los Miradores*. The first station can be reached from the town of Fortuna by heading west for 15 miles on

126

the only road leading in that direction, and then turning left at a crossroads that has a sign for the park. From here it is 2 kilometers to the station. To reach the new visitor's center, turn right (heading north) on the road in front of the entrance station and continue for about 2.1 kilometers. From the visitor's center, there is a 1-kilometer dirt road that leads out onto the peninsula and a scenic overlook affording views of the lake. The third station is in a tiny shack staffed until about 4 P.M., located on the north side of the Río Agua Caliente on the Sendero Los Tucanes. No camping was allowed in the park at the time of writing, probably to discourage people from attempting to climb the volcano when there are no park guards to stop them, but this could change.

There are plenty of hotels in Fortuna, plus one commercial campground. The owners of the La Catarata Ecotourist Lodge in Fortuna are an excellent source of information and other services. The lodge, which is part of World Wildlife Fund Canada, has a butterfly-breeding project, a paca-raising operation, and a medicinal plant garden on the grounds. The owners can arrange guides, taxis, and other services anywhere within the Arenal Conservation Area. The telephone number for the lodge is 479-9522, fax: 479-9178.

Please note that it is extremely dangerous, bordering on suicidal, to attempt to climb the volcano. In 1988, a tourist died while trying to reach the summit. There is at least one tour "operator" in Fortuna who offers to take people up the mountain illegally. Don't even think about it. Not only would you risk your own life in the attempt, but you could also jeopardize the lives of park personnel or Red Cross volunteers who might attempt a rescue.

Paca breeding project, La Catarata Ecotourist Lodge

TRAILS

Sendero Los Tucanes and Sendero Las Heliconias

Distance: 5.3 kilometers round trip
Hiking time: 2.5 hours
Elevation gain: Negligible
Map: 1:50,000 Arenal

This relatively easy hike (save for a bit of tricky footwork across some volcanic rubble) takes you through secondary forest and across a recent lava field, offering views of the volcano's south side. The trailheads are at the main park station and near the Arenal Observatory Lodge. After it leaves from the main park station, the trail passes through old pasture, which is growing back into secondary forest. The understory is dominated by **heliconias**, which look like little banana plants. In about 500 meters, the trail crosses a 500-meter dirt road leading to a shelter with a good view of the volcano. After crossing the road, you continue through old pasture for about 1 kilometer before reaching the edge of a lava flow. This flow is the result of an eruption in 1993, before the volcano became more active on the opposite or northwest side. The trail ascends for about 20 meters onto the lava field, which is strewn with sharp-edged boulders that can make walking a little tricky. The lava field is about 200 meters wide. Keep an eye out for the steel rods with yellow tips that mark the trail across the flow. At the point that the trail descends off the flow it is called the Sendero Los Tucanes, and it passes through secondary forest for about 1 kilometer before coming to the smaller of the two park stations. The trail then crosses a small river (the Río Danta) and out to the trailhead at the road. From here, it might be possible to hitch a ride back to the main park station (about 5 kilometers), but it may be easier to walk back the way you came.

TENORIO NATIONAL PARK

Size: Unknown
Distance from San José: 175 kilometers
Camping: Permitted, but no developed facilities
Trails: Yes
Maps: 1:50,000 Miravalles, Tierras Morenas, Guatuso
Dry season: December to May, relatively dry but windy; June to November are the rainiest months.
Transportation: It is possible to get to Bijagua by bus, but the schedule is erratic. Call the ICT at 222-1090 for the latest schedule.

Established in 1996, Tenorio is the country's newest national park. It is still being consolidated, and its exact area will not be known for some time yet; until then, Tenorio will most likely remain one of the best-kept secrets among Costa

Waterfall in the "Thermal River," Tenorio National Park

Rica's protected areas. It has thermal rivers, a diverse and largely unstudied fauna and flora, and a varied landscape containing a mix of premontane rain forest and features of the dry tropical forest on the side of the park facing the Pacific. The park contains little in the way of developed trails or other amenities for visitors, but this will certainly change in coming years.

ACCESS

The most convenient base for exploring the park is the Alburgue Cataratas near the small town of Bijagua in Guanacaste Province. This guesthouse, which is run by a cooperative of twelve families, is supported through a joint effort between World Wildlife Fund Canada and the Costa Rican Ministry of Environment and Energy. The lodge's staff is helpful, knowledgeable, and can arrange for transport or tours to various parts of the park. Call 383-8975 for more information.

Bijagua is 34 kilometers from a signed turnoff of the InterAmerican Highway, 7 kilometers north of Cañas. The Alburgue is about 2 kilometers up a signed, very rough road just as you get into town. The one developed trail in the park is located just behind the hotel.

Tenorio Volcano

TRAILS

Nature Trail
Distance: 1 to 8 kilometers
Hiking time: 45 minutes to 3.5 hours
Elevation gain: 40 meters for 1-kilometer loop, about 200 meters for longer trail
Map: 1:50,000 Miravalles

This trail passes through primary forest, and has the unusual and interesting feature of a short canopy walkway that gets you out over the treetops for a spectacular view. The trail is covered by a layer of bark mulch that makes for a comfortable walk. There is plenty of wildlife to be seen, and you shouldn't let the comfy substrate keep you from looking where you step; I have seen both **coral snakes** and **fer de lance** (*terciopelos*) snakes along the trail. You can do the short loop or take a longer route up onto a ridge and then down to a small lake. The trail begins just behind the hotel buildings, at either end of the parking area. At about the halfway point, you'll come to the elevated walkway anchored by cables to a large tree at the distal end. Only two people at the most should be on it at a time, and you might ask the staff at the Alburgue about its condition before venturing out.

About 100 meters before or after the walkway (depending on which end you started from) you'll come to an obvious trail leading slightly uphill. This trail passes through mostly primary forest for about 2.5 kilometers, and ascends onto a ridge before descending quickly to a seasonal lake that converts to marsh during the drier parts of the year. To get back to the Alburgue, go back the way you came.

Author on canopy walkway, Tenorio National Park

Sendero Altitudinal

Distance: Approximately 12 kilometers one way
Hiking time: Unknown at press time
Elevation gain: 1,500 meters
Maps: 1:50,000 Miravalles, Tierras Morenas, Guatuso

This trail was just beginning to be developed and marked in 1998. It's strongly suggested that you go with a guide, as the trailheads are nearly impossible to find and the roads leading to it are extremely rough, bordering on impassable. There is also a considerable amount of private land on both ends of the trail remaining to be purchased by the park, and local landowners are not terribly interested in having hikers wandering in their pastures looking for the overgrown trailheads. All caveats aside, this will be a fascinating trail once it is completed. It follows the Río Celeste, named for the weird, powder-blue color of its waters. This is the result of minerals dissolved in the water at the river's source, deep within Volcán Tenorio. The trail will lead to a saddle between Tenorio and Fila Chiquero, down onto the dry western slopes of the continental divide, and out to the road running between Highway 6 and the little farming community of Paraiso.

PEÑAS BLANCAS WILDLIFE REFUGE

Size: 2,400 hectares
Distance from San José: 115 kilometers
Camping: Permitted
Trails: Yes
Map: 1:50,000 Miramar
Dry season: January through April
Transportation: No public transportation available.

Peñas Blancas (White Cliffs) gets its name from the most prominent topographical feature in the area, a series of light-colored dolomite cliffs that are the result of volcanic uplift beneath them. The refuge was created primarily for watershed protection, and much of the area was selectively logged or otherwise disturbed before its protection. Some primary forest remains in the river valleys, however. You can find three types of forest represented here: tropical dry forest, semideciduous forest, and, in the higher altitudes, premontane moist forest. Because of the somewhat less than pristine nature of the forest, wildlife is not particularly common, although there is a fairly good representation of birds (seventy species counted) and the more common mammals, such as **kinkajous, howler monkeys**, and **peccaries**.

LOCATION AND ACCESS

The refuge is located near the town of Miramar, in southern Guanacaste Province. To get there, turn off the InterAmerican Highway at the town of Santa Rosa, 11 kilometers north of Esparza. There is only one road leading out of

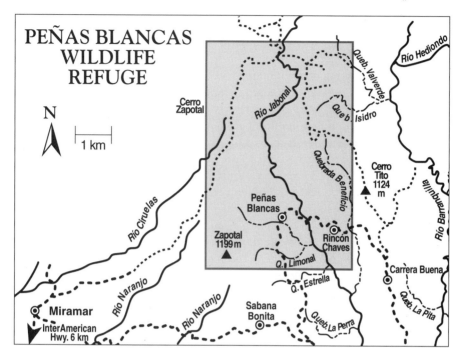

PEÑAS BLANCAS
WILDLIFE
REFUGE

N

1 km

Miramar, heading due east. In 8 kilometers, just past Sabana Bonita, you come to a T intersection; turn left here. In 5 kilometers you come to the small village of Peñas Blancas. The official boundary of the refuge starts shortly before the village. The road is rough in some places, and unless you have four-wheel drive, you should inquire in Miramar as to its condition during the rainy season.

VISITOR FACILITIES

There are no visitor facilities to speak of. It is possible to camp in the backcountry, along the river. The nearest hotels are in Esparza or Cañas.

TRAILS

Ridge Trail

Distance: 7 kilometers
Hiking time: 5 hours
Elevation gain: 560 meters
Map: 1:50,000 Miramar

This trail climbs rigorously up to a high ridge above the Río Jabonal. There is no water along this trail, so make sure you have plenty before setting out. In the lower elevations the trail passes through tropical dry forest vegetation with trees such as the **naked Indian** (*Bursera simaruba*) and the **spiny cedar** (*Bombacopsis quinatum*) predominating. It continues on through deciduous forest containing species typical of the tropical dry forest with the inclusion of some moisture-loving shrubs such as **piper curtispicum**. This plant is a member of the pepper family, and has distinctive elongated white flowers that are pollinated by **bats**. At the higher elevation, there is remnant premontane forest consisting primarily of **oaks** (*Quercus brenesii*). Oaks are an endangered genus all over Costa Rica because of the high-quality charcoal they produce, and the trees of this area have not been spared. Few mature specimens survive here.

The trail can be difficult to find. If you can, get someone to show you the entrance, or ask for the way to Cerro Tito. But if you want to try it on your own, continue on the road you came in on, over the Río Jabonal, through Rincón Chaves, and then past a second river, Quebrada Benificio. About 1.5 kilometers after the second river, there is a dirt track, more of a wide trail, leading due east. In another 0.5 kilometer, you'll come to a junction with a trail that appears to be more heavily traveled. Head left (north) steeply up a hill through open, hot, deforested country. In 0.75 kilometer there is another junction; bear left, continuing uphill. Continue climbing until you reach the summit of Cerro Tito, elevation 1,124 meters. From here you are afforded a view of the forested Jabonal river valley, and of the denuded hillside surrounding the reserve.

From here, the trail travels through patchy forest for about 4 kilometers before passing out of the refuge. The trail continues another 10.5 kilometers back to Miramar, but it's an open, hot hike. It would be a better route to mountain bike than walk, due to the long distance and relatively uninteresting countryside.

CAÑO NEGRO WILDLIFE REFUGE

Size: 9,969 hectares
Distance from San José: 291 kilometers
Camping: Permitted
Trails: Limited
Map: 1:50,000 Caño Negro
Dry season: January through April; March and April driest
Transportation: Bus from San José departs for Los Chiles at 5:30 A.M. and 3:30 P.M. from Calle 16, Avenidas 1/3; returns same times.

Caño Negro is gaining popularity with nature-oriented tourists. What draws them here are birds, and what brings the birds is a seasonal, 800-hectare lake. The lake fills at the beginning of the rainy season with runoff from the Río Frio. By the end of the short dry season, the lake dries up, with only a small pond in the deepest portion of the southeast corner containing water. The best way to see the refuge is by dugout canoe, which can be rented, or you can bring your own boat for more extended trips.

The lake is fortuitously located right in the center of the main part of the central flyway, attracting a wide variety of bird species. Notable species include the **American anhinga** (*Anhinga anhinga*), which often can be seen on the top of a snag drying its wings in the sun. A relative of the anhinga is the **neotropical**

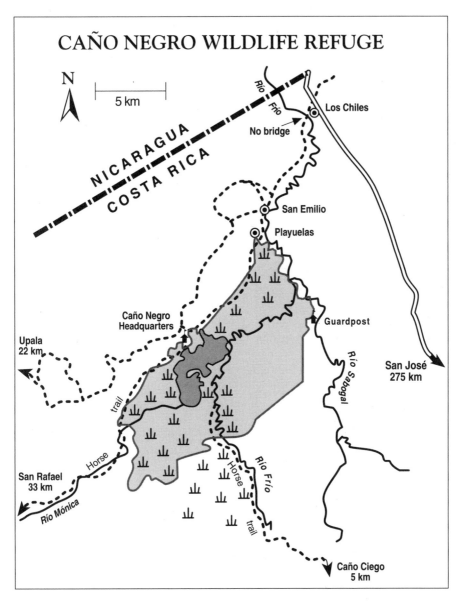

CAÑO NEGRO WILDLIFE REFUGE

N

5 km

Río Frío

NICARAGUA

COSTA RICA

Los Chiles

No bridge

San Emilio

Playuelas

Caño Negro
Headquarters

Guardpost

Upala
22 km

Río Sabogal

San José
275 km

trail

Horse

San Rafael
33 km

Río Mónica

Horse

Río Frío

Horse
trail

Caño Ciego
5 km

cormorant (*Phalocrocorax olivaceus*), the population here being the largest in Costa Rica. Other regularly seen water birds include the **roseate spoonbill** (*Ajaia ajaia*), the **northern jacana** (*Jacana spinosa*), and the **black-bellied tree duck** (*Dendrocygna autumnalis*). Hard-core bird listers take note: This is the only place where the **Nicaraguan grackle** (*Quiscalus nicaraguensis*) is found in Costa Rica.

Other interesting animals found here include a healthy population of the **spectacled caiman** (*Caiman crocodylus*), a relative of the alligator that is critically endangered in most of its range in the country. Their eye-shine reflecting the beam of a headlamp is a common, eerie sight from a canoe at night. Fishing is allowed in the refuge, and commonly encountered species are the **Caribbean snook** (*Centropomus undecimalis*) and the **gar** (*Atractosteus tropicus*), a species belonging to one of the first groups of bony fish to evolve. There used to be a population of **bull sharks** (*Carcharhinus leucas*) that migrated from the ocean up the San Juan River during the wet season. These large relatives of the great white shark have been badly overfished, and it is not known whether or not they still come here.

The vegetation surrounding the lake consists primarily of herbaceous plants with *Juncus sp.* and several species of grasses predominating. When the lake dries up, **gamalote grass** (*Paspalum fasciculatum*) covers the bottom. Small areas of forest within the refuge and the little that remain in the area outside it consist of flooded or seasonally inundated patches of **copaiba** (*Copaifera aromatica*) and **manni** (*Symphonia globulifera*). Palm groves grow in several places, consisting of **holillo** (*Raphia taedigera*), **corozo palm** (*Elaeis oleifera*), and **royal palm** (*Scheelia rostrata*).

LOCATION AND ACCESS

The refuge is located 165 kilometers north of San José, southeast of the town of Los Chiles near the Nicaraguan border. There are several ways of getting to the refuge headquarters in the small village of Caño Negro. The easiest way is to go by boat from Los Chiles, where boatmen on the Río Frio are available to take you by covered dugout on the five-hour trip to the reserve. Driving to the refuge is for the adventurous, requires a four-wheel drive, and may be completely impassable during the rainy season. The best road is the one from Upala, which heads southeast toward San Rafael. In 11 kilometers you will come to the tiny community of Colonia Puntarenas, where there is a signed turnoff for Caño Negro. From this point, it is 26 hard kilometers to the village. If you get stuck in the mud or break down, you are likely to have a long walk before you find anybody to help you.

VISITOR FACILITIES

You can arrange to stay in one of the outbuildings at the refuge headquarters, but space is limited, so call in advance. Unfortunately, there is no way of talking to the refuge directly; you have to call the Wildlife Directorate radio dispatcher (233-8112 or 222-9533). The safest thing is to bring a tent. You can also arrange to eat at the headquarters, as well as rent a canoe or hire a guide if you want. The rangers at the refuge don't see a lot of visitors, and are helpful and interested in telling you about their efforts to involve local people in the management of the refuge. Multiple-use is being studied, including the development of a sustainable fishery.

TRAILS

Most of the travel through the refuge is by boat. During the dry season, it is possible to do some walking around the lakebed. There is the possibility of trails being developed in the near future, so ask at the refuge headquarters.

DIRIÁ NATIONAL PARK

Size: 3,300 hectares
Distance from San José: 237 kilometers
Camping Permitted: No
Trails: Yes, but very poor condition
Map: 1:50,000 Santa Cruz
Dry season: December through May
Transportation: Four-wheel-drive taxi can be taken from Santa Cruz.

Diriá National Park may be one of the least visited of all of Costa Rica's protected areas. The park has yet to be consolidated into a cohesive single unit, and consists of two sections with several small farms scattered inside its boundaries. Vegetation in the park is classified as tropical premontane moist forests, interspersed with dry tropical forest patches. The park provides habitat for wildlife, which is becoming increasingly rare in the area, including **black guans**. The park's real claim to fame is its diverse variety of **orchids**, many of which have yet to be identified. Unfortunately, orchid poaching remains a serious problem. One of the nicest features of the park is a series of swimming holes along the Enmedio River.

LOCATION AND ACCESS

The park's station is located 14 kilometers south of Santa Cruz. Due to the park's remote character, the vagaries of local land ownership, the frequency of wildfires during the dry season, and extremely poor road conditions, it is necessary to arrange for transportation through the regional park office in Santa Cruz.

The regional office is located 200 meters to the south of the church in Santa Cruz. There is no telephone at the regional office or at the station itself, but you may be able to make advance arrangements via radio from the main park office in San José.

VISITOR FACILITIES

A rustic park station has been constructed utilizing an old farmhouse near the Enmedio River. It can accommodate 30 people at a time. This facility is primarily used by Costa Rican student groups. It may be possible to arrange for meals through the regional office. **Mango** and **lime trees** growing near the station add a nice touch. The water from the well is potable. The park has only one guard, who lives near the station.

TRAILS

The park has two main trails leading from the station that were under development in 1998. Once completed, they each will be approximately 4 kilometers in length. One follows the Enmedio River along a route that is reputed to be quite muddy and flooded in places in the rainy months and leads to a waterfall. The other will climb 1,000 meters steeply up a ridge to an example of orchid-rich tropical moist forest.

6
SOUTHERN PACIFIC REGION

Carara Biological Reserve
Manuel Antonio National Park
Ballena National Park
Mangrove Forest Reserve
Golfito Wildlife Refuge
Esquinas National Park
Corcovado National Park
Isla del Caño Biological Reserve
Isla del Cocos National Park

The widely dispersed parks located in this region protect the last intact lowland tropical forests on the Pacific side of Central America north of Panama, and a good cross section of the region's marine biodiversity. Here are the justifiably famous forests and wilderness coast of Corcovado, accessible by a well laid-out trail system that affords the visitor opportunities for extended tropical wilderness travel. The southern Pacific region also contains the small gems of Carara and Manuel Antonio, two of the smallest parks in the country but a delight to the tropical naturalist. Marine parks such as Isla del Caño and Ballena offer the visitor good diving and snorkeling opportunities. Costa Rica's most isolated park, Isla del Cocos, is also included in this region. The same isolation that makes it so difficult to reach also makes it a showcase for the process of evolution, giving it the nickname "Costa Rica's Galapagos."

CARARA BIOLOGICAL RESERVE
Size: 4,700 hectares
Distance from San José: 110 kilometers
Camping: Permitted
Trails: Yes
Map: 1:50,000 Tárcoles
Dry season: November through April
Transportation: Express bus from San José to Jacó departs at 7:15 A.M. and 3:30 P.M. from Calle 16, Avenidas 1/3; returns at 5:00 A.M. and 3:00 P.M.; Transportes Morales (322-1829).

This reserve is a must for anyone interested in tropical biology. Its high species diversity and ease of access make it a worthwhile day trip from San José,

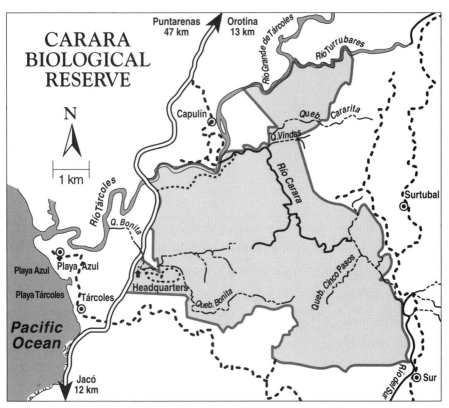

or on the way to parks farther south. Carara's diversity is a result of its situation in an "ecotone" or melding area between the dry forests to the north and the wet forests to the south. Added to this is the wide variety of soils in the reserve and, despite its relatively small size, the range of precipitation between different altitudes. The highlands in the interior receive an annual average of 3,200 millimeters of rain, while the more lowland areas receive around 2,000 millimeters. Carara is extremely important as a biological reservoir, which is amply evidenced by the denuded, eroded hillsides that surround it on all sides. Many threatened and endangered species live and breed here, including **American crocodiles** (*Crocodylus acutus*), **scarlet macaws** (*Ara macao*), and the **purpleheart tree** (*Peltogyne purpurea*).

The word *carara* is an indigenous term, reputedly meaning "river of crocodiles." The area where the reserve is located was occupied by an indigenous culture that is thought to have been allied with groups located in the Central Valley from 300 B.C. to 1500 A.D. Extensive tomb sites have been excavated here, and the burial places of people of high status are remarkably complex. They contain all that the occupants would need for a long journey, including wives, slaves, armaments, and large vessels of food.

Scarlet macaw mooching for treats

Carara was home to one of Central America's great indigenous heroes, the chieftain Garabito. Just before and during the Spanish conquests, he controlled a large territory that extended from Carara to the northern Gulf of Nicoya, the Central Valley, and the northern plains. Garabito's resistance to Spanish conquest is the stuff of legend. Around 1560, the Guatemalan High Court sent the brutal conquistadors Juan Vasquez de Coronado and Juan de Covallón to put a stop to Garabito's armed resistance. Garabito was apparently a brilliant tactician, and this, combined with his intimate knowledge of the landscape, allowed him to escape capture time and again. Once, the conquistadors did succeed in imprisoning his wife, Biriteka. Garabito asked one of his men to pose as the chieftain and allow himself to be captured. Knowing that the exhausted conquistadors would be busy celebrating the end of their task, he stole into their camp and rescued his wife. What happened to the imposter was not recorded.

Ultimately the indigenous population was extirpated through more indirect means: disease and massive settlement by Latino farmers. Eventually, Carara was included in the 18,000-hectare El Coyolar ranch, which was sold to an absentee North American landowner. In 1977, during the administration of a land-reform-minded president, the ranch was expropriated for a *campesino* resettlement scheme. Luckily, someone in the Institute of Lands and Settlements saw the tremendous conservation value of at least a portion of the forest, and arranged for the establishment of the reserve. It is fortunate that this biological treasure chest did not go the way of the rest of the area, a prime example of the unsuitability of many tropical soil types to intensive agriculture.

LOCATION AND ACCESS

The reserve is located 126 kilometers from San José, near where the Río Tárcoles empties into the Pacific Ocean—southeast of Puntarenas. The easiest route to get there is to take the main road to Puntarenas, exiting at Barranca for the road south to Puerto Caldera. From here, follow the signs for Jacó, and you'll have no problem. There are buses from San José to Jacó beach, south of the reserve, and you can ask the driver to let you off at Carara Biological Reserve headquarters. After passing over the Río Grande de Tárcoles bridge, the headquarters of the reserve is about 3 kilometers on your left. Stop in for your permit, and sign the visitors' register.

VISITOR FACILITIES

At the headquarters building, have a look at the reserve's small collection of preserved specimens, including several of snake species found here. The reserve staff are interested in talking with visitors about the problems of managing an ecological "island," along with other local environmental issues. It is possible to camp near the headquarters building, but it's pretty soggy during the rainy season and the mosquitoes can be bad. There are bathrooms and showers here. The closest hotels are in Jacó, 15 kilometers south.

TRAILS

Headquarters Loop Trail
Distance: 3 kilometers
Hiking time: 2 hours
Elevation gain: 30 meters
Map: 1:50,000 Tárcoles

This trail takes you through some magnificent primary forest. There are several huge emergent trees of a number of species, including **silk cotton** or **kapok** (*Ceiba pentandra*) and **espavel** (*Anacardium excelsum*). Telling the different

On the Headquarters Loop Trail, Carara Biological Reserve

species of trees apart can be difficult, particularly when the crown is 50 meters or more above your head! The bark of many tree species typical of the wet tropics is smooth (and thus useless for identification purposes) to dissuade vines and lianas, which might rob the tree of light or nutrients, from gaining a foothold. In addition, many tree leaves look superficially similar, having characteristic "drip tips" that keep water from building up on them, which would encourage the growth of fungus and other unwanted guests. The easiest way to identify trees is by fallen fruit and seedpods.

Kapok seeds are windborne, and the fluff in the seedpods was commonly used as a filling for flotation devices and sleeping bags during World War II. The smooth, oval-shaped pods are often found on the ground at the base of the tree. Kapok is also a good example of a "buttressed" tree. The buttresses are thought to support the massive trunk in damp soils, and some researchers claim that they are heavier on the side of the tree opposite the prevailing winds. Look for several large kapoks during the first kilometer of the trail.

The trail, marked by a sign, begins very close to the headquarters building. In about 0.75 kilometer you cross an intermittent streambed. During the dry season, many of the reserve's reptile species congregate here, including the notorious *terciopelo* or **fer de lance** (*Bothrops asper*). Remember that they are an interesting and ecologically important element of the tropical forests here, and if you are lucky enough to see one, don't molest it, just give it a very wide berth.

Now that you are anxiously looking down at your feet, you will probably encounter another interesting denizen of the forest here, the **black and green poison dart frog** (*Dendrobates auratus*). The trail winds around to the Quebrada Bonita, a tributary of the Tárcoles, and follows it for 0.5 kilometer. Notice how clear the water is here, where it comes out of undisturbed forest, as compared to the Tárcoles, which is choked with topsoil that has eroded off the deforested hills. Along the trail is a huge emergent tree that has fallen; this is the eventual fate of every large tree in the forest. The trail moves away from the river and loops back to the headquarters building.

Tárcoles River Trail

Distance: 4.5 kilometers
Hiking time: 3 hours
Elevation gain: 100 meters
Map: 1:50,000 Tárcoles

This trail follows an old road through a mixture of primary forest and secondary growth past marshes and viewpoints on the Río Grande de Tárcoles. Birding is excellent, particularly during the early morning and evening hours when the birds are moving to and from nesting and feeding areas. Check in at the headquarters to pay your entrance fee and sign in before walking the trail.

To get to the trail, head north on the main road back toward the Tárcoles river bridge. In 2 kilometers you should see a gated dirt road with a sign for the reserve stating that you need permission to enter. Park here and walk around the gate. On your left is an area of previously cutover pasture that is returning to forest. There are a couple of old dead trees that serve as roosting and possible nesting sites for **scarlet macaws**. If you are here during the evening, listen for their hoarse calls as they return from their feeding sites in the higher elevations and in nearby mangrove swamps. **Trogons** of several species and **spectacled owls** are also often seen here. The second-growth plants that have invaded the old pasture are host to a tremendous variety of insects, including at least two species of iridescent blue **morpho butterflies**.

In a little more than 1 kilometer you see a pond off to your left that was created by an enclosed meander or "oxbow" of the river. It is covered with **water hyacinth** (*Eichornia crassipes*), a plant in possession of a floating root system that provides ample cover for a tremendous variety of aquatic life. Shortly after the pond the trail comes to an open area on the riverbank, and **roseate spoonbills** and **crocodiles** are often seen on the sandbars in the river. The **American crocodile** is an endangered species in Costa Rica, and their presence here attests to Carara's great importance as a biological reserve. If you don't see them here, don't be disappointed; there are usually several on the sandbars and riverbanks near the Tárcoles River bridge that you came over from the north.

Crocodiles on the Tárcoles River, Carara Biological Reserve

The trail climbs up a hill, affording more views of the river, and then descends to a crossing of the Río Carara, at about 3.5 kilometers from the beginning of the trail. The river is too deep and swift during the rainy season to traverse by foot. The trail continues for another kilometer on the other side of the river before ending, but it travels through uninteresting territory that has been cut over. From the end of the trail, you have to go back the way you came, but you're certain to see something you missed on the way in.

MANUEL ANTONIO NATIONAL PARK

Size: 682 hectares
Distance from San José: 132 kilometers
Camping: Not permitted
Trails: Yes
Map: 1:200,000 Quepos
Dry season: December to March
Transportation: Express bus from San José to Quepos departs daily at 6:00 A.M., 12:00 P.M., and 5:00 P.M. from Calle 16, Avenidas 1/3, Coca Cola bus station; returns daily at 6:00 A.M., 12:00 P.M., and 5:00 P.M. Indirect bus from San José to Quepos departs daily at 7:00 A.M., 10:00 A.M., 2:00 P.M., and 4:00 P.M.; returns daily at 7:00 A.M., 10:00 A.M., 2:00 P.M., and 4:00 P.M.; call Transportes Morales (223-5567). Call the ICT at 222-1090 for the latest flight schedules.

Manuel Antonio National Park is one of Costa Rica's best known and most often visited parks, despite the fact that it's also the smallest. The park is an island of verdant wildness in a rapidly developing area. While visiting this little jewel of a place, with its intact wet tropical forest and abundant wildlife, you might consider how close the park came to being just another bunch of noisy restaurants and *cabinas*. The effects of the kind of development that the park was saved from can be seen in Quepos and its environs, where uninformed or ecologically disinterested developers have played havoc with the environment.

It was created in 1972, at a time when the area was poised for massive tourist development, funded primarily by foreign interests. The land constituting the park had gone through several foreign owners, all of whom managed to alienate and antagonize local people by blocking access to the area, even to the point of obstructing one of the main transportation routes to Quepos that passed close to the property. Things got increasingly ugly, to the extent that when the last private owner, a Frenchman, got wind of a proposed forced buy-out scheme by the government, he began to tear down trees, brought in large quantities of construction materials, and may have been responsible for dumping an unknown quantity of herbicide into the mangrove swamp, killing a small portion of it. Ostensibly, the idea was to render the area uninteresting as a protected area. Of course, these actions only served to speed up the expropriation process. Eventually it was discovered that the developer was planning to build a massive tourist

Above: Lower montane rain forest, commonly referred to as cloud forest

Right: The heliconia flower, with its water-filled bracts, is found in Costa Rica's rain forests.

Above: The red-eyed tree frog, peering out from bromeliad, inhabits the neotropical zones of Costa Rica.

Left: The Jesus Christ lizard, or basilisk, found in the lowlands, is so-called for its ability to run on the surface of the water.

Opposite, top: Beach and a small island of rain forest vegetation at Manuel Antonio National Park

Opposite, bottom: A squirrel monkey with a three-month-old youngster on its back leaps from a branch eighty feet above ground.

Above: Juvenile two-toed sloths in the Monteverde Preserve

Left: The Guaria Morada orchid, Costa Rica's national flower

Opposite: A blue-crowned motmot

Left: A leaf-cutter ant at work in La Selva biological station

Below: An arribada of olive ridley sea turtles emerges from the Pacific Ocean at dusk to lay eggs on Nancite Beach, Santa Rosa National Park.

Opposite, top: Golden toads, a rare and endangered species known only to Costa Rica

Opposite, center: The Leptophis nebulosis, a tree snake from the Columbridae family, feeds on frogs and lizards.

Opposite, bottom: A Ctenuchid moth on a flowering Senecio

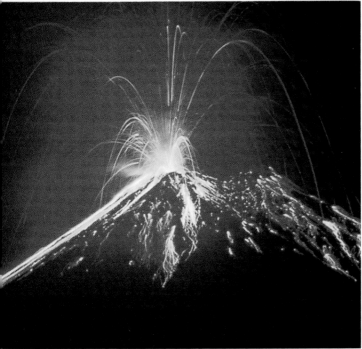

Above: The devastation of clearcutting, tropical rain forest adjacent to La Selva biological field station

Left: The eruption of Arenal volcano in 1991

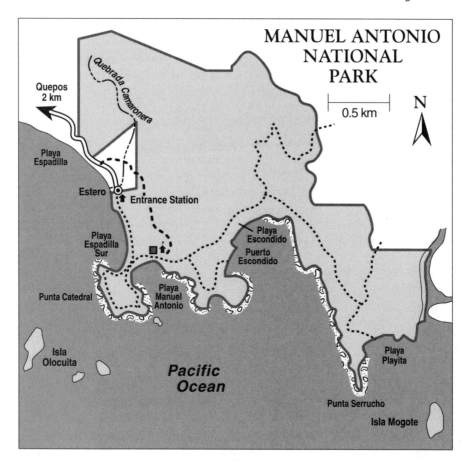

facility on the site, including a wharf, hotels, and at least twenty *cabinas*.

Today, the park protects a small but beautiful remnant of the tropical forest that once covered the region, as well as some sandy beaches and rocky headlands supporting a wide variety of marine life. Considering that this is the smallest national park in the system, Manuel Antonio has a remarkably long list of species inhabiting it: 353 species of birds, including **brown pelicans, brown boobies, tyrant hawk-eagles, gray-headed chachalacas, Solater's ant bird,** and **Baird's trogon.**

Mammal species are also quite diverse here. Ninety-nine species have been recorded for the park, fifty-nine of which are **bats.** Commonly seen are **three-toed anteaters, coatimundis,** and **two-toed sloths.** Less commonly seen but present are **ocelots, tyras** (a large predatory tree dweller related to weasels), and **gray foxes.** Three of Costa Rica's four species of monkeys occur here. **Squirrel monkeys** travel in troops of about thirty individuals, following patterns of movement dictated by time of day and seasonal food availability. **Howler monkeys** can be seen foraging for leaves and fruit in the canopy, and the males can be heard growling out their territorial calls. **White-faced monkeys,** which are direct competitors for food resources with squirrel monkeys during the dry season, are also common and easily seen as they move through the trees.

Commonly seen reptiles include **green iguanas** and **ctenosaurs**. Ctenosaurs, called *garrobo* in Spanish, look superficially similar to iguanas, but are gray to tan in color, and are smaller. **Snakes** of many species are found here, including a few venomous ones, so watch your step on the trails. **Sea turtles** nest on the beaches here, but in much smaller numbers than farther north.

Plant diversity is high here, too; preliminary studies show that at least 138 species of trees inhabit the park, despite its small size.

Safety note: Please be careful of riptides when swimming in the ocean here. Espadilla Beach (sometimes known as Beach 1), which abuts the park's western boundary, is extremely dangerous for swimming and many people drown here every year. Playa Espadilla Sur (Beach 2) and Manuel Antonio (Beach 3) are much safer, with Manuel Antonio having almost no surf or riptide danger at all. Don Melton, a longtime Quepos resident, has been pressing for a beach education program that would, among other things, put up signs warning visitors about the riptide and what to do if caught in one. Surprisingly, many Quepos businesspeople are in opposition to this, as they think that the warnings would scare off tourists. If you get caught in a riptide, which will feel like the water is strongly pulling you out to sea, try to stay calm. Swim across the tide parallel to the shore until you feel the current release you, then you can swim for shore. Do not fight the current; this will only lead to exhaustion. The vast majority of people who drown in riptides would not have died if they'd followed the procedure above.

LOCATION AND ACCESS

The park lies on the Pacific coast 7 kilometers south of the town of Quepos, which is between Damas and Matapalos. In Quepos, stock up on any food or drinks that you want to bring with you. There is regular bus service to Quepos from San José, and SANSA has flights leaving every day but Sunday. There is only one road that heads south out of Quepos, so it's impossible to get lost. There is an estuary at the end of the road where you can park your car or be dropped off by a taxi. You then have to cross the estuary. The water depth in the river ranges from ankle deep to 1.5 meters, so dress to get wet!

VISITOR FACILITIES

The park service has implemented a camping ban because of concerns about damage to the beach area and increases in the theft of items left in tents. The nearest hotels are in Quepos, but be careful when staying in very low-budget accommodations. Unfortunately, Quepos has a theft problem. Playa Dominical and Playa Hermosa to the south have a variety of accommodations and are convenient to Ballena National Park and Golfito Wildlife Refuge.

TRAILS

Punta Catedral, Manuel Antonio Beach, Escondido Beach, Punta Serrucho, and Playa Playita Trails
Distance: 7 kilometers
Hiking time: 3 hours
Elevation gain: 50 meters
Map: 1:200,000 Quepos

After crossing the estuary of the Quebrada Camaronera and heading south along the beach, you come to the entrance station. A bit later, you pass some restrooms. Near the second set of restrooms is a trail junction. One fork is the 1.5-kilometer side trail for Punta Catedral or Cathedral Point, which takes less than one hour to circle, but is covered with some of the oldest forest in the park. One of the more interesting tree species found here is the **cow tree** (*Brosimum utile*), recognizable by its large size and distinctive reddish gray bark (see Chapter 2, The Tropical Forest).

It's a short walk off the trail from the trail junction to Manuel Antonio Beach, named after a Spaniard from the early conquest years who was killed in a skirmish with the Quepos and buried here. For many years there was a small bronze plaque marking his grave, but the site has been lost. Also of historical interest is an ancient turtle trap constructed by the Quepo people. Located on the far right near where the beach ends, it's difficult to see except at very low tides after the full moon. The trap consists of rocks piled in such a way that turtles could swim over them at high tide and climb up on the beach to lay their eggs, but were unable to escape when the tide receded.

You will probably notice a sign warning visitors not to eat the fruit of the **manzanillo tree** (*Hippomane mancinella*). This tree grows in the sand of the beach and is easily recognizable by its brilliant evergreen leaves and by its fruit, which looks like a large yellow crab apple. The entire plant produces a white sap that is extremely poisonous if ingested, and can also cause inflammation and blisters on the skin. The smoke created by burning the plant is also dangerous. So many people have died from eating the tempting fruit of this plant that it is called "the tree of death" in Puerto Rico and Brazil. Local people say that victims of manzanillo poisoning are given tremendous quantities of bitter lemon juice, which would indicate that the toxins involved are strong alkaloids.

Another tree seen near the beach is the **copey** (*Copey clusia*), recognizable by its round, shiny leaves and spidery multiple trunks. This tree begins its life in a way similar to strangler figs: its seeds are dropped by birds in the crotches of trees that hold a little organic matter, where they germinate. They then grow on and around the host tree, eventually shading it out. The **beach almond** (*Terminalia catappa*) also grows in this area. This tree is native to the East Indies and Oceania, but has been transported all over the world because of its willingness to grow on barren sand and for its nuts, which are delicious but take a lot of work to open.

All of the rocky coastal areas of the park contain tide pools that provide close-up views of an amazing variety of sealife. Particularly nice pools are located on the western end of Manuel Antonio Beach. One survey counted seventeen species of **algae**, ten species of **sponges**, nineteen species of **coral**, twenty-four species of **crustaceans**, and seventy-eight species of **fish** living in them. You can poke around or snorkel in the tide pools, but please be careful if you venture out on the points where you are vulnerable to the waves.

Back at the junction with the Punta Catedral Trail, the other fork leads slightly inland along the beach, past the administrative buildings and the exhibition hall, and then passes up and over a headland. It then meets up with the side trail that descends to Escondido Beach. Past Escondido Beach, the trail travels to a junction with a trail that is growing over, leading off to your left. It goes to the park boundary. The right fork, which is also in poor shape, leads up and along the headland over Punta Serrucho, and down to Playa Playita, also known as Playita de Boca de Naranjo.

BALLENA NATIONAL PARK

Size: Undetermined
Distance from San José: 192 kilometers
Camping: Permitted on the beach only
Trails: None
Maps: 1:200,000 Quepos; 1:200,000 Talamanca
Dry season: January through March
Transportation: To Quepos, see Manuel Antonio National Park. From Quepos to Ballena National Park, no public transportation available.

This is one of Costa Rica's newest national parks. It was created in an attempt to conserve some of the marine resources of the southern Pacific region, which are under siege from overfishing and unchecked tourist development. This is a scuba diver's, snorkeler's, and beachcomber's park. It includes open ocean, islands, and beach up to the high-tide mark. Included in this area are Isla Ballena and Rocas las Tres Hermanas, two of Costa Rica's more interesting deep-water dive sites. Several rocky points offer snorkeling and tide-pooling possibilities. Several nice isolated beaches are situated in the park, including Playa Ballena and Playa de Arco.

The park gets its name from the Spanish word for whale, *ballena*. Several species of whales have been reported in or near the park, including **melon-headed whales** (*Peponocephala electra*), **sperm whales** (*Physeter catodon*), and **common, striped,** and **spinner dolphins.** More species are sure to be recorded here as more complete studies are carried out. None of these species have regular migration patterns as far as is known, so seeing them is a chance occurrence.

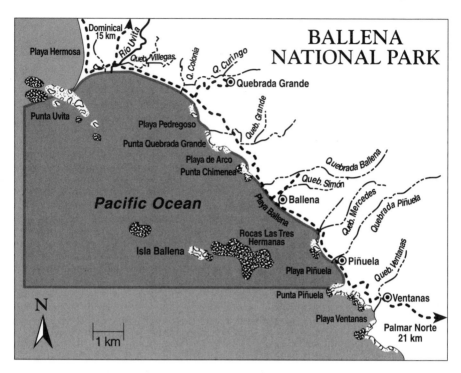

LOCATION AND ACCESS

Ballena National Park is bordered on the south by Punta Piñuela, extends out to sea for 9 kilometers, and heads north for 6 kilometers before coming back to shore at Punta Uvita on the southern end of Playa Hermosa. As of 1998, the only way to get to the park from the north was by four-wheel-drive vehicle. The road is rough, and there is a sizeable creek, the Río Uvita, that has no bridge across it. From the south, there are no major river crossings except right after a heavy rain, but the dirt road is rough from the village of Ventanas to the Río Uvita. It would be a nice area to tour by mountain bike.

VISITOR FACILITIES

Ballena doesn't even have a ranger station, much less any developed visitor facilities. Remember that the park ends at the high-tide line, and beyond that is private property. Consequently, there are no camping facilities per se. The closest hotels to the north end of the park are at Playa Hermosa, and to the south at Golfito, 60 kilometers distant. Some very basic supplies and water can be obtained in the towns of Piñuela and Quebrada Grande, but it is safer to bring food with you.

TRAILS

There are no trails in this park.

MANGROVE FOREST RESERVE

Size: 22,000 hectares
Distance from San José: 277 or 190 kilometers, depending on route
Camping: Permitted
Trails: Yes, but most travel within the area is via unmarked waterways
Maps: 1:200,000 Quepos; 1:200,000 Golfito; 1:50,000 Sierpe, Coronado, Terraba, and Changuena
Dry season: January through March
Transportation: Bus or plane to Palmar Norte, then bus or taxi to Sierpe. From Sierpe you need to arrange transport. See location and access below for details.

The Mangrove Forest Reserve, located at the mouth of the Terraba and Sierpe Rivers, contains Costa Rica's largest remaining mangrove forest. Despite the fact that mangrove swamps are essential spawning grounds for commercially valuable fish and shellfish, and are an important habitat for an amazing array of wildlife, they've been overharvested for dock timbers and charcoal and have been cut down to make way for shipping facilities all over the country. In fact, mangrove forests all over the tropics are in imminent danger of destruction. This reserve provides the adventurous traveler with opportunities to explore an extraordinary example of this fascinating and imperiled plant community.

Because of their dubious protective status, forest reserves are generally not described in this book. But because of its unsuitability for large-scale commercial timber exploitation (too soggy) and its recognized importance to the Costa Rican clam and shrimp industries, the Mangrove Forest Reserve is elevated to a conservation status at least slightly above the rest. The small, isolated communities that exist inside it (600 people total) are impoverished and undeveloped, making a living by producing charcoal (ostensibly regulated by the Forestry Directorate) and gathering clams and fish.

Mangrove forests are one of the most fascinating yet underappreciated ecosystems in Costa Rica. Most visitors see the edges of the reserve fleetingly as they power down the Río Sierpe on their way to the tourist lodges on the Osa Peninsula. This is a pity, as the mangrove forests, with their intense level of biological activity and their unique beauty, have immense potential appeal for tourists and biologists alike.

Mangrove Forest Reserve contains several unique species of plants and animals, including the **mangrove hummingbird** (which is found only in mangrove forests on the Pacific side of Costa Rica and Panama), and provides breeding and feeding grounds for other rare birds such as **mangrove vireos**, several species of **ibises, roseate spoonbills, herons**, and many others. The estuaries, channels, and other waterways are filled with an incredible variety of aquatic life, including huge **manta rays** which come to feed in the river, and which can be heard at night leaping from the water with a dramatic splash in an

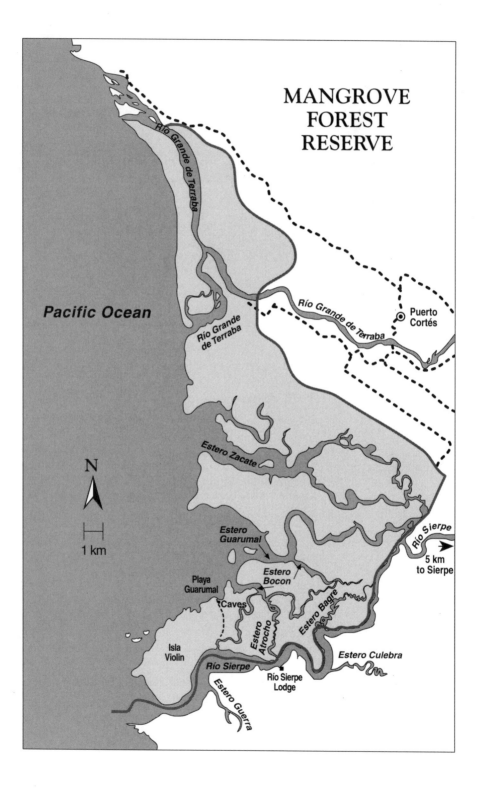

MANGROVE
FOREST
RESERVE

Pacific Ocean

Río Grande de Terraba

Río Grande de Terraba

Río Grande de Terraba

Puerto
Cortés

Estero Zacate

N

1 km

Estero
Guarumal

Estero
Bocon

Río Sierpe

5 km
to Sierpe

Playa
Guarumal

Caves

Estero
Atrocho

Estero Bagre

Isla
Violin

Río Sierpe

Río Sierpe
Lodge

Estero Culebra

Estero Guerra

The preferred form of transport, Mangrove Forest Reserve

attempt to rid themselves of skin parasites. **Crocodiles** and **caimans** are also found here, and can be viewed by traveling quietly in a canoe or kayak, or at night with the aid of strong light.

Besides mangrove forests, the reserve also encompasses some beautiful and nearly deserted beaches near the river mouths, and patches of wet tropical forest, most of which is second growth, but is nonetheless interesting. One note that should be of interest to birders: A **harpy eagle** was sighted several times along the Río Sierpe in 1994. The huge bird of prey actually came down to harass the chickens in the front yard of a local guide, Jorge Mora. Mr. Mora is a lay minister who has spent his whole life on the river, so there's little reason to doubt the veracity of his sighting. For more information about the ecology of the mangroves, see Chapter 2, The Tropical Forest.

LOCATION AND ACCESS

The reserve is spread out between the mouth of the Río Sierpe in the southeastern part of the country, just north of the Osa Peninsula, and the small village of Coronado in the north. The hot, sleepy town of Sierpe is the customary center of operations for trips in and out of the reserve. Sierpe has hotels, modest food stores, boats for hire to get downriver, and other services. Sierpe is reached via the town of Palmar Norte, located on Highway 18, by a 14-kilometer, rough, rocky road. Buses leave from San José to Palmar Norte seven days a week. Call the Tracopa Bus Company at 786-6511 for the latest schedule. SANSA has daily flights to Palmar Sur (right across the Terraba River from Palmar Norte) seven days a week. Call 786-6353 for the latest schedule. From Palmar Norte, buses travel down the bumpy road to Sierpe at least three times a day, leaving from in front of the Supermercado

Terraba. The latest schedule was 5:45 A.M., 9 A.M., 12 P.M., and 4:45 P.M., but these times are subject to change. You can also get a taxi from Palmar Norte to Sierpe. From Sierpe, unless you are paddling your own boats, you need to make advance arrangements with Mike Stiles of Río Sierpe Lodge, or another lodge owner, to get downriver.

VISITOR FACILITIES

There are no government-run facilities of any sort in the reserve. The best contact in the area is Jorge Mora, who can be reached through Mike Stiles. Río Sierpe Lodge is located about 23 river kilometers downstream from Sierpe, and is a convenient although somewhat rustic base of operations for travel into the reserve and down onto the northern Osa Peninsula. Jorge Mora, an extremely pleasant, knowledgeable guide, can take you through the creeks and estuaries in his small boat. Independent, non-motorized water travel is possible, but is complicated by the intensely tidal nature of the reserve's waterways. Kayakers should be strong paddlers skilled in the use of tide charts and topographical maps. Mike Stiles can arrange for rental kayak equipment. The message numbers for Sierpe Lodge are 284-5596 and (fax) 223-9945. Short trips also can be arranged through various tourist lodges in Sierpe, but if you want to really spend some time in the reserve you should make arrangements with Mike Stiles and Jorge Mora.

In preparation for kayak or hiking trips, remember that potable water is difficult to find here. This, along with the weather being hot all year, means that you're best advised to carry what you'll need. Another problem is that there is no ground firm enough in the mangrove forest to camp on, limiting your overnight stays to the dry edges of the reserve (some of which is private land) and to beaches on the ocean side. Biting insects are not a problem while traveling on the water, but if you plan to walk the one available trail or get out of your boat and into the mud of the mangrove forests, be prepared to fend off a few biting **flies, no-see-ums** (*purrujas*), and occasional **mosquitoes**. Mosquitoes (known locally as *zancudos*) are more of a problem on Isla Violín and dry land than in the mangroves. The brackish water in the creeks and estuaries is too saline and full of predators for mosquito larvae to last long.

TRAILS

Isla Violín Trail
> **Distance:** Approximately 4 kilometers round trip
> **Hiking time:** 2.5 hours
> **Elevation gain:** 260 meters
> **Map:** 1:50,000 Sierpe

This trail is the only walking route within the reserve. It travels through a mix of farmland, secondary forest, and patches of primary growth. The trail is

Natural arch, Isla del Violín, Mangrove Forest Reserve

rather difficult to find. It should also be noted that there is private land along the trail, and much of the ownership of Isla Violín is in dispute. Consequently, this route is best done with a local guide. The usual route to get to the north side of Isla Violín is to travel up the Estero Atrocho, which contains some magnificent mangrove forest, and out to the larger Estero Bocon. The trail is accessed by traveling almost to the mouth of the Estero Bocon and beaching your boat on the sand at the beginning of Playa Guarumal. You'll see a ramshackle house that may or may not be inhabited near where you should head inland. Before hiking the trail, you should have a look at the series of small caves and a natural arch that were created by the waves that pound the rocky headland at high tide. Make sure that you visit these during low tide, and don't enter the caves if there is seawater coming into them. The trail can be found by walking inland for about 200 meters until you come to an old banana plot; from here there is an obvious route uphill. The trail continues steadily uphill for a little over 0.75 kilometer and then descends to an overgrown promontory. At some point, this may be re-cleared to provide a view of the Río Sierpe. Return the way you came.

Water routes are potentially almost limitless, particularly if you are kayaking or if you hire a guide with a boat that is small enough to navigate the smaller creeks and estuaries. The forests in most of the reserve are pristine and beautiful. All of the waterways near the southern end of the Río Sierpe, including the Guerra, Bagre, Culebra, and Bocon Esteros, make for great day trips.

ESQUINAS NATIONAL PARK

Size: Approximately 5,000 hectares
Distance from San José: 298 kilometers
Camping: Not yet permitted
Trails: Yes
Map: 1:50,000 Golfito, Piedras Blancas, Golfo Dulce, Rincón
Dry season: January through March
Transportation: SANSA (233-0397) flies Monday through Saturday from San José to Golfito at 6 A.M. Travelair (232-7883) flies daily at 8:40 A.M. Buses leave San José from Calle 4, Avenida 18. Call the bus company, Empressa Alfaro, at 221-4214 or the ICT at 222-1090 for the latest schedules.

Esquinas National Park is one of Costa Rica's newest officially recognized protected areas. Besides protecting one of the last significant pieces of wet tropical forest on the Pacific side of the country, the park stands as an interesting example of cooperation between nonprofit citizens' organizations and governments in vastly different parts of the globe.

The Esquinas Forest in southern Costa Rica was declared a national park by presidential decree in 1991. This provided at least nominal protection to one of the last unprotected lowland tropical rain forests on the Pacific coast of Central America. However, since all land was in private hands and by law it could no longer be simply expropriated, Esquinas could only be cataloged as a "paper park" until it was bought and paid for by the government. The government honored logging permits issued before the declaration of the park, and deforestation continued for some time, inflicting considerable damage and jeopardizing the objectives of the decree.

Luckily, help was forthcoming from what might seem to be an unlikely source. Some time later in 1991, Michael Schnitzler, a well-known classical violinist from Vienna and part-time resident of Costa Rica, founded a nonprofit organization called Regenwald der Österreicher (Rain Forest of the Austrians) with the goal of raising funds to buy property in the Esquinas Forest. By 1997, more than 13,000 Austrian individuals had donated upwards of $1,000,000, enabling the purchase of over 25 square kilometers of rain forest. The purchased land was then turned over to the Costa Rican government for inclusion in the park. Today the park is a patchwork of land purchased by Regenwald der Österreicher and the Costa Rican government, along with a good deal of private holdings, some of whose owners hold valid logging permits. Some of the private land remaining within the idealized park boundaries is of high conservation value, and is in need of purchase. For more information on the park and how you can help, contact:

Michael Schnitzler
Regenwald der Österreicher
Sternwartestrasse 58
A-1180 Wien (Vienna) Austria
Fax and Telephone: (431) 470 4295

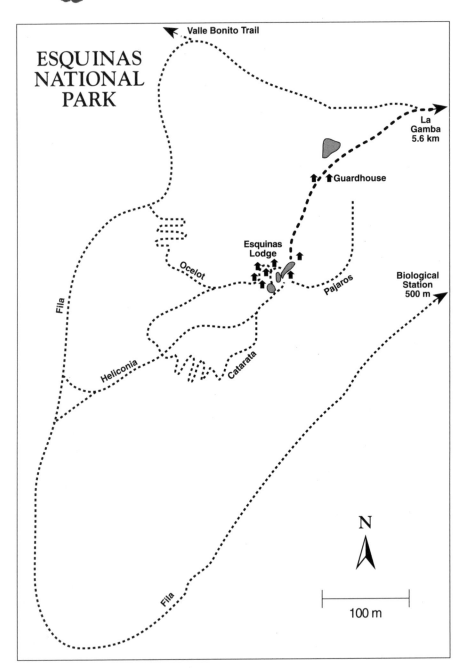

ESQUINAS
NATIONAL
PARK

Valle Bonito Trail

La
Gamba
5.6 km

Guardhouse

Esquinas
Lodge

Ocelot

Pajaros

Biological
Station
500 m

Fila

Heliconia

Catarata

Fila

N

100 m

Successive governments in Costa Rica since 1991 have shown little interest in solidifying protection of the park, largely leaving it for the Austrians to manage. Consequently, they need all the help they can get. Regenwald der Österreicher also runs a small, rustic biological research station located near the

Esquinas Lodge that is available to bona fide researchers doing field work in the area. Contact Regenwald der Österreicher for more information.

Biologically, the park has a number of interesting features. Much of the large and edible wildlife has been extirpated, but as the park is solidified and hunting brought under control, more of the forest's denizens should become common again. Some promising efforts are also underway to reintroduce native wildlife, including a project based at Playa San Josecito to reestablish **margays** and **ocelots**. The project manager, Sigi Wiesel, is happy to show visitors around. He can be contacted through Dolphin Quest at 775-1481.

LOCATION AND ACCESS

Esquinas is located northwest of Golfito, and roughly speaking is sandwiched between the Golfo Dulce and the InterAmerican Highway. There are two ways to access the park. The first is by land; the second is by water. All of the developed trails begin or end near the Esquinas Lodge located near the town of La Gamba. The lodge is reached by taking a fairly good road (passable to most two-wheel-drive vehicles all year) located on the west side of the InterAmerican Highway near the Kilometer 37 milepost, just south of the village of Briceno. From the InterAmerican, it's about 6 kilometers to the lodge. It is possible to have the bus drop you off at the turnoff and walk the rest of the way, but keep in mind that it is probably going to be a hot hike in the sun. Esquinas Lodge is run by Regenwald der Österreicher, and will be turned over to a Costa Rican/Austrian nonprofit organization called Progamba once the lodge starts to turn a profit. Money generated from the lodge will go back into protecting the park and to environmental education and development projects for the community of La Gamba. The park starts as soon as the manicured grounds of the hotel end. It is possible to hire a guide through the lodge, and the managers are a good source of information about trail conditions and the status of the park. Call 775-0515 or 775-0131 for the Golfito office, fax 775-0631, or try the cellular phone number, 382-5798, to reach the lodge directly.

Regenwald der Österreicher Research Station, Esquinas National Park

To reach the park from the coast, you need to either hire a boat in Golfito or make arrangements with one of several lodge owners to take you in their boats, which generally are reserved for their guests. A trail leading from the coast at Playa San Josecito to Esquinas Lodge may be finished by the time you arrive (see the Trails section to follow). Call Rainbow Lodge (U.S. number: 503-690-7735) or Dolphin Quest (Costa Rica number: 775-1481) for transportation options and support services for the area. The trip from Golfito to Playa San Josecito takes about 45 minutes.

VISITOR FACILITIES

Visitor facilities are confined to those provided by private lodges located on either side of the park.

TRAILS

Fila, Ocelot, Heliconia, Catarata, and Pajaros Trails

Distance: Variable depending on route
Hiking time: 1–5 hours
Elevation gain: 300 meters maximum
Map: 1:50,000 Piedras Blancas

The trail system that begins at Esquinas Lodge offers a tremendous variety of possible day hikes and, given that they are relatively short, all routes are described here. Remember to bring plenty of water before setting out as it is always hot, particularly when hiking uphill!

The Heliconia and Catarata Trails begin right behind the swimming pool. The Catarata Trail (1.5 kilometers, requiring about 1.5 hours hiking time) follows a small creek for the first 100 meters and offers a series of small waterfalls during the wet season. It then climbs steeply for another 200 meters before coming to a junction with the Heliconia Trail. After the junction it descends to another creek and past a couple of small waterfalls that flow seasonally before meeting the Ocelot Trail. The Ocelot Trail ascends steeply to a junction with the Fila Trail. An interpretive booklet (in German only) for this trail is sometimes available at the lodge. The Heliconia Trail passes through rather uninteresting second growth forest and scrub, but provides a quick descent back to the lodge from the ridge top. The Pajaros Trail leads through a section of flat, scrubby second growth, but can provide some productive birding, particularly in the morning and evening hours. The Fila Trail is about 2.7 kilometers long and takes most people at least four hours to complete—remember that you have to climb up to the top of the ridge. It is not well maintained, and the sections that pass through secondary forest can be quite open and hot. The trail affords some good views down into the forested valley that surrounds the lodge, but it is mostly closed in by the regenerating canopy.

Valle Bonito Trail

Distance: 5 kilometers
Hiking time: Approximately 8 hours one way
Elevation gain: 300 meters maximum
Map: 1:50,000 Piedras Blancas, Golfo Dulce

This trail is still in development, and consequently won't be described in great detail here. Its proposed route passes through land that is still in private hands, and there are active logging concessions within these private parcels. If it can be solidified, it will provide access from the network of trails around Esquinas Lodge to the coast at Playa San Josecito. Check with the staff at Esquinas Lodge or with one of the tourist lodges at Playa San Josecito as to the trail's progress and condition.

GOLFITO WILDLIFE REFUGE

Size: 1,309 hectares
Distance from San José: 342 kilometers
Camping: Permitted
Trails: Yes
Map: 1:50,000 Golfito
Dry season: January through March
Transportation: SANSA (233-0397) flies from San José to Golfito Monday through Saturday departing at 6 A.M. Travelair (232-7883) flies daily at 8:40 A.M. Buses leave San José from Calle 4, Avenida 18. Call the bus company, Empressa Alfaro, at 221-4214 or the ICT at 222-1090 for the latest schedules.

This refuge was created primarily to protect the watershed for the town of Golfito, which it surrounds on three sides. Due to its close proximity to town, the forest has been damaged in places by illegal activity, and large, edible wildlife species have suffered from poaching, but it's still worth visiting if you are in the area. Birding is good due to a road that gets you up on a ridge affording views above the thick canopy, and there are a few trails.

The refuge has several points of interest for the botanically minded. There are a number of rare species here that have been extirpated in the rest of the Golfo Dulce area and, in a few cases, in the rest of the country. One such species is a tree in the **avocado** (*Lauraceae*) family belonging to the genus *Carydaphnopsis*. This genus has only been recorded in the Golfito Wildlife Refuge and in the Peruvian Amazon, the rest of the genus being confined to southern Asia. Its presence here constitutes an example of how plate tectonics has isolated closely related species in different parts of the world. Another interesting plant found here is a species of **cycad** (*Zamia fairchildiana*). Cycads, which look like small, compact palm trees, are some of the oldest plants on earth. Members of this group are well represented in the fossil record and were flourishing at the beginning of the Cretaceous period when dinosaurs walked the earth.

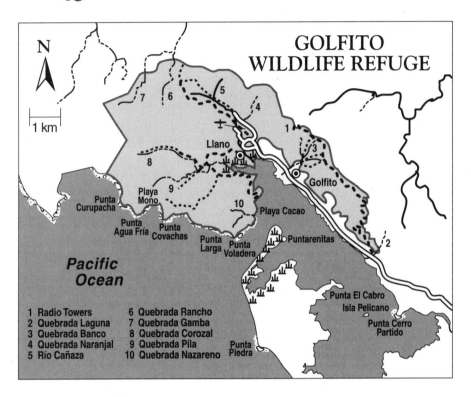

GOLFITO WILDLIFE REFUGE

Pacific Ocean

1 Radio Towers
2 Quebrada Laguna
3 Quebrada Banco
4 Quebrada Naranjal
5 Río Cañaza
6 Quebrada Rancho
7 Quebrada Gamba
8 Quebrada Corozal
9 Quebrada Pila
10 Quebrada Nazareno

LOCATION AND ACCESS

The refuge, as well as the town of Golfito, is located on the Golfito Peninsula in Golfo Dulce. The refuge surrounds the town of Golfito on three sides, with the fourth side fronting the ocean. This makes it one of the most accessible refuges in the system; trails are still unmarked, however. Once you arrive in the town of Golfito, getting to the park is just a matter of walking out of town in one of several directions.

VISITOR FACILITIES

The headquarters building is in town in the University of Costa Rica building. Camping is officially allowed, but due to the refuge's close proximity to town, you should pick your site with caution. Since you need to get permission to camp from the refuge administration, ask them what areas are considered safe. Otherwise, hotels in Golfito range from cheap pits to moderately priced rooms.

TRAILS

Radio Tower Trails

Distance: 8 kilometers without car, 1 kilometer with car
Hiking time: 5 hours without car, 3 hours with car
Elevation gain: 505 meters
Map: 1:50,000 Golfito

The drive or walk up the gravel road to the microwave tower station offers rewarding birding and affords views above the canopy. The road starts behind the first soccer field off the main road when you come into town. It ascends for 7 kilometers to the towers, where it's at least slightly cooler and windier than in town. **Toucans** are commonly seen here, as are mixed flocks of **tanagers** and many other species. Three trails, each about one kilometer long, lead off the gravel road and descend into town. The entrances are often overgrown and difficult to find. If you are interested in walking to the towers from town, have someone show you the entrance.

Playa Cacao Trails
Distance: 2 kilometers one way
Hiking time: 2 hours
Elevation gain: 240 meters
Map: 1:50,000 Golfito

There are also three trails off the road to Playa Cacao. The first two are reached by taking the right-hand fork in the road. This takes you to another fork. A right takes you to a 1-kilometer trail up the Quebrada Corozal; a left takes you to a shorter trail up the Quebrada Pila. Back at the first fork on the main road, continue about 0.5 kilometer farther for the longest trail, a worthwhile 2-kilometer (one way) hike with views of the Golfo Dulce from a high ridge top. Here again, the entrance is sometimes obscured, so it's best to ask directions. The hike is short, but hot.

CORCOVADO NATIONAL PARK
Size: 41,788 hectares
Distance from San José: 335 kilometers
Camping: Permitted
Trails: Yes
Maps: 1:200,000 Golfito, 1:50,000 Carate, 1:50,000 Rincón, 1:50,000 Golfo Dulce
Dry season: January through March
Transportation: SANSA (233-0397) flies from San José to Golfito Monday through Saturday departing at 6 A.M. Travelair (232-7883) flies daily at 8:40 A.M. Buses leave San José from Calle 4, Avenida 18. Call the bus company, Empressa Alfaro, at 221-4214 or the ICT at 222-1090 for the latest schedules.

Corcovado National Park is certainly one of the most interesting in the system. The tropical wet forests contained within its boundaries are widely considered to be the most species-rich in Central America. More than 500 species of trees are found here, including huge specimens of **silk cotton** or **ceiba** (*Ceiba pentandra*) and **espavel** (*Anacardium excelsum*) that reach nearly 70 meters in height. A

Two "Tarzan wannabes,"
Corcovado National Park

wide array of plant communities is found here, including **montane, swamp**, and **holillo forests; marshes; mangroves;** and **beach** communities. Some 6,000 species of insects of every imaginable shape and size have been identified, and this number is expected to rise above 10,000 species with further study. There are 367 species of birds, 140 of mammals, 117 of reptiles and amphibians, and 40 of freshwater fish. Species found here that are critically endangered or absent in the rest of the country include **jaguar, American crocodile, scarlet macaw, caiman,** and **Baird's tapir. Harpy eagles,** which are probably extinct as a permanent resident in the country, have been sighted on several occasions.

If Corcovado sounds like a tropical naturalist's paradise, it very nearly is. There are a few drawbacks that you should be aware of, however. One is the park's remoteness relative to others in the system. You need to walk for at least a full day to get to the headquarters at Sirena, or fly in from Golfito or Puerto Jimenez, which is expensive. It is also hot, with average temperatures being about 26 degrees Celsius, and humidity, even in the drier season, hovers near 100 percent. Trails in the rainy season become almost impassable because of the almost supernaturally slick clay that underlies most of them. The biting insects, chiggers, and ticks are bad, particularly during the rainy season, necessitating repellents and long clothing. But for the stalwart visitor who is prepared for a little privation, this ecological gem is well worth the trouble.

This park constitutes one of Costa Rica's greatest conservation success stories. The area's uniqueness was well known by the time the parks department was created in 1970, but the department lacked the funds to buy and manage such a large and remote tract of land. The issue of Corcovado's protection was pressed in 1975 when settlers, who had been arriving in large numbers to "squat" on the lands of a large North American/Japanese timber firm in what is now the park, threatened to consolidate their holdings by cutting trees down or "improving the land" as the law requires. The timber firm and the squatters

162

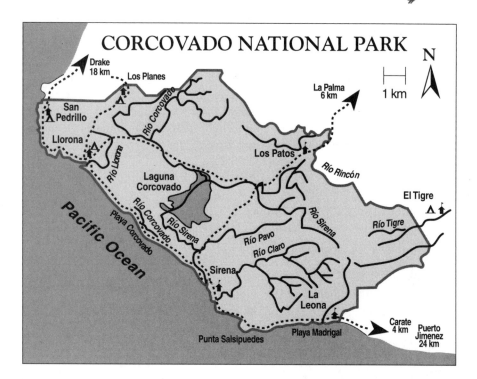

were poised to engage in massive deforestation to settle the dispute, and it took some very fancy footwork on the part of then-President Daniel Oduber Quirós and the world scientific community to come to an agreement that would make everyone happy. The squatters had to be compensated and resettled and the timber company had to be paid, all in a matter of months. For his herculean efforts, President Oduber was awarded the Albert Schweitzer Award in 1977.

Something else has brought people into the park besides its biotic riches, and that something is gold. In the 1930s, hunters found lumps of the metal on the surface near present-day Playa Madrigal, and this set off a gold rush that was to last several decades. When the park was created, many people were still working gold in the Río Claro area. The supervisor at the time was instructed to tell the miners that they could continue their activity in the park as long as they did not bother wildlife. This policy, seen as necessary for the greater good of the nation, resulted in conflict. In 1986 it was realized that well over 1,000 people were working the Río Claro area, causing damage to the river, deforestation, and destruction of wildlife. Some were found to be using mercury in the mining process, and this was leaching into the river. After considerable trouble, resources were marshaled and hundreds of police were shipped in to evict the miners. Considering that both sides were armed, it is remarkable that no one was killed. Today, mining within the park is illegal. Park officers make as many armed patrols as possible to guard against incursions, which unfortunately still occur, though on a much smaller scale than before.

LOCATION AND ACCESS

The park is located on the Osa Peninsula in the southwest corner of the country. The easiest way to the central guardpost and biological station at Sirena is to get to Golfito (see Golfito Wildlife Refuge in this chapter) and then fly from Golfito. There are several companies that do this, usually in one-engine Cessnas that can take three people and gear. During the dry season you can expect to pay up to $500 per planeload for the 10-minute flight. This is a real gouge, but if enough people attempt to bargain perhaps the price will come down. One company that is presently cashing in is VEASA (232-1010).

Here is a rundown of your options to walk into the park:

1. Puerto Jimenez to La Leona

There used to be a ferry that went between Golfito and Puerto Jimenez—which is where the park headquarters is located and from which two of the walking routes originate—but this was discontinued several years ago. Now you need to get someone to bring you in a private boat at a cost of around 6,000 colones, and you might have to arrange this a day in advance if you're not in Golfito early in the morning. From Puerto Jimenez, it's possible to get a taxi to the mining town of Carate and walk 3.4 kilometers to the park boundary at La Leona. There is said to be a truck that leaves Carate for Puerto Jimenez on Monday, Thursday, and Saturday at 10:00 A.M.

2. La Palma to Los Patos

From the town of La Palma, 35 kilometers north of Puerto Jimenez, there is a trail that leads to the Los Patos station about 10 kilometers distant. There is a once-a-day bus that leaves during the morning (erratic hours) from Palmar Norte to La Palma via Rincón.

3. Palmar Norte to San Pedrillo

Palmar Norte is located about 230 kilometers south of San José. You can walk or take a taxi the 35 kilometers from Palmar Norte to Drake and from there walk down the beach 18 kilometers to the park boundary at San Pedrillo.

4. Sierpe to San Pedrillo

It is also possible to hire a boat in the town of Sierpe in the Valle de Diquis that will take you down the Río Sierpe, through part of the Mangrove Forest Reserve, and along the coast to San Pedrillo. This trip takes between six and eight hours and is not cheap; expect to pay at least 8,000 colones.

VISITOR FACILITIES

If you don't have a tent, the place to stay is in the central park station at Sirena. This is an interesting area with a number of trails, and you could easily spend several days exploring here. Visitors are usually housed in the "attic" or second story of the main building. It's dry here, but open on the sides and you will definitely need a mosquito net at night. The park usually has extras, but if you have one, bring it. Research or tour groups often use the station in the dry season, so it is doubly important that you call the headquarters in Puerto Jimenez (735-5036) to make a reservation. You can also arrange for meals if you do so in advance; they are reasonably priced and good, especially considering that what is not grown on the premises is flown in or brought by boat.

TRAILS

Shorter trails around the station at Sirena are described first, followed by trails leading to and from Sirena. One cautionary note: **collared** and **white-lipped peccaries**, animals related to pigs, are relatively common in Corcovado. They travel in large bands (in former times they could number up to 500 individuals but now usually average about 30), rooting up everything edible with their large teeth. Although their aggressiveness has been grossly exaggerated, they should be given a wide berth when encountered. They are often seen in the secondary forest along the trail to Los Patos. Usually you will smell them before making a sighting; a large herd produces quite a funk. They have bad eyesight, and it's remarkably easy to approach them or have them walk closely past you if the wind is right. When alarmed, they clack their jaws together, producing a sound not unlike two coconuts or deer antlers being sharply hit together. At this point it's advisable to back up and wait for the herd to pass, keeping an eye out for a suitable tree or rock to climb. If you give them enough time to smell or hear you, they almost always retreat.

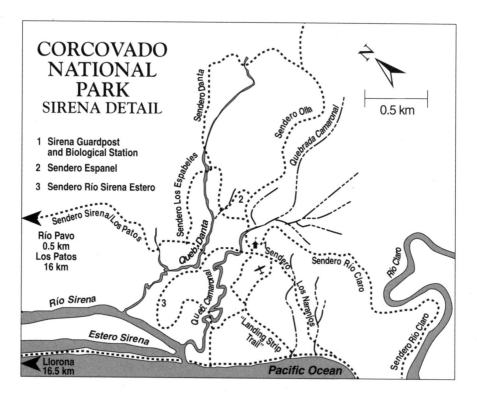

Trails around Sirena

You could easily spend several days on the trails and river courses around Sirena, particularly if you're interested in birding, wildlife watching, or botanizing. **Scarlet macaws** are remarkably common and visible around the station, and **tapirs** are reputed to occasionally come out onto the lawn and airstrip in the evening. All four of Costa Rica's monkey species occur here and can be easily observed.

Remember that it is hot and that even short hikes require a high water intake!

Short Trails Leading to and from Sirena

Sendero Río Claro

    Distance: 3.5 kilometers
    Hiking time: 2 hours, 30 minutes
    Elevation gain: 200 meters
    Map: 1:200,000 Golfito

This trail, one of the short trails near the station, really stands out. It can be done in a morning or afternoon, with plenty of time for exploring. The Río Claro trail starts from behind the station and heads southeast. The trail climbs onto a ridge and follows it for a little over 1 kilometer before descending to the river (there are very nice swimming spots in a couple of places) and then coming out to the beach at the estuary of the river. Look for tapir and cat tracks in the sand along the estuary; tapir tracks consist of three "toes" and are at least as big as your hand. From the estuary you can walk back along the beach to the sign for the Sendero al Estacion, which is actually the Sendero los Naranjos, or go a little farther to the landing strip trail.

There's another option if you have footwear that you don't mind getting wet, which is to walk up the Río Claro. This clear, pristine tropical river makes for a fascinating day hike or backpack. It is unusual among rivers in the region in that it has long stretches that are without meanders, affording views of 1 kilometer or more straight upstream. Birding is great along the banks. Several species of **kingfishers** are common, including the **ringed, Amazon,** and **pygmy** species. Walking along the sandy banks and through the water is slow going, and whether you are out for a short hike or a three-day backpack trip, count on having to take a lot more time than usual to get from point A to point B. As this is one of the areas of the park that occasionally attracts fugitive gold miners, you should check with the park guards to make sure that it has been recently patrolled before setting out for the upper reaches of the river.

Sendero Olla

    Distance: 2.5 kilometers
    Hiking time: 2 hours
    Elevation gain: 200 meters
    Map: 1:200,000 Golfito

Another interesting short trail that starts close to the Sirena station is the Sendero Olla. This trail starts across from the northeast corner of the station. In 0.2 kilometer there is a junction with Sendero Los Espabeles to the left, and in another 2 kilometers there is a junction with the Sendero Espavel, also to the left, where there is a magnificent **cedro tree** (*Cedrela sp.*). The Sendero Olla climbs up to a ridge, traveling through some of Corcovado's justifiably famous upland tropical wet forest. Keep all of your senses primed, and you will start to get an appreciation for the beauty and complexity of this area. There are a couple of places along the trail where you will smell a strong musky odor; these are very probably scent-marking sites for a jaguar or puma. These majestic predators need tremendous amounts of territory (jaguars need at least 100 square kilometers each) to assure themselves an adequate food supply and access to mates, and they mark the boundaries of this territory with urine.

There is much of botanical interest along the trail. Although it is difficult to see into the crowns of the forest giants that tower over your head, they do drop their seeds and fruits onto the ground. One of the interesting species common along the trail is **wild nutmeg** (*Virola sebifera*). The seeds, which are about 10 millimeters long, are encased in a heavy capsule that opens into two halves when the seed is ripe. The sweet-smelling, bright red covering of the seed is called an aril. It is attractive to birds such as toucans who swallow it whole, digesting the aril and vomiting up or passing the seed in a new location. In commercial nutmeg, which is native to Southeast Asia, the aril is the spice known as mace. Other common trees are the **cow tree** (*Brosimum utile*), which has a drinkable latex sap (see Chapter 2, The Tropical Forest), and the **silk cotton** (*Ceiba pentandra*). Silk cotton trees are easy to recognize because of their stout, planklike root buttresses and their smooth gray trunks. One specimen near the end of the trail is at least 60 meters in height.

The trail follows the ridge for about 2 kilometers before coming to a huge tree-fall blocking the path; the trail is overgrown after this point. The circular route that utilizes the Sendero Danta has also grown over, but you might ask the park rangers if it has been cleared. If the Sendero Danta is clear, then it is 2.5 kilometers back to the station from its junction with the Sendero Olla. If the Sendero Danta is not clear, you must return the way you came.

Sendero los Espabeles and Sendero Río Sirena Estero

Distance: 5.5 kilometers
Hiking time: 2 hours
Elevation gain: Almost none
Map: 1:200,000 Golfito

Among other worthwhile trails around Sirena is the Sendero los Espabeles, which begins at its junction with the Sendero Olla and circles around to meet the Sendero Danta, then the Sendero Sirena/Los Patos. This route meets up with the Sendero Río Sirena Estero (1.7 kilometers). The estuary trail takes you through some secondary forest and down to a couple of good birding spots at the mouth of the Río Sirena. The trail empties out onto the beach. Take a left and you come to the "Airstrip" Trail in about 1.25 kilometers, and the Sendero los Naranjos (marked with a sign reading Sendero al Estacion) about 0.5 kilometer farther.

Short Trails from San Pedrillo

The San Pedrillo ranger station is a pleasant place to camp, with bathroom facilities, showers, and dependable drinking water. There are also two interesting short trails that are worth spending a day exploring.

San Padrillo Waterfall Trail

Distance: 4 kilometers round trip
Hiking time: 2 hours
Elevation gain: None
Map: 1:50,000 Llorona

This short trail leads up a nameless creek that begins just behind the ranger station. There are quite a few cycad plants along its banks, and at least a few small caimans in the creek. The trail ends at a lovely waterfall and some good wallowing pools.

Río Pargo Trail

Distance: 6.5 kilometers
Hiking time: 3 hours
Elevation gain: 100 meters
Map: 1:50,00 Llorona

To reach this trail, walk 1.75 kilometers south on the main trail leading away from the San Pedrillo ranger station. Shortly before coming to the mouth of the Río Pargo, you will see an unmarked trail entrance to your left. The trail climbs uphill for about 0.5 kilometer, passing through a piece of forest that is in the process of regeneration, the land here having served as a small farm before the formation of the park. After a short, steep climb, you'll come to the top of the ridge, and walk on relatively flat ground for about a kilometer before descending back to the main trail along the coast. From here you are about 0.5 kilometer south of the Río Pargo, from which you'll take the main trail back to San Pedrillo.

Long Trails Leading to and from Sirena

Coastal Trail from San Pedrillo to La Leona

Distance: 33 kilometers
Hiking time: 2 or 3 days, if you can make all of the river crossings at low tide
Elevation gain: 50 meters
Map: 1:200,000 Golfito

Beach hiking here is open and hot; you need to have at least three quarts of water-carrying capacity per person, and more if you have it. The rivers are quite brackish, and you need to carry enough to last you between park stations. If you can work it with the tides, walking at night is a more comfortable option than doing it during the heat of the day.

Pay your entrance fee at the park station at San Pedrillo and jot down the low tide times that they should have posted. You can camp near the station if you've arrived late in the day and intend to start hiking the next day. For an interesting side trip from the park station, the nearby San Pedrillo River can be waded and swum up to a 30-meter waterfall.

The trail to Llorona starts on the beach then travels inland through some interesting primary forest dominated by **cedros marias trees** (*Cedrela mexicana*), and finally through some old banana farms that are returning to forest. After 6 kilometers you come to the park station at Llorona. This makes a good stopping point for the first day. You can camp here and do the interesting, long day hike (10 kilometers each way) to the park station at Los Planes. About 1 kilometer from Llorona on this side trail is a huge **ceiba** or kapok tree that may be the largest tree in the park, measuring nearly 70 meters in height and having buttresses almost 10 meters tall. The side trail continues through mostly virgin lowland forest to the outpost at Los Planes, where you can get water for your return—or you can camp at the station.

The other side trail that leads out of Llorona is a 20-kilometer route that passes behind Laguna Corcovado, meeting the Los Patos Trail at a point known as *Cedral*. This trail is limited to research use, and special permission is required to travel it. It is not often used, and if you do wangle permission, a guide is recommended. The Laguna Corcovado is the remains of what was once an ocean inlet that existed for a time at the end of the last ice age. While the **herbaceous marshes** and **holillo palm swamps** that surround it are of interest to botanists, and the lake provides habitat to many rare and unusual animal species, it is ridden with biting insects and is difficult to get to. Stable populations of **crocodiles, caimans**, and **jabiru storks** are found here, flourishing in the lagoon's isolation.

Back at Llorona on the main trail heading south on the beach, you soon come to the estuary of the Llorona River, which must be crossed at low tide. From here it's a long, hot beach walk, no way to get around it. In about 7 kilometers from Llorona (about 13 kilometers from San Pedrillo) you come to the second estuary crossing at the Río Corcovado. In another 6 kilometers (19 kilometers from San Pedrillo) you come to the Río Sirena, and after that there is another 1.5 kilometers (20.5 kilometers from San Pedrillo, 14.5 kilometers from Llorona) before you come to the trail to the station at Sirena. This is a good place to camp on your second night. If you want to set up your tent, ask the rangers where they want you to put it (see Visitor Facilities in this section).

From Sirena heading south, you cross the Río Claro estuary, which is the last river crossing that needs to be done at low tide. The main attraction of the

Beach near the mouth of the Río Claro, Corcovado National Park

following section of beach is the small cave at Punta Salsipuedes (5 kilometers from Sirena, 25.5 kilometers from San Pedrillo), which translates as "get out if you can," testimony to the many ships that have wrecked off the point. The cave is home to large numbers of **bats** and has some small cave formations (stalactites and stalagmites) near the back. Its mouth is accessible only at low tide.

From Punta Salsipuedes the trail follows the beach for a time and then moves inland a little before coming out at Playa Madrigal, about 6 kilometers from Punta Salsipuedes (11 kilometers from Sirena, 31.5 kilometers from San Pedrillo). From Playa Madrigal, it's another 1.5 kilometers to the official boundary of the park at La Leona (12.5 kilometers from Sirena, 33 kilometers from San Pedrillo).

Sendero de los Patos

Distance: 18 kilometers
Hiking time: 1 day
Elevation gain: 200 meters
Map: 1:200,000 Golfito

This is the one noncoastal route in and out of the park. It passes through some interesting primary forest with good opportunities for wildlife observation. You can hike the 32 kilometers from Sirena all the way to the town of La Palma in eight or nine hours if you are used to the heat.

The trail begins across the airstrip from the Sirena headquarters building. It starts in secondary forest before passing into typical lowland tropical wet forest. In about 4 kilometers the trail crosses the Río Pavo and then continues on over level ground for about 5 kilometers more. The trail begins to climb into slightly drier, more upland forest before crossing the Río Sirena and then, shortly after, at about 13 kilometers from Sirena, coming to the junction with the trail to Llorona via Laguna Corcovado, which heads off to your left. The trail crosses another small river and then passes through forested ridges another 5 kilometers to the station at Los Patos on the border of the park (18 kilometers from Sirena). You can camp here, or press on to the town of La Palma, 14 kilometers and about four hours distant. The trail should be obvious until you come to the first river crossing (the Río Rincón). The trail to stay on is the one that follows the riverbed.

Stream-walking on the Río Claro, Corcovado National Park

ISLA DEL CAÑO BIOLOGICAL RESERVE

Size: 300 hectares of land; 5,800 hectares of sea
Distance from San José: 311 kilometers
Camping: Yes, with advance permission from the parks authority (735-5036)
Trails: Yes
Map: 1:200,000 Golfito
Dry season: January through March
Transportation: No public transportation available

Isla del Caño is actually the tip of a huge underwater mountain, made up of rocks formed more than 40 million years ago as a product of the Cocos and Caribbean plates pushing against one another. It is surrounded by a rocky shoreline and a few small beaches that are almost inundated at high tide. Five coral reefs made up of more than fifteen species of stony corals and containing a profusion of fish, mollusks, and other sealife surround the outer shore, and most of the people who come to visit this park do so to dive or snorkel.

It also has archaeological importance, apparently having served as an offshore burial ground and ceremonial site for people of the Diquis cultural group who inhabited the Golfo Dulce until the arrival of the Spanish. Besides tombs (mostly plundered before the creation of the reserve), the evidence for this consists of large stone spheres found out in the open in many places. They range in size from 7.5 centimeters to almost 2 meters in diameter and their significance is unclear, but the nearly perfect spherical form they possess must have been quite a chore to produce with primitive tools. There also seems to have been a purposeful planting of **cow tree** (*Brosimum utile*) orchards, particularly in the center of the island. They might have been planted as a food source (see Chapter 2, The Tropical Forest) or perhaps they had some ceremonial purpose.

Wildlife on the island is scarce. There are relatively few species of insects present; these include **carpenter bees** and two species of brightly colored, metallic-looking bees of the genus *Euglossa*, one red and the other green. It is estimated that the richness of insect species is about 1 percent of that of similar habitat in Corcovado on the mainland. The reasons for this are unclear, but the seasonal climate here (very wet in the rainy season and very dry the rest of the year) and the lack of opportunity for insects to escape to suitable microclimates probably have a role. It has also been theorized that so much of the original vegetation was planted into cow tree orchards and disturbed for burial sites by the indigenous visitors that the island cannot support many species.

There is one species of **mosquito** on the island that probably breeds in **bromeliads** and does not seem to have nearly as much predation on its larvae as on the mainland. Consequently they are very common during the rainy season, necessitating the liberal use of repellents in the forest.

Besides three species of frogs and a couple of small lizards, vertebrate life consists of **pacas** (large nocturnal rodents), **opossums**, and a few species of birds, some of which, such as **cattle egrets**, commute from the mainland. **Feral pigs** released long ago, perhaps by visiting pirates in the eighteenth century, have caused some damage and there is an effort now to hunt them out.

If you can visit the island to experience its *Robinson Crusoe*-like tropical isolation or to snorkel its pristine reefs, you have a number of Costa Rican conservationists to thank. In 1973 the whole island was in danger of being mauled by tourist development when the government rented it to a foreign company planning to build a number of hotels and other facilities. While the battle for the island's preservation was waged between the Costa Rican Association of Biologists, the development company, and congressional representatives for both sides, the company cleared some of the forest near the present-day ranger station for a wharf and marina. This scar has been slow to heal. A restraining order was placed on the company, and the island was included as a part of Corcovado National Park in 1976. A few years later, it was accorded biological reserve status.

LOCATION AND ACCESS

Isla del Caño lies about 10 kilometers off the Osa Peninsula, northeast of the San Pedrillo Station in Corcovado National Park. Due to the difficulty of arranging for transportation from the mainland, most people come here as part of an organized tour. Proyecto Campanario (282-5898) runs trips to the island. You can try to arrange a trip independently from Palmar Norte, but round-trip transportation is expensive from there.

VISITOR FACILITIES

Advance permission to camp must be obtained from the National Parks office in Puerto Jimenez (735-5036). You can camp on the island near the ranger station, where there is also water. Ask the rangers to show you where they want you to put your tent.

TRAILS

Mirador and Archeological Area Trail

Distance: 4 kilometers
Hiking time: 2 hours
Elevation gain: 30 meters
Map: None

There is one trail open to visitors. From the ranger station, it climbs steeply for about 100 meters before coming to the top of the ridge. At this point there is a signed trail junction, with one trail that is for researchers only going to the lighthouse, and another heading off to your left. After about 0.5 kilometer you'll come to another Y and a trail sign. One trail leads 0.75 kilometer to a *mirador* or lookout with a view of the ocean. The other fork leads 0.75 kilometer to an "archeological area" where a number of plundered graves are surrounded by bits of pottery, stone spheres, and other artifacts. Please leave these where you found them.

ISLA DEL COCOS NATIONAL PARK

Size: 2,400 hectares of land, 18,575 hectares of sea
Distance from San José: 600 kilometers
Camping: Not permitted
Trails: Yes
Map: 1:200,000 Quepos
Dry season: January through March
Transportation: No public transportation available

Cocos Island is often called Costa Rica's Galapagos. The similarities are its great distance from the mainland, its endemic species (those found nowhere else), and the great expense involved in getting there.

This isolated island, located more than 500 kilometers from Costa Rica's Pacific Coast, is of volcanic origin. Its great distance from possible sources of colonizing plants and animals has made it a natural laboratory for evolutionary biologists. Surveys have revealed the presence of 235 species of plants (seventy endemic), eighty-five species of birds (three endemic), two endemic species of lizards, three species of spiders, and 351 species of insects (sixty-five endemic).

Endemic terrestrial invertebrates include the **Cocos Island flycatcher** (*Nesotricus ridgwayi*), **Cocos Island finch** (*Pinaroloxias inornata*), **Cocos Island cuckoo** (*Cocyzus ferrugineus*), **Cocos gecko** (*Sphaerodactylus pacificus*), and **Cocos Anole** (*Anolis townsendi*). The two lizard species must have arrived on rafts of vegetation. Both species have close relatives living in Central and South America. There is also at least one endemic species of freshwater fish, *Cotylopus cocoensis*. It too has relatives on the mainland, in Panama to be exact, but the only conceivable way that its ancestors arrived here would be as eggs on the feet of birds.

The island is covered with extremely dense premontane rain forest, in which almost every tree is covered with **bromeliads** and other epiphytes. On the upper elevations of Cerro Iglesias, the vegetation is considered to be of the montane rain forest life zone. All this luxuriant growth is supported by more than 7,000 millimeters of rain a year. One of the interesting endemic plants here is the **Roosevelt palm** (*Rooseveltia frankliniana*), named after U.S. President Franklin Roosevelt, who visited the island four times between 1934 and 1940. It grows in dense stands on the drier slopes near the rocky cliffs that form most of the perimeter of the island.

Many of the visitors who are lucky enough to be able to come to Isla del Cocos do so to dive its turquoise waters and reefs. There are 18 species of **corals**, 57 of **crustaceans**, 118 of **mollusks**, and more than 200 species of **fish** found in the waters around Cocos. **Hammerhead** and **white-tipped sharks** are also quite common, and divers should be well versed in how to behave around these animals.

Unfortunately, all is not completely well for Cocos' unique biological community. Plant and animal species that have been introduced by humans pose particularly difficult problems. Pigs, cats, goats, and white-tailed deer have all done considerable damage. Pigs, which were introduced by pirates in 1793, are probably the worst offenders. They loosen so much soil in the process of rooting for food that they have been implicated in causing the death of coral on some of the reefs. Cats are a problem, as they kill and eat anything that moves. Less obvious but serious threats are introduced plants such as coffee and guavas, which replace the less aggressive native understory plants. (Guavas are also a terrible problem on some of the Galapagos Islands in Ecuador.) Illegal fishing has been a terrible problem, depriving nesting seabirds of food and causing other disruptions to the marine ecosystem. Compounding all of this is the lack of money for enforcement (there are no guards on the island) and the difficulty of doing even cursory patrols from the mainland. Perhaps the best bet for the preservation of Cocos would be for pirate treasure to be found here, and a portion allocated for management of the island.

The first reference to Cocos was on a map dated 1541. From that point on, the abundance of fresh water, coconuts, and pigs made the island a favorite stopping place for whalers and pirates. Included among the latter was the infamous Benito "Bloody Sword" Bonito, who is said to have hidden fabulous treasures on the island. The English pirate James Thompson also made Cocos a frequent stopping point, and is said to have hidden the famous "treasure of Lima" here. Apparently, near the end of a successful peasant revolt, the clergy, aristocrats, and royalty of Lima, Peru, desperate not to have their riches fall into the hands of the underclass, entrusted Thompson with the task of transporting their money and valuables to a safe port. Thompson and his crew promptly killed the Peruvian guards posted on the ship to guard the treasure, and sailed for Cocos. Thompson was later captured by the Spanish, but his life was spared and he was released in hopes that he would lead them, unwittingly, to the treasure. He ducked his pursuers, and it is not known whether or not he ever made it back to the island.

Many attempts have been made to find the treasure of Lima and other caches left by buccaneers. All have turned up little or nothing. In 1992, a wealthy American treasure hunter gained permission to mount a multimillion-dollar search using highly sophisticated sonar and ultralight airplanes. Once again, nothing was found.

LOCATION AND ACCESS

Isla del Cocos is located far offshore at a northern latitude of 5 degrees, 30 minutes, 34 seconds, and a western longitude of 37 degrees, 18 minutes, 6 seconds. Access is either by boat or with a private company.

VISITOR FACILITIES

The guardpost has toilets and potable water, but no camping is allowed on the island; visitors are required to sleep on their boats.

TRAILS

There are a couple of trails, one to the viewpoint on Cerro Iglesias and the other to Cabo Dampier. They are steep and muddy; have someone guide you.

7

CENTRAL HIGHLANDS REGION

Poás National Park
Juan Castro Blanco National Park
Braulio Carrillo National Park
Irazú National Park
Guayabo National Monument
Tapantí Wildlife Refuge
Chirripó National Park
La Amistad National Park
San Vito Wetlands

This is a region of contrasts. It contains Costa Rica's most populous area, and the country's largest park. The Central Valley, where the cities of San José, Cartago, and Heredia are situated, contains 60 percent of the country's three million people. Consequently, many of the parks and reserves are small, though interesting nonetheless. They include active volcanoes and a well-known archaeological site. In contrast with the hustle and bustle of the Central Valley are two of Costa Rica's great wilderness parks, Braulio Carrillo and the vast (by Costa Rican standards at least) La Amistad.

POÁS NATIONAL PARK

Size: 5,599 hectares
Distance from San José: 37 kilometers
Camping: Not permitted
Trails: Yes
Map: 1:200,000 San José
Dry season: December through April
Transportation: From San José, a bus leaves at 8 A.M. from Parque de la Merced (Avenida 2, Calle 12). From Alajeula, buses leave Sundays at 8 and 9 A.M. from Parque Nacional. Weekdays, a bus leaves Alajuela to San Pedro de Poás at 11 A.M.; take a taxi from there to the park. Check with bus drivers about return times.

Volcán Poás is one of the two easily accessible active volcanoes in the region, the other being Irazú. Both are among the few active volcanoes in the Americas whose summits are easily reached by car.

Poás National Park is one of Costa Rica's most visited parks, attracting thousands of people on an average dry-season weekend. Except for birds, wildlife is relatively sparse, but there are a number of unusual plant communities represented within the park, including an unusual form of stunted cloud forest.

Volcán Poás has a long history of eruptions, dating back as far as 11 million years. Poás, along with Volcán Barva, created the first "floor" of the entire Central Valley during the Pliocene epoch and has been showing at least some amount of volcanic activity ever since. Probably the largest event occurred in 1910, when an eruption early in the morning of January 25 sent an estimated 640,000 tons of ash falling on the Central Valley. More recently, in 1974 Poás sent a column of volcanic ash that rose to 10,600 meters in elevation, and for most of 1989 the park was closed due to the intensity of volcanic activity. Generally, the mountain now restricts itself to occasional rumbles and periods of geyserlike activity. Poás is considered to be a "composite" volcano, and nine distinct craters have been identified on its surface. The largest of these, visible only from an airplane, is more than 4 kilometers across.

LOCATION AND ACCESS

The park is located northeast of the city of Alajuela, which is situated near San José in the Central Valley. To get to Poás from San José, a bus leaves from Parque de la Merced (Avenida 2, Calle 12) at 8 A.M. From Alajeula, buses leave Sundays at 8 and 9 A.M. from the Parque Nacional. Weekdays, buses leave Alajuela for San Pedro de Poás at 11 A.M. It is necessary to take a taxi from San Pedro de Poás to the park. You should check with the bus drivers about the return times, as these seem to vary from day to day. If you are driving, the most direct route from San José is to go to Alajuela and ask near the Hotel Alajuela for the correct road to the park. Once you get on the right road, it's a straight shot to the national park.

VISITOR FACILITIES

The visitor center has interpretive displays and a snack/drink stand. Fundación Neotropica, a conservation group, runs a gift shop above the visitor center. Camping is not allowed in the park, and the closest hotels are in Alajuela.

A diverse group of visitors to the Poás Volcano, Poás National Park

TRAILS

Crater Overlook and Botos Lake Trails

Crater Overlook Trail
    Distance: 0.75 kilometer
    Hiking time: 15 minutes
    Elevation gain: None
    Map: None

Botos Lake Trail
    Distance: 7.5 kilometers
    Hiking time: 20 minutes
    Elevation gain: 50 meters
    Map: None

To get to the crater, walk past the visitor center on the 400-meter, two-lane asphalt "trail" for about fifteen minutes. If you get there early enough in the morning before the clouds roll in, you'll get an impressive view down into the bottom of the crater, 300 meters below. The milky green color of the lake at the bottom is a result of sulfur suspended in the water. The lake is prone to periods of geyserlike activity, sending plumes of steam and water up to 250 meters high. This occurs when water seeps into the shaft of the volcano and vaporizes. When the pressure inside the shaft becomes greater than that of the water on top of it, a geyser results.

Just before the crater overlook is the 20-minute side trail to Botos Lake. The 1.5-kilometer trail passes through an unusual stunted forest. The diminutive aspect of the vegetation is caused by a combination of cold (it gets down to freezing here), cloud cover, and acid rain from the volcano.

The dominant tree here is the **wild mamey** (*Clusia odorata*). You might recognize some of the shrubs as belonging to the **blueberry** genus (*Vaccinium sp.*). The trail ends at the overlook for Botos Lake, which fills one of Poás's extinct craters.

Escalonia Trail

    Distance: 1 kilometer
    Hiking time: 30 minutes
    Elevation gain: None
    Map: None

There is another short walk that starts from the picnic area. The 1-kilometer Escalonia Trail takes you 30 minutes through forest that is of much larger stature than that found near the active crater. Interesting trees found here include the **Poás magnolia** (*Magnolia poasana*), which is restricted to this and other volcano forests in Costa Rica. Another is the **escalonia** (*Escallonia poasiana*). This tree, which has a distinctive, pagodalike shape, is an indicator of the frost line in Costa

Rican forests. Several species of oaks are also common. Commonly seen birds here include Costa Rica's national bird, the **clay-colored robin**, and several species of **hummingbirds**. The **clay-colored robin** is a drab bird with an almost supernaturally beautiful courtship song. The choice of this bird as a national symbol was meant as a metaphor for how something beautiful could come of humble beginnings.

JUAN CASTRO BLANCO NATIONAL PARK
Size: 14,285 hectares
Distance from San José: 95 kilometers
Camping: Not permitted
Trails: Extremely limited
Map: 1:200,000 San José
Transportation: None

This park was created in 1992, primarily to protect the watersheds of several cities in the Central Valley from logging and to ensure adequate flow for hydroelectric dams in the area. The park contains some extremely species-rich premontane and montane wet forests flanking the peaks of Volcán Platanar (2,183 meters) and Porvenir (2,267 meters).

LOCATION AND ACCESS
This park, despite its close proximity to the cities of the Central Valley, is extremely difficult to access. You can skirt the fringes by driving north from the town of Sarchi for 18 kilometers until you reach the village of Bajos del Toro, located on the park's southern flank. There are a couple of short, unmarked footpaths and horse trails that lead into the park from Bajos del Toro, but most travel in the park is for those willing to bushwhack with map and compass.

VISITOR FACILITIES
None in the park. The closest lodgings are in Zarcero and Alajuela.

BRAULIO CARRILLO NATIONAL PARK
Size: 44,099 hectares
Distance from San José: 23 kilometers
Camping: Permitted
Trails: Yes
Map: 1:200,000 San José
Dry season: January through April—last two weeks of July and December usually dry, many parts of the park remain wet year-round
Transportation: A bus from San José to Limón departs hourly every day from 5:00 A.M. to 7:00 P.M. from Calle 19, Avenida 3. Get off the bus at the Carrillo ranger station at the northerly point on the road inside the park. Returns are the same times. The bus company is Coop Limón (223-7811).

The precipitous forested slopes along the Siquirres Highway, Braulio Carrillo National Park

After a couple of days of the noise and diesel exhaust of San José, you might find it hard to believe that a large block of nearly untouched wilderness lies only 20 kilometers away. Many parts of Braulio Carrillo National Park, with its precipitous terrain and heavy forest, remain unexplored. Other parts are easily accessible, and the short trails that have been developed give a fascinating window into tropical nature.

Braulio Carrillo National Park was named after the third president of the country, Braulio Carrillo Colina. He served the last two years of a term when his predecessor resigned, and then returned to power via a military coup in 1838. In 1841, after he named himself president for life, he was removed from office and exiled to El Salvador, where he was assassinated. Although Costa Ricans deplore dictators, the park was named after him because of his efforts to build roads to both coasts and end Costa Rica's economic isolation.

During his tenure, he succeeded in pushing a road from the Central Valley to the then tiny port of Puntarenas, but a road to the Atlantic proved a more difficult undertaking. It took more than 30 years to finally finish the "Carrillo road." Most of the original route has returned to forest, but a section can still be walked that parallels the present modern highway to Siquirres (see Trails in this section).

In 1973 the idea of a more direct and easily maintained route (than what existed) to the Atlantic surfaced. The route that was planned passed through one of the largest unprotected wilderness areas left in the country, and a fierce battle ensued between conservationists and pro-development elements. In 1978 an agreement was reached that created Braulio Carrillo National Park, protecting the land that the road passes through.

Examples of seven distinct life zones are contained within the park. The precipitous volcanic terrain and the diversity of soil types have provided for a diverse group of organisms. At least 6,000 species of plants are found here, and preliminary studies have counted 333 species of birds. Rare and interesting species that are found here include **quetzals** and **bare-necked umbrella birds**. Despite its proximity to San José, much of the park remains unexplored.

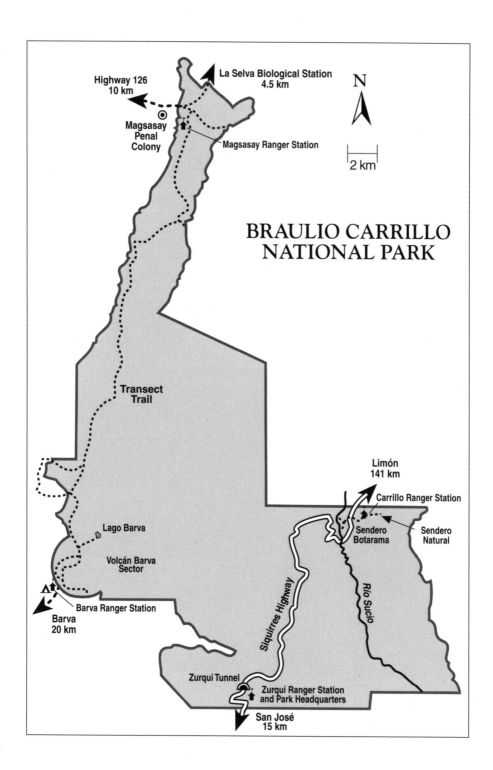

Highway 126
10 km

La Selva Biological Station
4.5 km

N

Magsasay
Penal
Colony

Magsasay Ranger Station

2 km

BRAULIO CARRILLO
NATIONAL PARK

Transect
Trail

Limón
141 km

Carrillo Ranger Station

Sendero
Botarama

Sendero
Natural

Lago Barva

Volcán Barva
Sector

Siquirres Highway

Río Sucio

Barva Ranger Station

Barva
20 km

Zurqui Tunnel

Zurqui Ranger Station
and Park Headquarters

San José
15 km

LOCATION AND ACCESS

Braulio Carrillo National Park is located 20 kilometers northeast of San José. The part of Braulio Carrillo that most people see is the southern area on either side of the Siquirres Highway on the way to the Atlantic coast. If you're coming from San José, the road to Limón is marked as the Siquirres Highway. The park headquarters is located less than 1 kilometer before the Zurqui Tunnel on the right side of the highway.

A four-wheel-drive vehicle with high clearance is necessary for the trip to Volcán Barva. The route starts in the city of Heredia, easily reached from San José. From Heredia find the road to the town of Barva. The turnoff is near the old church in the center of town, but you will probably need to ask in order to find it. From Barva head for Sacramento. The paved road has a series of forks and you need to turn in this sequence: left, right, right. Take a left at the fourth fork and travel steeply uphill to a group of hotels known as the village of Porosati. From here the road, although still pavement, gets steadily worse. At the next fork go left. You then come to a T intersection with a sign directing you to the park, 8 kilometers away. In about 4 kilometers the pavement ends and the road gets truly horrendous. Eventually you come to a gate and the park station.

In the northern area, near the Magsasay penal colony, there is a park ranger station that is usually occupied. This area may be worth visiting when trails become better developed, or as a way to get to the lower reaches of the Transect Trail (see Trails in this section). To get there, a four-wheel-drive vehicle with high clearance is necessary, but, depending on the amount of rain that the area has received, the road may be impassable even then. To get to Magsasay, drive from San José to Alajuela and take Highway 126 out of Alajuela. In 38 kilometers, after passing through the village of Bosque, you come to a dirt road off to the right. If you get to the town of La Virgen on Highway 126, you've missed the turn. Almost as soon as you turn off the highway, there is a fork in the dirt road; take the left fork. Magsasay is reached in 10 kilometers. Ask here for directions to the unmarked trail, which takes at least four hours to hike. Another option is to come in from La Selva Biological Station on an unmarked trail that also takes about four hours to hike. Call the La Selva station manager (240-5033) well ahead of time to get permission for this. They require that you have a La Selva-trained guide with you. To sum it up, the trails in this remote sector are for adventurous and seasoned hikers.

VISITOR FACILITIES

At the park headquarters near Carrillo, at the north end of the road through the park toward Limón, there are some natural history displays, and the staff is knowledgeable and helpful. There is another station at the other end of the road near the Zurqui tunnel, but it is not always occupied. Camping is not permitted at either station or in their vicinity.

The Volcán Barva sector in the park's southwest corner has a station where camping is permitted and it can be used as a base for day hikes. Ask the station

Hikers en route to Barva Lake, Braulio Carrillo National Park

personnel where they would like you to camp. Barva is an interesting town in that it was the first impermanent Spanish settlement in Costa Rica, and the one-story buildings that line the central square are the oldest in the country. Barva is named after the leader of the tribe of indigenous people who inhabited the area before being displaced to make way for the settlement.

TRAILS

Sendero Botarama

> **Distance:** 1 kilometer
> **Hiking time:** 2 hours
> **Elevation gain:** 25 meters
> **Map:** 1:200,000 San José

A couple of short trails are near the ranger station that is closer to the eastern end of the park. The Sendero Natural Botarama (named after a species of tree) is a 1-kilometer dirt road that is closed to traffic and leads to the Río Sucio. In 1998 the park personnel were discouraging use of this trail because of the high number of car break-ins that have occurred here.

Sendero Natural

> **Distance:** Approximately 3 kilometers
> **Hiking time:** 2.5 hours
> **Elevation gain:** 200 meters
> **Map:** 1:200,000 San José

This loop trail, which begins from the parking lot at the Carillo ranger station, was still being developed in 1998. It is quite steep and muddy in places. Check into its condition at the station if you are not feeling adventurous.

Lago Barva Trail
Distance: 3 kilometers
Hiking time: 2.5 hours
Elevation gain: 50 meters
Map: 1:200,000 San José

The route starts as a continuation of the road that you came in on. For about 1 kilometer, it passes through old pasture with some ancient **oaks**. Oaks of this size are rare in Costa Rica, most having been burnt for charcoal. Due to the cool temperatures and frequent cloud cover, these trees are very slow-growing, and some of the giants that you see here are perhaps 600 years old.

In about 2 kilometers the road ends at a trail leading off to the right. This trail takes you to Lago Barva, about 1 kilometer away. Lago Barva, really a large pond, is situated in an extinct crater. Despite its inviting appearance, the water is apparently too acidic for fish, but there is an abundance of aquatic insect life.

There is a faint 2-kilometer trail from an old shelter located about 0.5 kilometer from the Barva ranger station, on the road to the Lago Barva Trail. It starts behind the building and winds through old pasture that has good birding. **Scintillating hummingbirds** are common. There is also an interesting ground cover plant with tiny red berries that grows in some of the more open areas. If you take one of these berries and squeeze it between your fingers, you will notice that it contains two seeds that look like coffee beans, and, indeed, it is a member of the coffee family. Most likely you won't be able to pick through the maze of old cow trails that cross the pasture, but if you luck out, you will meet up with the road farther up toward the Lago Barva trailhead.

Transect Trail
Distance: 40 kilometers
Hiking time: 3 to 4 days
Elevation loss: 2,866 meters
Map: 1:200,000 San José

A rarely used trail, often called the Transect Trail, leads out of the Barva area, down the slopes of the volcano, and north to the area of La Selva Biological Station in the lowlands. The total distance is about 40 kilometers and the trip would take four days. The elevation at the beginning of the trail is 2,900 meters, and it descends to 34 meters. There are a series of shelters along the way.

The reason that it is not discussed at length is that you need a local guide to show you the way. Used as a horse-pack route by the former landowners, it is poorly maintained and has numerous turnoffs. You can ask about someone to guide you at the Zurqui ranger station and park headquarters, or at La Selva Biological Station. The rangers at the ranger station in the Volcán Barva sector may pretend that the trail does not exist; they view the trail as unsuitable for foreign tourists. This trail has tremendous potential though. The lower sections of the trail are accessible from the park guardhouse near Magsasay.

IRAZÚ NATIONAL PARK

Size: 2,309 hectares
Distance from San José: 54 kilometers
Camping: Not permitted
Trails: Yes; very limited
Map: 1:200,000 San José
Dry season: December to April
Transportation: No public transportation available

Irazú is the highest volcano in Costa Rica, with an elevation of 3,432 meters. It is easy to reach from San José or Cartago, and a well-maintained paved road goes all the way to the summit. If you're at the summit as close to dawn as possible, you might be able to see both oceans. It can be extremely cold (the record low temperature was 3 degrees Celsius and the average is 7.3 degrees Celsius in the daytime), so dress warmly.

Volcán Irazú has a long and tumultuous history of eruptions, with the earliest written account dating to 1723. The largest eruptions in recent memory occurred between 1963 and 1965. You can still see some of the damage that the city of Cartago sustained during this period. There were massive mudslides, and great loss of life and property occurred. One of the volcano's explosions sent a boulder weighing several tons onto one of the farms on the northwest side of the mountain, and the impact created a hole 3 meters deep and 4 meters wide. During U.S. President John F. Kennedy's visit to San José in 1963, the volcano celebrated by belching forth a huge cloud of ash that covered the city in gray

The principal and active crater of Irazú Volcano, Irazú National Park

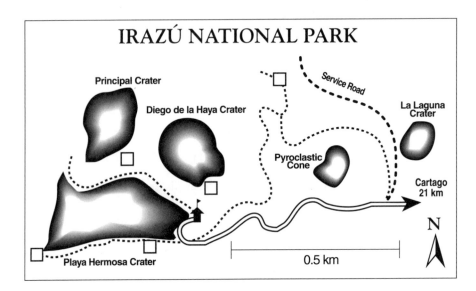

IRAZÚ NATIONAL PARK

Principal Crater

Diego de la Haya Crater

Service Road

La Laguna Crater

Pyroclastic Cone

Cartago 21 km

Playa Hermosa Crater

0.5 km

N

grit centimeters deep in places. But Irazú has given something back to the region by creating some of the best agricultural land in the country, and the pasturage on its flanks supports a large dairy industry. Recently, Irazú has started rumbling again, but there isn't any indication of a major eruption anytime soon.

It's a pity that Irazú's vegetation has been severely affected by human activity, as its steep gradient and high altitude must have presented a striking gradation in plant communities. Now, original plant cover is found only in the most inaccessible ravines and river courses. Above 2,000 meters the vegetation is typical of the tropical montane wet forest, a community that is restricted primarily to Irazú and consists mostly of **oaks** (*Quercus sp.*). The plant life at elevations above 3,100 meters has elements of the *paramo* community, a life zone that is typical of the high Andes Mountains of South America. Plants living at this elevation are slow-growing and stunted by the cold, and volcanic activity has made life even harder for them on Irazú. The shrub **Castelleja Irazúensis** is typical of this zone and is recognizable by its showy red flowers.

Wildlife was once very abundant in the region, and there is record of a ranch on the upper reaches of the volcano that closed down in 1855 solely because of predation by **jaguars**. Those days are long gone, and now the most common mammalian residents of the park are **rabbits** (*Sylvilagus brasilensis*) and **coyotes**. A few birds live in the rarefied air of the summit, including **sparrow hawks**, **volcano juncos**, and a few species of **hummingbirds**. Hummingbirds go into a state of hibernation on cold nights, allowing them to exist at high elevations despite their high metabolism.

There are four craters at the summit: the closest, Diego de la Haya (extinct); the principal and presently active crater farthest to the west; and two small inactive craters southeast of the main crater. The principal crater is the largest, measuring slightly more than 1 kilometer in diameter and 300 meters deep. Peering into it as it rumbles and issues steam and sulfurous fumes is like looking into the deepest bowels of the earth.

LOCATION AND ACCESS
The park is located near Cartago, a city east-northeast of San José, and the entire trip from San José takes a little over ninety minutes. From Cartago, take Highway 8 all the way to the park. Take it slow and be careful of cows in the road. You can also take a taxi from Cartago, or hitch a ride.

VISITOR FACILITIES
There are numerous *pensiónes* (almost all dumps) in Cartago, or you can stay at an interesting alpine-style hotel that's impossible to miss on the way up.

TRAILS
There are several short nature trails around the crater area. On the trail to the principal crater, look off the road to your left before you reach the park station to see a structure known as a pyroclastic cone, made up of chunks of volcanic material that solidified before it was issued forth from the volcano. It used to be possible to walk around the main crater, but this route was closed off due to safety concerns.

GUAYABO NATIONAL MONUMENT
Size: 217 hectares
Distance from San José: 84 kilometers
Camping: Permitted
Trails: Yes
Map: 1:200,000 San José
Dry season: December through April
Transportation: Bus from San José to Turrialba departs hourly from 6:00 A.M. to 10:00 P.M. daily from Calle 13, Avenidas 6/8; returns at the same times. Call Transtusa at 556-0073. Bus leaves Turrialba Monday through Saturday at 5:15 P.M., returns Tuesday through Sunday at 5:40 A.M.

Guayabo National Monument is Costa Rica's only archaeological park. Well-preserved stone mounds, roads, and aqueducts mark the site of what probably was an important commercial and perhaps religious center dating from 800 to 1400 A.D. A knowledgeable and helpful staff of archaeologists and interpreters is on hand to guide you through the ruins, and some speak rudimentary English, having attended an archaeological residency program in New Mexico. In addition to the ruins trail (which you are not allowed on without a guide), there is a short nature trail with mediocre wildlife-viewing opportunities.

On this trail, the nests of **Montezuma oropendelas**, large birds in the oriole family, can sometimes be seen in the trees near the path. These pendulous structures are woven of grass and other vegetation and can be almost 1 meter long. Oropendelas usually nest in groups and often very near the nests of several species of aggressive **predatory wasps**. The reason for this is that the young oropendelas, although well protected from predation in their pouchlike nests on the very ends of branches in the canopy, often fall prey to **botflies**. These insects lay their eggs on the nestlings, and the larvae burrow into the bird's skin, eventually killing it. But when the oropendelas construct their nests near the nests of certain species of **wasps** and **stingless bees**, these wasps or bees kill any botflies in the vicinity while leaving the birds unmolested. It is thought that the bees and wasps are sensitive to the sound of the fly's wing beats, which sound very similar to those of the types of flies that parasitize their young, and they consequently won't tolerate its presence. You can examine some oropendela nests up close at the interpretive center near the administrative building, or near the center of the ruins where workers put them up on the fence when they find them blown down after a storm.

Because of the small size of the reserve and the fact that all but an inaccessible 20 percent is in secondary forest on abandoned coffee plantation land, Guayabo has limited value as wildlife habitat. Still, it provides an interesting glimpse into Costa Rica's pre-Columbian past.

A number of mysteries surround Guayabo, some of which may be answered as excavation progresses. Although there is plenty of evidence to suggest that the site had been inhabited as early as 1000 B.C. and at its peak period maintained a population of up to 10,000 people, it was suddenly abandoned sometime in the early fifteenth century A.D., before the arrival of the Europeans. Whether political instability, ecological disaster, disease, or some combination of these factors led to Guayabo's abandonment is, as yet, unknown.

LOCATION AND ACCESS

Guayabo is located 18 kilometers from the town of Turrialba, which is 64 kilometers east of San José. There are several buses to Turrialba per day from San José, and it is possible to catch a bus from there to Guayabo. These run infrequently and inconsistently, so it is easier to take a taxi. A paved road begins on the west side of Turrialba, followed by a short stretch of gravel road that is passable year-round. Signs alert you to the turnoff for the monument.

VISITOR FACILITIES

It is possible to camp at the monument, near the headquarters building. Call the monument in advance (333-5473) to make sure that there will be room. There is at least one *pensión* in the town of Guayabo less than 1 kilometer away, and several hotels in Turrialba. The monument is also an easy day trip from San José, where accommodations are plentiful.

If you arrive after the gate opens at 8:00 A.M. but before your guide is ready to take you around the ruins, you can have a look at the interpretive center located across the road from the office. It contains artifacts representative of the various stages of the site's cultural evolution, and some natural history displays.

TRAILS

Nature Trail
Distance: 1 kilometer
Hiking time: 1 hour
Elevation gain: Almost none
Map: 1:200,000 San José

All access to the ruins is strictly controlled, and visitors are not allowed in them unaccompanied. However, there is a circular 1-kilometer nature trail that passes through a remnant secondary forest. Wildlife is relatively scarce, but it's a worthwhile short hike.

Ruins Trail
Distance: 1.5 kilometers
Hiking time: 2 hours
Elevation gain: 30 meters
Map: 1:200,000 San José

The trail through the ruins is only about 1.5 kilometers long, but in the company of one of the monument's knowledgeable interpretive guides, you can easily spend two hours walking it. You pass tombs, aqueducts, and a monolith with a depiction of the spirit of water (a caiman or crocodile) carved into one side and the spirit of the forest (a jaguar) on the other. You climb up a gently graded hill to a lookout point, and then descend to the ruins.

The most obvious features of the site are stone mounds (*montículos*) that are thought to be the foundations of conical thatched-roof buildings, probably built during the Middle Period (800 to 1000 A.D.), during the site's period of peak population. Also from this period are cobbled roads (*calzados*) that are thought to stretch out from the site for several kilometers and connect with trade routes coming from the Atlantic lowlands and the central plateau. A large spring emanates from the ground here, and its output and the aqueducts leading from it are still an important part of irrigation systems serving the surrounding farms and communities. Less obvious but just as interesting as these structures are several petroglyphs carved into paving stones along the road, including one that seems to be a celestial calendar used to predict the onset of the wet and dry seasons. Many finely crafted stone objects, including tables and gravestones, were excavated in the 1820s and can be viewed at the national museum in San José.

TAPANTÍ WILDLIFE REFUGE

Size: 4,715 hectares
Distance from San José: 35 kilometers
Camping: Permitted
Trails: Yes
Map: 1:50,000 Tapantí
Dry season: January through March
Transportation: Bus from San José to Cartago departs every 10 minutes from Calle 13, Avenidas Central/2; returns same times. Bus from Cartago to Orosi leaves hourly from the church ruins and returns at the same times. Call 551-6810 for information.

This refuge provides the visitor a chance to walk through an example of montane rain forest or cloud forest close to the cities of the Central Valley. There are excellent opportunities for wildlife watching, picnicking, and some of the best trout fishing in the country. Originally set aside to protect the watershed of an important hydroelectric dam, it is also home to at least 211 species of birds, including **three-wattled bellbirds.** In the higher, largely inaccessible and partially unexplored interior, **quetzals**, **jaguars**, and **ocelots**, along with a variety of other mammals, are found. There is also a diverse array of **amphibians**. This refuge constitutes a valuable biotic resource for the Central Valley, the most heavily populated area of the country, and is well worth the trip from San José. Remember that the refuge receives up to 7,000 millimeters of rain annually, so bring your rain gear!

LOCATION AND ACCESS

The refuge is located close to the town of Orosi, which is about 20 kilometers slightly southeast of San José. Cartago is easily reached from San José. From Cartago, take the road on the east side of town that goes to Paraiso. The road to Orosi descends steeply into the Orosi River valley, crosses a bridge, and then ascends toward the refuge. Signs mark the way from Orosi to Tapantí, and everyone in town knows the way to the refuge. Unfortunately, it is difficult to get there by bus; the best one can do is to take the bus from Cartago to Orosi and the tiny town of Río Macho, but this still leaves you with a 9-kilometer walk to the refuge. It is easy to get a taxi from Orosi, however, and you can arrange to be dropped off and picked up the day after, leaving you ample time to explore.

VISITOR FACILITIES

Your first stop will be at the visitor center (which opens at 6:00 A.M.) to pay your entrance fee and to get your camping permit. A nice camping and picnic area is close to the Río Grande de Orosi, occasionally stocked with trout. Even if you have no interest in fly-fishing, the river is a lovely place to bird-watch. There are a couple of hotels in Orosi, and a number of rather dumpy *pensiónes* in Cartago.

A poor man's umbrella plant and an admirer, Tapantí Wildlife Refuge

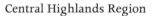
TRAILS

Sendero Arboles Caidos

Distance: 2.5 kilometers
Hiking time: 2 hours
Elevation gain: 200 meters
Map: 1:50,000 Tapantí

There are only three trails in the reserve, all short. About 1 kilometer up the road from the ranger station, an unmarked trail comes off the road on the left side. This is the entrance or exit to the semicircular Sendero Arboles Caidos (Fallen Trees Trail), about 2.5 kilometers in length. The trail climbs steeply for about 0.25 kilometer, travels along a ridge top, and then steeply descends back to the road. It takes you through an example of the tropical montane rain forest. **Tree ferns** (families *Cycantheaceae* and *Dicksoniacea*) are common, and indicate that some disturbance in the recent past has occurred here, either by wind or human intrusion. Tree ferns are usually pioneer light-gap species in high-elevation wet forests, and are interesting not only for their unusual appearance, but also because they are utilized as a renewable rain forest resource in Guatemala and Hawaii. The corklike outer layer of tissue on the "trunk" of the plant is stripped off in such a manner as to not injure the fern, which will grow another layer, for use in orchid culture. Tree ferns are an ancient group of organisms, and dinosaurs fed upon species similar to the ones that you see here.

Sendero Oropendela

Distance: 1 kilometer
Hiking time: 1 hour
Elevation gain: Almost none
Map: 1:50,000 Tapantí

Near the far end of the Sendero Arboles Caidos, on the opposite side of the road, is the Sendero Oropendela, which takes you about 1 kilometer along the river, past the picnic area.

Sendero la Pava and Lookout Trail

Distance: 0.5 kilometer
Hiking time: 20 minutes
Elevation gain: 75 meters
Map: 1:50,000 Tapantí

Another 3 kilometers farther up the road from the Sendero Oropendela, on the right side, is the Sendero la Pava (Turkey Trail), which descends 0.5 kilometer to the river and a nice fishing or swimming spot if you choose to brave the chilly water. A common but spectacular plant that grows along the road is the **poor man's umbrella** (*Gunnera insignis*), which looks like rhubarb on steroids.

Another 2 kilometers beyond the Sendero la Pava you will see a wooden sign with an eye on it; here there is a short trail up a hill to a lookout from which you can see a spectacular waterfall coming down from the high forest. From this vantage point it's easy to see how Tapantí's forests are responsible for the creation of 150 separate creeks and rivers draining into the Orosi and down into the Atlantic watershed.

CHIRRIPÓ NATIONAL PARK

Size: 50,150 hectares
Distance from San José: 151 kilometers
Camping: Permitted
Trails: Yes
Map: 1:200,000 Talamanca
Dry season: December through March
Transportation: Bus from San José to San Isidro departs hourly daily from 5:30 A.M. to 5:00 P.M. from Calle 16, Avenidas Central 1/3; returns the same times; Call Musoc at 222-2422. Bus from San Isidro to San Gerardo de Rivas departs at 5:00 A.M. and 2:00 P.M.; returns 7 A.M. and 4 P.M.

What could be more pleasant after backpacking or boating in the hot lowlands than a visit to the cool plains of the Andes Mountains? Chirripó National Park, which boasts the highest peak in the country, comes pretty close. The upper reaches of the park, often cold and almost always cloaked in mist, contain the northernmost example of the *paramo* life zone, which is typical of high-elevation plains much farther south. The park also contains extensive areas of lower montane and montane rain forest, offers excellent opportunities for wildlife observation and nature photography, and is one of the few areas suitable for technical rock climbing in Costa Rica.

Before setting out, you should be aware that the park authorities allow only 40 people in the park at any one time, and a reservation system has been instituted to protect the area from overuse. Call the parks department in San José at 233-4160 to make a reservation. Do so as far in advance as possible, as the park is quite popular with *Ticos* (Costa Rican citizens) as well as tourists. The peak season for use is around Easter, when *Ticos* have vacation time. Accommodations are available in huts (*refugios*) in the high peak region, though they are a bit run-down and smoky; they also provide a good base for day hikes. Enjoying this fascinating place involves some dues paying, however. The 15-kilometer, 10-hour hike to the summit area borders on grueling. This trial can be ameliorated somewhat by hiring a horse-packer from San Gerardo de Rivas to take your gear up; a horse can carry up to three packs and costs about 3,000 colones. This service is only available during the dry season from January through March to save wear

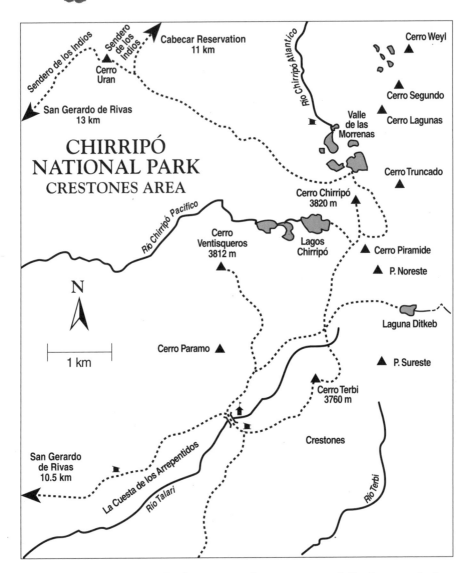

on the trails. If you opt to do this, you need to carry enough food, warm clothes, and water for the day. If you are carrying your own gear, you can also make the trip easier by staying at the first *refugio*, a little more than halfway up the trail.

One note about equipment: If you want to cook your meals or make hot drinks, you should carry a stove (see Chapter 1, Preparing for Your Trip, What to Bring). Although there are wood-burning stoves at the *refugios*, they are inefficient and smoky and there is some question as to whether burning even the previously fire-killed vegetation from the high-altitude areas of the park is a good idea—the practice may be discontinued altogether.

Chirripó experiences wide temperature variations. It can be as warm as 24 degrees Celsius during the day and then drop to freezing at night. Nights below freezing are common, and the all-time record low was 9 degrees Celsius. You'll need a warm sleeping bag, a warm hat, and a sweater, and long underwear and gloves are not a bad idea. The altitude change between sea level and the high country is severe enough to give some people altitude sickness, particularly if you've just spent a week or two in a dugout canoe or lying out on the beach. It is best to plan your trip to Chirripó after having spent at least a week hiking at a mid-elevation place such as Rincón de la Vieja or Monteverde to begin the process of acclimatization. Symptoms of altitude sickness are chronic headache, nausea, lack of appetite, and sleeplessness. The only cure is to tough it out for a few days or to descend until symptoms disappear. Altitude sickness at this elevation is rarely dangerous, but if you or a member of your party experience severe versions of the symptoms described above, you should descend.

LOCATION AND ACCESS

The park is located near San Isidro, which is 100 kilometers southeast of San José. There are buses running every hour from San José to San Isidro. From San Isidro, an all-weather gravel road takes you 9 kilometers to the town of San Gerardo de Rivas. The main route into the park is located northeast of San Gerardo de Rivas. A bus runs from San Isidro to San Gerardo de Rivas. Make sure you specify San Gerardo de Rivas, as there is another San Gerardo in the area.

VISITOR FACILITIES

There are several cheap places to stay in town. La Posada del Descanso is highly recommended (774-0433, extension 106). The owner, Francisco Elizondo, offers several grades of accommodation, including possibly camping in his back-yard if all else is full. Mr. Elizondo can answer virtually any question that you might have about the natural and human history of the park. His wife can cook fine meals at a very reasonable price with just a few hours' warning, and either one of them can arrange for pack horses during the dry season or taxis back to San Isidro at the end of your hike. Because the hike up to the park usually takes at least ten hours, get an early start out of San Gerardo de Rivas.

Paramo vegetation, Chirripó National Park

TRAILS

Refugio Base Crestones and the Summit Region

Distance: 16 kilometers one way to Base Crestones, 22 kilometers to Chirripó summit
Hiking time: 2 or 3 days, allow more for exploring the Crestones area
Elevation gain: 2,200 meters to Base Crestones, 2,520 meters to Chirripó summit
Map: 1:200,000 Talamanca

Fill up on water in San Gerardo de Rivas, as the next reliable source is 8 kilometers uphill. To get to the trailhead, get back on the only road passing northeast through town, the continuation of the one you came in on. Continue up the hill past the church, until you reach a fork in the road; take the right fork. Continue on until you come to a very elaborate sign marking the trailhead. The trail climbs up into a pasture, and then to a fence. Look for an unmarked right turn that goes very steeply uphill at 1.5 kilometers from the trailhead. The trail you were following continues along the fence, following level ground for a short time before descending toward the pastures. If you start to walk downhill along the fence, you've missed the turn.

After climbing the first major hill and passing through a stand of secondary vegetation, you'll come to another fence-line with a steep pasture on one side. **Swallow-tailed kites** are very commonly seen here as they soar and hover over the hillside seeking lizards, insects, and small rodents, their principal prey. This is also a good place to view the erosional effects of grazing cattle on such a steep grade, and to witness further deforestation as it creeps up the mountainside to the very border of the park. **Dung beetles** are usually present in this and other pastures near the park boundary, making the best of a bad situation by pairing off, male and female, and rolling a ball of cow dung off to a suitable location where eggs will be laid in their prize before it's buried.

The trail continues steadily uphill through the lower montane rain forest past the park boundary at 4.5 kilometers. In another 2.5 kilometers you crest a hill and walk for a short distance over level ground before descending to the first *refugio*, at about 6 kilometers from the trailhead. Park service employees often use this as a base while doing trail work, so it's often full. Please don't eat food or use fuel that you may find here, as it most likely belongs to the workers and all of it is brought up by foot or horseback. There is a spring with a plastic pipe and holding basin carved out of a tree stump on the northeast side of the building off the trail.

From here, the vegetation begins the transition from lower montane rain forest to montane rain forest. The tree species begin to be weighted toward several species of **oaks**, and **dwarf bamboos** and other high-elevation plants begin to dominate the understory. This is the domain of the **quetzal**, but although the park is home to one of the largest populations of these iridescent, emerald green birds, they are shy and difficult to see near the trail during periods of heavy

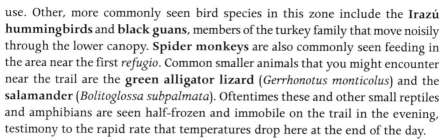

use. Other, more commonly seen bird species in this zone include the **Irazú hummingbirds** and **black guans**, members of the turkey family that move noisily through the lower canopy. **Spider monkeys** are also commonly seen feeding in the area near the first *refugio*. Common smaller animals that you might encounter near the trail are the **green alligator lizard** (*Gerrhonotus monticolus*) and the **salamander** (*Bolitoglossa subpalmata*). Oftentimes these and other small reptiles and amphibians are seen half-frozen and immobile on the trail in the evening, testimony to the rapid rate that temperatures drop here at the end of the day.

From the first *refugio*, you'll climb three more major hills. The first is the Cuesta de la Agua (Water Hill), so called because it becomes a small river during a hard rain. This is followed by the Monte Sin Fe (Mountain of No Hope). You descend slightly into a small, enclosed valley and should see a sign for the REFUGIO NATURAL, at about 7.5 kilometers from the trailhead. This is a small natural rock shelter that can be used in an emergency if you are totally exhausted or get caught out in the dark, but it's quite cold and damp.

From this point it is 3.5 kilometers, mostly uphill, to the Base Crestones huts. As you gain elevation, the vegetation becomes more dry and stunted. The last major climb is called La Cuesta de los Arrepentidos (Repentance Hill), and shortly after its crest you should be in sight of the huts, reachable after a short descent.

As you near the last hill, you will notice that most of the stunted trees are burnt and all of them are dead. This is the result of a fire that swept through most of the *paramo* and near-*paramo* vegetation in 1976. Thought to have been set intentionally by a disgruntled local resident, this fire burned 90 percent of this vegetation type within the park. The actual *paramo* within the Crestones area has recovered well, although a few species may have been extirpated, but the stunted trees surrounding the basin had yet to really regenerate even as late as 1998.

After a brief descent, you come to three huts situated by the Río Talari, at about 11 kilometers from the trailhead. The largest cabin is the most comfortable. If the cabins are intolerably smoky (the wood stoves let in more smoke than is carried out by the pipes), you can also camp anywhere around them. The ranger's cabin is located about 100 meters farther up the valley.

The cabins are located at the foot of the valley where the true *paramo* begins. On the way down the hill to the cabins, you might see some familiar-looking plants that have North American relatives, including **paintbrushes** (*Castilleja sp.*), **blueberries** (*Vaccinium sp.*), and **purple gentian** (*Gentiana sp.*). Mixed in with these are many species native to South America, including the **piñuela** (*Puya dasiliroides*), a plant that grows in marshy areas and generates a showy spike of blue flowers from an agavelike base. Because of the *paramo*'s harsh environment, only eight of the park's seventy-three recorded bird species are found there. These include the **volcano junco, rufous-crowned sparrow, sooty robin,** and **red-tailed hawk**.

To get to the summit of Mount Chirripó, pick up the only trail that gains elevation, traveling northeast. After passing turnoffs for short side trails to Cerro Ventisqueros, Laguna Ditkeb, and Cerro Terbi, you come to a saddle and see a turnoff for the short walk to the small but picturesque Lagos Chirripó, really not more than a series of ponds. The main trail takes you onto the short side trail for a steep climb from here to the summit. From the top on a clear day, you can see both oceans and most of the major high-elevation landmarks within the entire country. To the east are San Isidro and the InterAmerican Highway. To the north, the closest peak is Mount Uran at 3,819 meters, and to the northeast is Volcán Turrialba on the right and Volcán Irazú more to the left.

The summit is also an excellent place to contemplate the geological history of the region and the peculiar glacial geomorphology of Chirripó. During the Upper Jurassic period, 135–150 million years ago, pressure caused by the Atlantic and Pacific plates squeezing together caused an upwelling of the seafloor and unleashed a series of volcanic eruptions that formed cones that reached above the surface of the water. It wasn't until the Miocene period, 15–20 million years ago, that the Talamanca range, of which Chirripó is considered a part, completely emerged. The nascent land mass of Central America was not connected to North and South America until the Pliocene period, about 11 million years ago. The glacial component of the geomorphology of the landscape came into play during the Wisconsin glaciation, some 25,000 years ago. During this period, glaciers carved out signature U-shaped valleys and left such features as cirques (rounded depressions at the heads of valleys that often contain lakes or marshy areas) and moraines (piles of rounded stones and other material left by the receding glacier). Pinnacles and the sharpened summit ridges are also testimony to glacial action.

There is another *refugio* located on the northwest side of Chirripó peak. This building is closed to tourists, reserving it for scientific research. The main trail continues from the junction with the summit side trail, heading around the east side of the peak, then northwest across the *paramo* and descending to Cerro Uran, about 11 kilometers distant, before leaving the park and returning to San Gerardo de Rivas, another 11 kilometers farther. This circular route is about 35 kilometers from San Gerard and back. The trail is very indistinct and irregularly maintained. If you are interested in taking this route, check with the park people to see if it is clear enough to follow.

Lago Chirripó, Chirripó National Park

It is possible, although difficult to arrange, to get into the park through the Cabecar Reservation by going to the town of Paseo Marcos, meeting a guide, and hiking to the village of Chirripó Arriba and from there onto the backside of the park via the Sendero de los Indios. This takes you through some very remote territory that even local indigenous people will not traverse when the weather is bad. This trip takes a minimum of three days. To find out how you might be able to arrange this trip, talk to the people at Selvamar. Contact: Walter Odio and Pérez Zeledón, Apdo. 215-8000, San Isidro de El General. Telephone: 771-4582; Fax: 771-8841; e-mail: selvamar@sol.racsa.co.cr

LA AMISTAD NATIONAL PARK

Size: 193,929 hectares
Distance from San José: 410 kilometers
Camping: Permitted
Trails: Limited
Maps: 1:200,000 Talamanca; 1:200,000 Limón
Dry season: Effectively none, but December through March is dryer on the western slope
Transportation: Express bus leaves San José for San Vito from Calle 14, Avenida 5 at 2:40 P.M. daily, returns 5 A.M. Call Tracopa bus lines at 221-4214 for the latest schedule. Bus from San Vito to Las Mellizas departs daily at 9:00 A.M., 2:00 P.M., and 5:00 P.M. Helechales bus from San José to San Isidro departs hourly 5:00 A.M. to 5:00 P.M. daily from Calle 16, Avenidas 1/3; returns the same times. Call Musoc at 222-2422. Bus from San Isidro to Buenos Aires departs at 6:30 A.M., 8:30 A.M., and 12:30 P.M. Bus from Buenos Aires to Potrero Grande departs at 6:30 A.M. and 12:00 P.M.

La Amistad extends along the backbone of Costa Rica's Talamanca range, from the eastern boundary of Chirripó National Park all the way to the Panamanian border. There are several points of access into the park, none of them easy. The best routes are through private reserves located on the fringes of La Amistad proper. The Zona Protectora Las Tablas is composed of the private holdings of some of the largest landholders in Costa Rica, who receive substantial tax breaks for keeping most of their land under forest. A few of these landowners have begun ecotourism businesses, providing places to stay and guide services through their lands and into La Amistad. The Zona Protectora Las Tablas borders the park near the frontier with Panama in the southwestern corner of Costa Rica. This is a fascinating and sparsely visited part of the country, and one could easily spend months exploring there. However, in keeping with the wilderness character of the area, logistics are difficult. Guides are an absolute necessity unless you are very skilled with map and compass and willing to get lost. This is premontane and montane rain forest, high and sometimes cold. A medium-weight sleeping bag and long underwear are a good idea in the higher altitudes.

LOCATION, ACCESS, AND VISITOR FACILITIES

The center of operations and main access point for the Zona Protectora and for the relatively accessible parts of La Amistad is the pleasant town of San Vito, located about 85 miles from San Isidro de General on the InterAmerican Highway. This is where you will want to buy food and other supplies. An excellent place to stay in the San Vito area is the Wilson Botanical Gardens, located 6 kilometers south of town. The gardens (also known as *Las Cruces*) are a facility of the Organization of Tropical Studies, and are directed by the preeminent tropical biologist Luis Diego Goméz. Both luxuriant and basic dorm-style accommodations are available here, although the dorms are often in use by student groups. Wilson is known the world over as a birding hotspot, and you should make reservations well in advance if you have your heart set on staying there. The 10 hectares of gardens contain tropical plant species from around the world, and there are 148 hectares of late-succession, second-growth forest, most of which is open only to researchers. In 1998, the charge to get into the gardens was $8 per day. Call 773-3278 for more information.

There are three park stations in the Zona Protectora and the southern part of La Amistad. They all operate intermittently (there are only two park rangers responsible for the entire southern half of La Amistad) and the roads leading to them range from bad to impassable. Unmaintained, unmarked trails lead from these stations, and it is usually possible to camp near them. All three of the stations are accessed through San Vito.

Progresso is the most accessible of the three. Take the most easterly road out of San Vito toward Sabalito, 8 kilometers distant. Turn left at the only gas station in town. From here, it's about 18 kilometers over rough gravel roads (watch for oil-pan-smashing rocks jutting from the roadbed) to the village of La Lucha. An extremely rough 5-kilometer "road," actually a wide horse trail that is possibly impassable during the wet season, leads to the station. It may be necessary to walk.

The Santa Maria Pittier Station is 31.5 kilometers by extremely bad road (four-wheel-drive only, and cross your fingers even then) and horse trail from San Vito. It is best to ask about the road's condition in the village of Colonia Gutierrez Braun before proceeding. In 26 kilometers, you'll come to the little village of Agua Caliente, from which it is about a 5-kilometer walk uphill to the park station. You could conceivably camp here, and explore the unmarked trails around Cerro Pittier. Again, this is an extremely remote place, and you'll need to bring your compass and all your wits to prevent getting lost.

The third station, Altamira, is located 11 kilometers outside the town of Portrero Grande. It is best to ask in Portrero Grande about the latest road conditions, but it has been reported that the road has deteriorated to a horse path. You will probably have to walk.

There is an express bus at least once a day from San José to San Vito. Call Tracopa bus lines at 221-4214 for the latest schedule. From San Vito, you can hire a four-wheel-drive taxi to take you where you want to go. In general, the dirt roads in this part of the world are horrendous, with large protruding rocks, mud, and dust all conspiring to make things difficult for you. Take people's warnings concerning road conditions very seriously. When a local tells you that a road is bad, it is. You can save yourself a lot of potential grief by hiring local four-wheel-drive taxis to take you where you need to go.

An excellent base from which to explore the area is the La Amistad Lodge, located in the Zona Protectora near the town of Mellizas. It is situated in the middle of a large working farm surrounded by forest. From the lodge, you can arrange for local guides to take you into the more remote parts of Las Tablas, La Amistad, and even over the border into Panama. You can call the lodge directly (289-7667, fax: 289-7858) or make arrangements through Horizontes Tours in San José (See Appendix 1 for contact information). You can also camp at the farm of Miguel Sandi, which is outside of the village of Las Tablas on the border with Panama. Mr. Sandi is reputed to be one of the best guides in the area, but he is not always easy to get ahold of. You can ask the staff at La Amistad to help you find him, or you can write him in advance (in Spanish) at: Miguel Sandi, La Lucha, Sabalito, Coto Brus 8257, Costa Rica. Access to his farm can be achieved by four-wheel-drive only, and during rainy periods you will also need chains. His place is difficult to find, so it is best to either arrange in advance for him to pick you up (about $50 from San Vito) or take a taxi. You can also check with the staff at the Wilson Botanical Gardens to see if he's any easier to reach by the time you get there; he might even have a telephone by then.

LAS TABLAS AREA

1842 m
Cerro Pittier

Las Tablas

Santa Maria Pittier

5 km

Agua Caliente

Progreso

Mellizas

5 km

Altamira

Colorado

El Carmen

Santa Elena

F. Naranjo

Fila Tigre

La Lucha

4.5 km

13.5 km

11 km

Portrero Grande

San Luis

18 km

San Miguel

34 km

Colonia
Gutierrez
Braun

La Union

13 km

N

8 km   Sabalito

San Vito

(Not to scale)

*Measurements
in kilometers
indicate distances
between asterisks.*

Another interesting place in the area is the Las Alturas Field Station, located at the foot of Cerro Echandi, which is managed by the Wilson Botanical Gardens. It is generally not available to individual travelers, being used primarily for student and birding groups. However, you can plead your case with Luis Diego Goméz to see if an exception may be made.

TRAILS

Unmarked trails branch out from all three park stations described above. These require the use of map and compass, and guides are strongly recommended. In addition, there is one long route that you might consider undertaking if you're feeling adventurous.

TransContinental Trail

Distance: 70 kilometers
Hiking time: 10 or 11 days
Elevation gain: 2,700 meters
Map: 1:200,000 Talamanca

One of the most interesting and strenuous long trails in the country begins in the town of Ujarrás on the Ujarrás-Salitre-Cabagra Indigenous Reservation 9 kilometers from Buenos Aires. The very strenuous, 70-plus-kilometer, ten- or eleven-day route passes through the reservation, into La Amistad, and up onto the central ridge of Cerro Abolado at more than 2,700 meters before descending. On the descent, the trail passes through the Cabecar Reservation to the town of Kichuguecha, into the Valle de Talamanca, and then out at the town of Caroma.

Waterfall, Zona Protectora Las Tablas

The trail is extremely difficult to follow, and perhaps more so since a 1991 earthquake caused quite a bit of damage. The route marked on topographical maps bears very little resemblance to the real one. Also, there have been reports of a clandestine but thriving industry in marijuana production on the Atlantic slope, hidden away in patches carved out of the forests near remote villages along portions of the trail. These "gardens" are to be avoided, as their owners will not be happy to see you. For many years, few people were willing to guide visitors on this arduous, ten-day trip. However, a number of changes have taken place since the publication of the first edition of this book that make the journey a good deal more tenable. The Talamanca Conservation Organization (ATEC) has identified at least one indigenous guide who knows the trail well, has some first-aid training, and is apparently reliable. His name is Zenon Villanueva Vargas and he lives in the small village of Bajo Coen by Coroma. He has an ongoing agreement with indigenous leaders from both reservations, meaning that the complicated advance permissions and arrangements described in the first edition are no longer necessary. Mr. Vargas can be reached through the Talamanca Conservation Association at:

ATEC
Puerto Viejo de Talamanca
Limón, Costa Rica
Telephone/fax: 750-0188
E-mail: atecmail@sol.racsa.co.cr

You should begin to make arrangements with ATEC at least a month before your visit, as communication between ATEC and Mr. Vargas is complicated by his lack of a telephone. Visitors should bring their own food, and be prepared to feed Mr. Vargas and perhaps one assistant guide. Because of the trip's length and the arduous topography, it would be wise to bring some freeze-dried food and other lightweight provisions. You should also bring a complete array of first-aid supplies. There are a number of stream crossings, including one that is reputed to be dangerous. It may be a good idea to bring a 9mm rope and some knowledge of how to use it to cross streams safely. According to Mel Baker of ATEC, the trip can be undertaken from either the Atlantic side, beginning at Caroma, or the Pacific side, leaving from Ujarras. Both require a steep, six-to-eight-hour climb. The advantage of doing the trip from the Pacific side is that the climb is done the first day while you are relatively fresh, whereas from the Atlantic side the climb occurs around the third day. The Pacific side is also buffeted by strong gusts of wind that sometimes force you to lie down so as not to get blown off the trail, also something that may be better endured early in the trip. On the other hand, there is probably less chance of the trip being botched due to miscommunication if the departure point is closer to the home of the guides and ATEC's office. However, Mr. Vargas is willing to guide a trip from either side. Be prepared for everything from heat to near-freezing temperatures at night at the higher elevations, along with rain and high winds. The trip can be done at any time, but the best weather is probably in March and April.

SAN VITO WETLANDS

Size: 10 hectares
Distance from San José: 233 kilometers
Camping: No
Trails: No
Map: None available
Dry season: December through March
Transportation: No public transportation; take taxi from San Vito.

Birders spending a little time in San Vito will probably want to visit the San Vito wetlands, also known as the wetlands of San Joaquin. This area is located on private property, but the owners have formed an agreement with the government not to develop the marsh for the near future. Officially, it is administered by a local organization called the Association for the Protection of the Natural Resources of Coto Brus and is included in the La Amistad Biosphere Reserve. In the early 1990s a Canadian conservation organization donated some money to build a lookout tower, which in 1998 was in a dangerous state of disrepair. Despite their small size, the wetlands attract large numbers of water birds, including **purple** and **common galinules, white-throated crakes,** and **least grebes.**

LOCATION AND ACCESS

To reach the wetlands, take the road heading out of San Vito northeast toward Lourdes. You will pass a landing strip on your left. Continue on for about two hundred meters, where you will need to take a left turn on a dirt road. You may be able to see the marsh from the road, depending on the height of the grass. Park at the bottom of the hill and walk up to the house, where you'll need to pay a nominal entrance fee. From here you can walk through the pasture around the edge of the marsh. Be careful when climbing the tower, as the wooden steps and floorboards may be rotten.

VISITOR FACILITIES

None. There are several hotels in San Vito and you can also stay at the Wilson Botanical Gardens; see the La Amistad section for details.

8

CARIBBEAN REGION

Barra del Colorado Wildlife Refuge
Tortuguero National Park
Cahuita National Park
Gandoca-Manzanillo Wildlife Refuge
Hitoy-Cerere Biological Reserve

The Caribbean region is one of the country's most diverse, in terms of both natural history and human culture. The parks and reserves of the area provide visitors with ample opportunity for the exploration of both. Sea turtle nesting beaches, canals and quiet rainforest backwaters, coral reefs, and extensive mangrove estuaries are all here, with examples of each contained in the region's protected areas. The region's cultural variety comes from a melding of three major influences: English-speaking Caribbean blacks, several indigenous tribal groups, and, most recently on the scene, Spanish-speakers from other regions of Costa Rica and Nicaragua. The region is experiencing what is probably the most rapid rate of change in the country, particularly in its southern portion. Tourism, expansion of the banana industry, the demise of chocolate crops (from a fungal disease), and logging and mining interests are all pressing change upon the land and its people. The populace's response to these changes and the need to prioritize values make this a fascinating area for visitors interested in development issues.

BARRA DEL COLORADO WILDLIFE REFUGE

Size: 92,000 hectares (on paper; in reality it's much smaller)
Distance from San José: 99 kilometers via aircraft
Camping: Permitted
Trails: Limited, most travel within the reserve is on water
Map: 1:200,000 Barra del Colorado
Dry season: February, March, and April are driest, but there really is no defined dry season
Transportation: SANSA (233-5330) flights from San José to Barra del Colorado depart at 6:00 A.M. on Tuesday, Thursday, and Saturday; return on the same days at 7:00 A.M.

The size of this seemingly huge reserve is deceptive; much of the area was cut over and settled even before officials in San José drew up its boundaries, and the forest is still under siege from illegal logging and settlement by both Costa

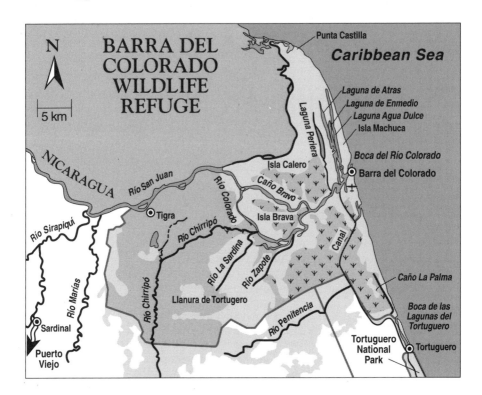

Rican and Nicaraguan refugees. This is particularly the case for the western part of the reserve where whole towns are springing up. Much of the rest of the area is still in private hands or has been leased to timber companies. The wet portions of the reserve, however, remain largely untouched, and one could spend many days exploring its swamps, sloughs, and backwaters. There is also good potential for extended unintentional exploration if you're not good with map and compass! For the independent traveler with a sea kayak and navigational skills, trips of several days or weeks are possible, particularly if combined with exploration of the Tortuguero National Park area, or you can arrange for guides and transportation without too much trouble.

For notes on the natural history of the river and its environs, please see Tortuguero National Park in this section. One interesting phenomenon peculiar to the Río San Juan is the migration of **bull sharks** (*Carcharhinus leucas*) from the saltwater of the Atlantic Ocean upriver to Lake Nicaragua. It's not known why these very large relatives of the great white shark make the trip, or exactly how they deal with the change in salinity so quickly. They pose no danger to travel on the river, and no attacks have been recorded on it. They may be essentially extinct anyway from overfishing near the mouth of the San Juan and perhaps from changing conditions in the river itself.

The two sides of the river are remarkably different. The Nicaraguan side is covered with dense primary rain forest, partially contained within the massive

Indio Maiz reserve. This is in sharp contrast to the Costa Rican side of the river and the banks of the Sirapiquí, where the forest has long ago fallen before the chainsaw and been chewed back by the mouths of hungry cows. The reasons for the difference are the result of Costa Rica's higher population and the relative freedom that the lumber industry has been given (by virtue of previously unenforced timber laws) to cut where it wanted. Things are improving, but for this area the change has come too late. The river itself has suffered in that there is good evidence to indicate that navigation on it is becoming increasingly more difficult because of siltation. This problem has been building for some time; there are old reports of pirate vessels sailing up the Río San Juan all the way to Lake Nicaragua in the eighteenth century. Nowadays there are times when even the *lanchas* have problems. On the more positive side, there is a movement afoot to consolidate what is left of Barra del Colorado and administer it with more intensity and forethought. Hopefully the forces of reason will prevail, and all of it won't look like the south bank of the San Juan.

LOCATION AND ACCESS

The Barra del Colorado Wildlife Refuge is located in the northeast corner of Costa Rica, on the border with Nicaragua. The easiest way into the refuge is to fly on SANSA to the town of Barra del Colorado from San José. You can also travel one or both ways on the San Juan and Sirapiquí Rivers to or from the towns of Barra del Colorado or Puerto Viejo, bearing in mind that the trip upriver takes six to seven hours and the trip down about four hours. Starting from Barra del Colorado, the route takes you up the Río San Juan, which is actually Nicaraguan territory, though Costa Rica has unlimited use of it. You will have to stop at one or two Nicaraguan checkpoints before reentering Costa Rican territory at the mouth of the Sirapiquí. All of the boatmen who make the trip are well known by the border officials, and passengers are rarely asked to produce documents since the cessation of Contra war hostilities in the region.

VISITOR FACILITIES

The easiest place to arrange for trips into Barra del Colorado and down to Tortuguero via the canals is at the Tarponland Lodge and Restaurant located right off the runway. Be careful to firmly set prices for trips so that there are no surprises on the river when you run out of gas and the guide looks to you to buy it. The owner of the lodge knows everyone on the river in both Costa Rica and Nicaragua, and can arrange boat transportation and guides for trips all the way to Limón or Puerto Viejo. He can be reached by telephone at 221-9932.

The recently created Canadian Organization for Tropical Education and Rainforest Conservation (COTERC) has a small research-oriented field station in the refuge on Caño la Palma. COTERC offers basic dormitory accommodations for 13 people at a time. Write in advance to P.O. Box 335, Pickering, ON L1V 2R6 Canada (905-683-2116).You can also take your chances and just show up; if you have a tent you will probably be able to stay on the grounds if the dorms are full.

Caño la Palma is 16 kilometers south of Barra del Colorado via the canal. It flows into the canal from the east, and is the first stream to the north of Cerro Tortuguero. About 1 kilometer upriver you will see a large sign for the field station on the bank near the dock.

TRAILS

The land owned by COTERC includes some lovely primary forest, and has trails to an interesting upland tract on Cerro Tortuguero to which field station personnel are happy to guide people. Nearby are some important turtle nesting beaches that have yet to be discovered by the ecotourism industry. You should be able to hire motorboats and a guide through COTERC.

TORTUGUERO NATIONAL PARK

Size: 18,946 hectares
Distance from San José: 254 kilometers by land or water
Camping: Permitted
Trails: Very limited
Maps: 1:200,000 Barra del Colorado; 1:200,000 Limón; 1:50,000 Tortuguero; 1:50,000 Agua Fria; 1:50,000 California
Dry season: February and March
Transportation: No public transportation available.

Nature tourists on the Tortuguero Canal, Tortuguero National Park

TORTUGUERO NATIONAL PARK

N

5 km

Barra Del Colorado
27 km
Caño Palacio
Isla Chira
Isla Quatro Esquinas
Caño Chiquero
Cerro Tortuguero
119 m
Casa Verde Turtle Research Station
Tortuguero
Nature trail
Caño Sérvulo
Caribbean Sea
Río Tortuguero
La Fortuna
Mata de Limón
Maquilla
Millon
Cariari
Astua y Pie
Sagrada Familia
Curia
San Cristobal
Esperanza
Pueblo Nuevo
Cruce
Guapiles
20 km
Guapiles
20 km
Lomas de Sierpe
Laguna Del Tortuguero
Caño Sierpe
Río Sierpe Viejo
Caño California
Jalova Ranger Station
Laguna Jalova
Boca del Río Parismina
Río Parismina Canal
Limón
42 km

Tortuguero is one of Costa Rica's best-known parks, and not without reason. It provides visitors a chance to view a diverse array of wildlife while traveling by boat on a series of waterways, including a section of the famous Limón-to-the-Nicaraguan-border canal. The canal was constructed in the 1930s to provide a more economical and safe way of transporting timber than the old method, which was to tie logs together and tow them to Limón via the ocean. The park protects examples of a surprisingly diverse array of plant associations, including swamp forests, lowland rain forests, and beaches. It's also one of the best places in the country to witness sea turtles nesting, the beaches here being one of the most important sites for the **green sea turtle** in the Caribbean.

The word *tortuguero* means "turtle catcher" in Spanish. The lives of turtles and people have been intimately intertwined here at least since the arrival of the first indigenous tribal group, relatives of the Mayans, several hundred years ago. These people and other indigenous groups such as the Zambo-Misquito who arrived later, utilized turtles in a sustainable manner and all was in balance until the first settlement of Europeans in 1541. The large-scale exploitation of the adult turtles and their eggs soon followed, reaching its peak around 1912, when commercial ships loaded to the underside of the decks with turtle products made

regular departures from Limón to the United States and Europe. One ship, the *Vanguard*, was recorded to have left Limón with eighteen tons of turtles in its hold. The trade in whole turtles declined with the advent of the practice of taking only the "calipee" (a cartilaginous substance found under the plastron or lower shell of the turtle that was used to make soup), and leaving the poor animals to die a slow, miserable death on the beach.

But the calipee and egg trade continued, reaching another peak in the 1950s. (The eggs are still in demand today as *bocas*, or snacks, eaten in bars, and are erroneously believed to have aphrodisiacal properties.) The situation looked so grim for the survival of the turtles that in 1959 Dr. Archie Carr, a respected herpetologist and conservationist, began the Brotherhood of the Green Turtle and its subsidiary, the Caribbean Conservation Corporation (CCC), to address the problem. They started out primarily as research organizations along with engaging in the protected hatching and release of turtles, but soon found themselves advocating new protective laws and finally the creation of the park. The park was signed into being in 1970, ending a long period of unsustainable exploitation of both the forest and the turtles. Today the CCC, now headed by Dr. Carr's son, is still an important player in the struggle for conservation in the area. You may be able to visit them near the town of Tortuguero if you arrange it with them in advance.

Observing nesting turtles is an unforgettable experience. From August to November the most common of the four species that occur here, the **green turtle** (*Chelonia mydas*), come ashore at night. They grow to a length of 1 meter and adults weigh between 75 and 200 kilograms. They are herbivorous, eating turtle grass and algae, and are as efficient at digesting cellulose as cows. Because of this, there has been a lot of interest in trying to domesticate them, but so far to no avail. The **hawksbill turtle** (*Eretmochelys imbricata*) is much smaller than the green, measuring between 65 and 90 centimeters and weighing between 35 and 75 kilograms. Hawksbills are the source of the "tortoiseshell" ornaments that you can still find for sale on the streets of San José and that are in such great demand in Japan. This species is critically endangered, and it is unfortunate that more do not nest within the park. While they are supposedly protected in Costa Rica, some are still poached both within the country and farther north, and their shells all too often end up in the hands of tourists.

The **loggerhead turtle** (*Caretta caretta*) is a very infrequent nester here, and is easily recognizable by the large size of its head, about twice that of a green turtle in proportion to its body, and its relatively small flippers. The **leatherback turtle** (*Dermochelys coriacea*) nests here from mid-February to the end of April. It can attain a length of as much as 2 meters and weigh more than 700 kilograms. (See Chapter 2, The Tropical Forest, for more information on this species.) Even though fewer than 300 leatherbacks nest in the park per year, the nesting sites at Tortuguero are still important for their survival in the region.

If you are interested in seeing the turtles, you are now required to go with a guide who has been trained by the parks department and is a part of the local guides cooperative. You can make arrangements for doing so at the information kiosk (see visitor facilities, below). During turtle nesting season, non-researchers are not allowed on the beach after 10:00 P.M. To ensure that the turtles are not unduly disturbed, your guide will follow good turtle-watching etiquette. Flashlights must be kept off until the turtle is located and she has finished the laborious process of excavating her nest and is in the process of actually laying her eggs. Turtles are extremely cautious creatures and straying from this protocol will probably cause the turtle to turn around and go back into the ocean. While they will most likely come back out to lay again, it places undue stress on the animals.

Other interesting species found here include the endangered **manatee, jaguar**, and at least 309 species of birds. Bird life on the canal is varied, to say the least. Many species that are difficult to see in the forest are much easier to observe. During the fall and spring migration periods, spectacular numbers of North American species pass through the area en route to South America. These include **orioles, warblers**, and large numbers of **Swainson's hawks**. Permanent residents include several species of **kingfishers, herons**, and **rails**. Less commonly seen species include the **great green macaw**, which replaces the **scarlet macaw** of the Pacific side of the country. Both species are endangered, and Tortuguero is one of the great green's last strongholds. They can sometimes be seen crossing the canal, particularly in the evening and early morning as they move from feeding to roosting sites in raucous flocks of up to fifteen individuals.

One of the goals held by many visitors to Tortuguero is to see a **three-toed sloth** (*Bradypus griseus*). While they are common in the canopy beside the canal, it takes an experienced eye to spot one. Besides being slow moving, sloths grow their own camouflage in the form of algae in their fur, giving them a gray-green cast. Sloths are host to several species of beetle and a moth that live in their fur and nowhere else, and all of these deposit their eggs in the sloth's dung when it comes down to the ground once a week to defecate and urinate. Why they descend to do this, opening themselves to attack by predators on the ground and expending a lot of energy, is still a mystery. **White-faced** and **howler monkeys** are also commonly seen.

The water around you is home to many interesting species. These include the **gar** (*Atractosteus tropicus*), a fish that qualifies as a "living fossil." The genus that it belongs to dates back to the Cretaceous period, about 90 million years ago. They reach a length of 2 meters and have a javelin-shaped body covered with heavy scales, and their long mouths are equipped with a fearsome-looking set of crocodile-like teeth. They are shy creatures, however, and are eagerly sought as a food fish by locals. Gars are particularly prone to predation by humans during June and July, when they migrate into shallow, flooded areas to breed.

If you are really lucky and are traveling one of the quieter backwaters, you may see one of Costa Rica's most endangered mammals, the **manatee** or **sea** cow (*Trichechus manatus*). These huge but defenseless, totally aquatic animals were formerly hunted for food by locals, but nowadays mortality is usually caused by injuries from powerboat propellers. They are important for keeping the waters here navigable, because one of their main food items is the **water hyacinth**, a species that floats on the surface and can completely close a creek to boat traffic.

LOCATION AND ACCESS

The park is located in the northeast part of Costa Rica, on the Atlantic coast. The traditional way to reach the small town of Tortuguero, where the park headquarters, accommodations, and other services are located, is to take the canal trip from the port of Moin near Limón. There used to be regular launch service from Limón to Tortuguero, but this was discontinued when the canal became too shallow for large boats, a result of silt runoff from deforestation. Private boatmen will take you from Moin (near Limón) to Tortuguero for about $65 per person. The trip takes about seven hours. Alternately, you can fly into Barra del Colorado on SANSA (for details, see Barra del Colorado Wildlife Refuge in this section) and then hire a boat to take you south to Tortuguero, usually a five-hour trip. The wildlife watching seems to be better coming from the north, probably because of the rapid rate of deforestation taking place in the unprotected portions of the forest near the banks of the canal. (The timber companies were requested by the government to leave a 15-meter-or-so corridor of trees along the bank for the benefit of tourists plying the canal when people began complaining about the lack of wildlife along some sections of it. Obviously, the animals are not fooled by this cosmetic approach to conservation.) Recently, a road was proposed that would link the village of Tortuguero with the Atlantic lowlands. To their credit, the people of the village voted in a referendum overwhelmingly against the project.

VISITOR FACILITIES

There are several places to stay in the town of Tortuguero, from basic to luxurious. However, the area is increasingly popular, so you should make reservations well ahead of time. You can also camp near the park headquarters at the north end of the park on the canal. The fee for camping is $2. Information about guides for turtle watching, or where to rent *cayugas* (dugout canoes), can be obtained either from the park office or at the information kiosk in the center of town.

The Sierpe Hills sector (Lomas de Sierpe) at the western end of the park can be reached via a paved road from Guapiles through Cariari to about 4 kilometers before Mata de Limón. The road from the turnoff to the village of Maquilla is dirt (or mud) and passable only to four-wheel-drive vehicles. From here you have to walk to the even smaller village of La Fortuna. From La Fortuna ask for the trail to the Agua Fria ranger station. A trail that leads to the station can be reached from off the Río Tortuguero, but you will probably need a guide to find it. From the river, it's about 4 kilometers to the station.

TRAILS

Tortuguero Nature Trail

Distance: 2 kilometers
Hiking time: 1 hour
Elevation gain: None
Map: 1:50,000 Tortuguero

The only dry-land (and this just barely) trail in the more accessible eastern end of the park is the 2-kilometer nature trail located just north of the headquarters building near Tortuguero village. There are quite a few mosquitoes, so bring your repellent. The trail takes you through examples of five of the plant communities in the park. The forested parts of the trail are in **cativo** forest, named after the dominant tree species *Prioria copaifera*. This community is marshy and sometimes inundated with water, enough of the time at least for the tree to distribute its seeds by floating them away. The trail has signs numbered to correspond to a trail guide put out by the park service, but it is rarely available in Tortuguero.

The trail comes out onto the beach, where **coconut palms** and the **purple beach pea** (*Mucuma sloanii*) are representative species in this plant community. You can walk back to town via the beach. You can also walk along the beach for about 20 kilometers to the park border near the Jalova Ranger Station. The ranger station, however, is surrounded by water on three sides and cannot be accessed from this point.

The Sierpe Hills

Distance: 7 kilometers
Hiking time: 3 hours
Elevation gain: 100 meters
Map: 1:50,000 Agua Fria

There is a poorly cleared and sometimes obscure 7-kilometer trail from the Agua Fria Ranger Station to and around one of the outlying hills of the Lomas de Sierpe. The trail itself goes through previously cutover forest and is not that interesting, but it does get you into the Sierpe Hills. The Sierpe Hills, which are of volcanic origin, rise to an elevation of 311 meters and are covered with tall, old-growth tropical wet forest. There are no trails on the eastern slope of the hills, so this is map and compass territory.

CANAL AND RIVER TRIPS

Barra del Colorado to the Tortuguero Canal

Distance: 100 kilometers
Paddling time: 6 days
Maps: 1:200,000 Barra del Colorado; 1:200,000 Limón; 1:50,000 Colorado; 1:50,000 Tortuguero; 1:50,000 California

Quiet backwater, Tortuguero National Park

Strong paddlers who bring their own craft with them to Costa Rica may want to consider doing trips in the Tortuguero–Barra del Colorado region. There are some definite advantages to taking a small boat from Barra del Colorado south to Tortuguero. You can get up into some of the quieter creeks and backwaters for a more intimate view of the vegetation and wildlife than is possible on a big boat that stays to the canal. The entire canal from Moin to Barra del Colorado is a little more than 100 kilometers with little current. There is not much in the way of distinguishing landmarks along the canal itself, the sides being lined with low and medium-height marsh forest and stands of **raffia** or **holillo** palm, a water-loving species. One interesting landmark is Cerro Tortuguero, located 5.5 kilometers north of the town of Tortuguero. This 119-meter hill is the remnant of a volcanic cone that predates the sediments that make up the Tortuguero plain, and sticks up like the tip of an iceberg through the alluvium.

Río Sierpe
Distance: 25 kilometers
Paddling time: 1 or 2 days
Map: 1:50,000 Agua Fria

Sidetrips that you can attempt with your own boat or with a rented motorboat and guide include the Río Sierpe. This river takes you through some of the last untouched territory in the region and if you are an adept "poler," you can get to the Sierpe Hills, about 25 kilometers from the mouth of the river. The Agua Fria map is essential for this trip.

Caño Chiquero

Distance: 17 kilometers
Paddling time: 1 or 2 days
Map: 1:50,000 Tortuguero

Two kilometers northwest of the town of Tortuguero is the Caño Chiquero, a creek that takes you through patches of virgin forest mixed with cutover areas. There is good birding to be had on the Chiquero, and anyone with a dugout and motor can get you there.

CAHUITA NATIONAL PARK

Size: 1,067 hectares
Distance from San José: 211 kilometers
Camping: Permitted
Trails: Yes
Map: 1:50,000 Cahuita
Dry season: January through March
Transportation: Bus from San José to Sixaola departs at 6:00 A.M., 2:30 P.M., and 4:30 P.M. from Calles Central/1, Avenida 11; returns at 5:00 A.M., 8:00 A.M., and 2:30 P.M.; call Transportes Mepe at 257-8128. Bus from Limón to Cahuita departs at 5:00 A.M., 10:00 A.M., 1:00 P.M., and 4:00 P.M. from the Radio Casino; returns at 5:00 A.M., 10:00 A.M., and 3:00 P.M. Timetables are notoriously changeable, so call for latest schedule.

Cahuita (from the indigenous words *kawe* or mahogany and *ta* or point) National Park was created in 1970 to protect the country's largest coral reef. One hundred twenty-three species of fish have been listed here, along with a variety of corals and other invertebrates. The park also protects an example of tropical moist forest, along with swamp forests and marshland.

Much of what you see exposed at Punta Cahuita was well under water before the 1991 earthquake, and nowadays you must walk some distance to get to the ocean. The quake constitutes the latest disaster to befall the reef; it has other problems as well. Silt from deforestation in the Talamanca Mountains behind the park, as well as soil and pesticide runoff from the expanding banana industry, is killing the reef. Besides outright suffocating the **coral polyps**, silt also interferes in the symbiotic relationship that many corals have with **blue-green algae** that live within the animals' tissues and provide them with a good deal of their food. Silt blocks the light that the algae need to photosynthesize, eventually killing both algae and polyp. There is still a lot worth saving in Cahuita, and it is hoped that the government will become more interested in the problems that threaten Costa Rica's only mature coral reef.

The most common coral species include **moose horn coral** (*Acropora palmata*),

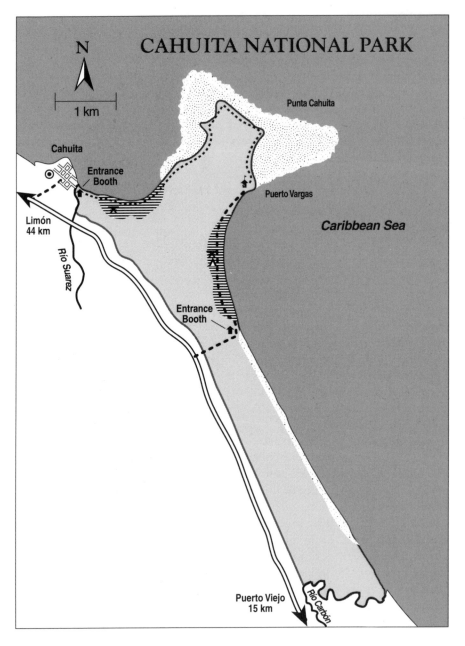

which grows in flat shelflike formations and has a reddish tinge; **deer horn coral** (*Acropora cervicornis*), yellowish gray in color; and **brain coral** (*Diploria crivosa*), which looks remarkably like its namesake and can grow quite large, one specimen on the outer edge of the reef being 2 meters in diameter.

In deeper water the **fan coral** (*Gorgonia flablellum*) can be found, swaying gently in the current. It's not a true coral, as its skeleton is made of chitin rather than calcium carbonate. **Black sea urchins** (*Diadema antillarum*) are unfortunately common and have to be watched for. The spines are very painful and difficult to remove, but you can slowly dissolve them with full-strength vinegar. In the outer reef, you may still come across a **spiny lobster** (*Panulirus sp.*), but these have become rare over the years from poaching.

One of the more commonly encountered of the 123 species of fish on the reef is the **blue parrotfish** (*Scarus coerulens*). This fish can be seen and quite clearly heard crushing live coral with its immensely strong "beak" made up of fused teeth. The fish ingests the coral, exoskeleton and all, and excretes the hard part in the form of sand. Most of the white sand on the local beaches was formed in this way.

One object of historical interest located near the outer reef is the wreck of an eighteenth-century slave ship. It has been pretty well picked over (illegally) by curio seekers, but manacles and other objects made in England point to its origin and purpose. While there's not much of it left, you can probably get one of the locals or park people to show you where it is.

Cahuita provides an interesting case study in community relations and conservation. Unfortunately, the park service started out on the wrong foot with the local populace by expropriating the land for the park, mostly from small landholders, without seeking their consent, and, even worse, in some cases without compensation. This was done during a less enlightened period in the evolution of the park service bureaucracy, but most compensation cases are still pending and the land values in the area are obviously rising, making it difficult for the government to come up with the money. People from the towns of Gondoca and Manzanillo have watched this process with some dismay, and it has caused resistance to the creation of the Gandoca-Manzanillo Wildlife Refuge farther down the coast. Cahuita locals, particularly those old enough to remember the whole process of the park's creation, are more than happy to talk to you about the issue.

LOCATION AND ACCESS

The park is located just south of the town of Cahuita, about 43 kilometers south of Limón. You can take the bus that leaves three times a day from San José to Sixaola, or you can get a bus from Limón. You can also drive from San José via the Siquirres Highway.

VISITOR FACILITIES

Camping is allowed at the park's well-organized campground, which has water, toilets, and grills, but it's quite crowded on weekends and holidays. There are many hotels in the town of Cahuita and farther south in Puerto Viejo. Masks and snorkels can be rented in both towns, but there is no scuba equipment for rent outside of San José.

TRAILS

Cahuita to Puerto Vargas and Río Carbón (park boundary)

Distance: Puerto Vargas, 7 kilometers one way; park boundary, 14 kilometers one way
Hiking time: Puerto Vargas, 2 hours; park boundary, 4 hours each way
Elevation gain: None
Map: 1:50,000 Cahuita

The trail starts at the south end of Cahuita. After crossing the Río Suarez, you are in the park. There's a park entrance station here. The trail starts as an old road and basically follows along the beach. The most obvious wildlife on this section of the trail is the **amiva lizards** (*Amiva quadriliniata*) scurrying to get out of your way. These small reptiles are active foragers, using their sensitive olfactory sense by licking the ground and at the air and transferring particles to a structure called Jacobson's organ, located in the roof of the mouth. Also common here is the **basilisk** or **Jesus Christ lizard** (*Basilicus basilicus*). This relatively large brown lizard gets its common name from its habit of running on its hind legs with such speed as to carry it across water for short distances.

The trail takes you through a mixture of swamp forest and tropical moist forest. **Howler monkeys** are often heard but rarely seen because of the heavy undergrowth. The territorial calls of the males, produced with a bony resonating chamber around the larynx, can be heard for more than 1 kilometer, even in dense forest. **Three-toed sloths, raccoons,** and **coatimundis** are also common.

At 3.5 kilometers, the trail comes out of the forest to Punta Cahuita and the reef. As the trail rounds the point, the shoreline becomes less sand and more coral rubble. This area contains good tide pools. Organisms, including several species of **chitons**, flat mollusks with a dorsal shell divided into separate plates, and **hermit crabs** (*Pagurus sp.*), are common. In 7 kilometers the trail arrives at Puerto Vargas and the park's administration area. From Puerto Vargas you can hike a short trail to the entrance booth on the road, and walk or hitch back to Cahuita, 7.5 kilometers via the road.

Or to continue on from Puerto Vargas, it's another 5.5 kilometers to the border of the park at the Río Carbón, which you will need to wade if you are backpacking down to Puerto Viejo, 15 kilometers distant. It's a hot, exposed walk on the beach and there is no water along the way, so if you have run out, the Carbón is it. Trees along the beach, besides the ubiquitous **coconut**, include the **beach almond** (*Terminalia catappa*), a species that is instantly recognizable by its large spatulate leaves and green, almond-shaped fruit. This tree is not a native; it is indigenous to the East Indies and has been transported all over the tropics. The nuts are edible, but it takes a tremendous amount of work to separate them from their fibrous encasement and then break open the tough shell.

GANDOCA-MANZANILLO WILDLIFE REFUGE

Size: 5,013 hectares of land; 4,436 hectares of sea
Distance from San José: 241 kilometers
Camping: Permitted
Trails: Yes
Map: 1:50,000 Sixaola
Dry season: February, March, June, September, and October
Transportation: Bus from San José to Sixaola departs at 6:00 A.M., 2:30
P.M., and 4:30 P.M. from Calles Central/1, Avenida 11; returns at 5:00 A.M.,
8:00 A.M., and 2:30 P.M.; Transportes Mepe (257-8128). Bus from Limón to
Sixaola departs at 5:00 A.M., 10:00 A.M., 1:00 P.M., and 4:00 P.M. from the
Radio Casino; returns at 5:00 A.M., 10:00 A.M., and 3:00 P.M. Timetables are
notoriously changeable, call for latest schedule.

The Gandoca-Manzanillo Wildlife Refuge contains a few of Costa Rica's last
living **coral reefs** and the last **orey** (*Camprosprma panamensis*) swamp in the
country. It also contains the only intact mangrove swamp on the Atlantic coast,

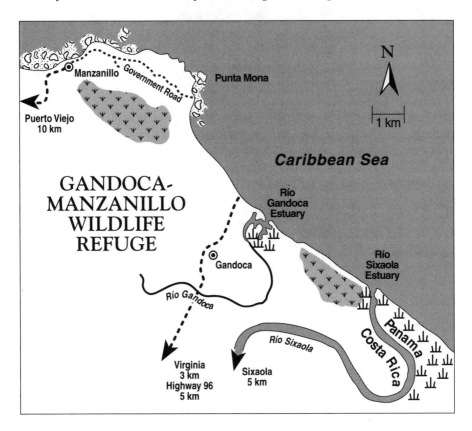

an important turtle-nesting beach, and extensive tracts of **cativo** forest and **holillo** swamp. Some 358 species of birds have been identified here, 40 percent of which are considered "rare" in neighboring Panama. Two of the country's more notable bird sightings in recent years were the appearance of a **harpy eagle** in 1985 and 1986 on the southwest side of the refuge. This huge raptor is probably extinct in Costa Rica due to deforestation and hunting pressure, but these transient sightings are cause for a little hope that the species could return or be reintroduced. Other endangered species found here include **American crocodiles, tapirs,** and **manatees.** Besides being a very important wildlife habitat, the refuge contains considerable scenic beauty around the coast, with nearly deserted beaches and large coconut groves.

Terrestrial hermit crab, Gandoca-Manzanillo Wildlife Refuge

One organization that was instrumental in the establishment of the refuge and maintains a continuing interest in it is the Asociación de los Nuevos Alquimistas (ANAI). ANAI was created by a group of people formerly associated with the New Alchemy Institute in the United States who were interested in advancing appropriate technology and agriculture in the tropics. They saw the need to protect the biotic resources in the area that is now the refuge and pressed for its protection. The refuge still has problems with poaching and incursion by squatters, and tourism developers have been slavering to get at some of its beachfront property, so the people at ANAI have to stay continually vigilant. To get more information about ANAI's work and to write to them with questions, observations, or suggestions about the reserve, or to donate funds (always put to good use), write to ANAI, 1176 Bryson City Road, Franklin, NC 28734, U.S.A. You can also do them a favor and send them copies of whatever letters you send to the Wildlife Directorate or ICT that concern the park. ANAI has a base in Gondoca, but you need to write ahead of time to arrange a visit.

LOCATION AND ACCESS

The refuge is located about 12 kilometers southeast of Puerto Viejo, just south of the small village of Manzanillo. There are several ways to get there. There is a once-a-day bus from Puerto Viejo. This will get you to the Punta Mona trailhead near Manzanillo and to the coral reefs. You can get to Puerto Viejo by taking the Sixaola bus and getting off at the gravel road into town, at a point called *El Cruce*. From here you have to hitch or walk about 4 kilometers to Puerto Viejo.

To get to the mangrove area on the Panamanian border, take the Sixaola bus from San José all the way to Sixaola, where you then need to hire a boat. You can also get taxis from Puerto Viejo to Manzanillo. The road from Puerto Viejo is rough but passable to two-wheel-drive vehicles, though you should check on its condition in Puerto Viejo to make sure, particularly after heavy rains.

If you are interested in trying to get to the estuary of the Río Gandoca, you can get to the town of Gandoca with your own four-wheel-drive vehicle via a rough dirt road from the plantation areas of Daytonia and Virginia passing through Highway 96, west of Sixaola.

VISITOR FACILITIES

Camping is allowed in the refuge, but is best done on or near the beach because of heat and biting insects inland. There is one hotel in Manzanillo, but it is very basic. There are many places to stay along the road to Puerto Viejo and in town. The most interesting is Cabinas Chimuri, owned and operated by Mauricio Salazar. He can arrange tours by horseback or by foot into the indigenous people's reserves in the area, and is very knowledgeable about the natural and human history of the area, as well as the environmental problems the Talamanca region faces.

Snorkeling equipment can be rented in Puerto Viejo at several places, or you

can try Willie Burton in Manzanillo, who also takes people out diving and fishing. ATEC can put you in contact with many people in the area, including local naturalists, herbalists, fishermen, and farmers who lead tours for visitors.

TRAILS

Manzanillo to Punta Mona (Monkey Point)

Distance: 5.5 kilometers one way
Hiking time: 5 hours round trip, minimum
Elevation gain: 100 meters
Map: 1:50,000 Sixaola

This trail takes you to several lovely, secluded beaches and passes through a mixture of mostly secondary forest with some tropical moist forest. It's hot and muddy, and the mosquitoes and other biting insects can be bad, so bring repellent and remember to fill up your water bottles in Manzanillo, as there is no reliable water along the trail.

Coconut palm grove, Gandoca-Manzanillo Wildlife Refuge

The route starts on the northeast side of the village of Manzanillo, where you walk along the beach for 1 kilometer or so. Stay as close as possible to the ocean. The last house that you pass is that of Willie Burton, and you'll then have to cross a creek before entering a grove of coconut trees. From here, you pick up the trail, which climbs up a small bluff that has a wonderful view of the ocean and the reef. You can snorkel in this area, if you're careful about the waves; there is also reputed to be a swift current on the outer edge of the reef. The species composition of the reef here is similar to Cahuita's, but if you snorkel both you will notice that there is more live coral here. This is because the siltation is not as bad this far down the coast. The reef here is less mature than the one at Cahuita, allowing a lot more of the waves through to the shore and permitting more of a current. Hopefully, Gandoca-Manzanillo's reefs will be better managed than Cahuita's, and will be here long enough to grow as old as its beleaguered relative farther north.

The trail drops twice down to small beaches before climbing a steep hill and heading slightly inland at about 1 kilometer from the trailhead. These beaches have a remarkable variety of shells on them, attesting to the relative health of the reef. As this is part of a protected area, please look and admire, but don't take them home; leave them so that future visitors will also be able to enjoy them. There are hundreds of species, but some of the more common ones are several species of **cone snails**, predatory mollusks that are part of a family that has members in the tropical Pacific venomous enough to kill an adult person, although local ones are harmless. Other species include delicate **bubble shells** and several species of **cowrie shells**, recognizable by their coffee-bean shape.

Watch your footing on the bluffs between the beaches, as they are slick and steep. One hill is known locally as Breakneck, for obvious reasons.

The trail comes up over a bluff and at 1.5 kilometers meets with a dirt (mud, really) track known as "the government road." Take a left here. You pass through a couple of extended hog wallows before coming up a hill and into a squatter settlement, assuming that these people have not been relocated. This is (was?) an area of beautiful tropical wet forest, with large buttressed trees. There are several side paths into the forest off the main road, and you can take these as long as you mark your turns.

The forest is showing signs of damage from **feral pigs**, but there is still a fantastic array of bird life. Keep an eye out for **chestnut-mandibled** and **keeled-billed toucans**, particularly in the remnant trees in the pasture on the right side of the road. You might think that the huge, gaudy bill that these birds carry around with them would be an encumbrance, but they are actually extremely light, being almost hollow and crisscrossed with thin supportive structures throughout. Also commonly seen on this section of trail are poison dart frogs (*Dendrobates auratus* and *D. pumilio*), the **black and green** and **strawberry poison dart frogs**, respectively. For information on the natural history of these fascinating amphibians, see Chapter 2, The Tropical Forest.

The trail continues through mostly secondary growth containing large patches of a bananalike plant called *bananillo* by the locals. It is actually a member of the **heliconia** family, and **hummingbirds** are attracted to the plant's gaudy red flowers. In the thickets along the trail, you may hear strange buzzing and other noises, followed by a loud "pop." These are the territorial or courtship calls of one of several species of **manakins**, small colorful birds that almost never come out into the open. They produce the sound with stiff, modified feathers on their wings.

The trail rises up a short hill, from which you can see your destination, Punta Mona. From the pleasantly shady beach, reached in 5.5 kilometers from Manzanillo, you can see well into Panama, about 8 kilometers to the south. There is some live **coral** right off the point, but be careful of the currents on the outer edge of the reef.

RIVER TRIPS

Río Gandoca

Distance: 5.5 kilometers from Gandoca
Cruising time: 5 hours
Map: 1:50,000 Sixaola

The mouth of the Río Gandoca has some immature mangrove forest mixed with swamp forest, and can be reached from Manzanillo (this can be a little rough for those prone to seasickness) or by hiring a dugout from Gandoca. **Manatees** or **sea cows** have been reported from the estuary, as have small **crocodiles** and **spectacled caimans**. The birding is also very good.

Río Sixaola

Distance: 30 kilometers round trip
Cruising time: 3 to 6 hours by motorboat
Map: 1:50,000 Sixaola

It is somewhat difficult (but not out of the question) to get to the mangrove forest at the mouth of the Río Sixaola. It is not reachable from the ocean, as there are some very dangerous currents that local boatmen are usually unwilling to run. Go to the town of Sixaola and ask around for someone who has a boat equipped with a strong motor to get you there and, more important, back again. It's about 30 kilometers round trip to the estuary. The **mangroves** there are a continuation of the massive mangrove swamps farther south in Panama and are the last on the Atlantic side of Costa Rica. They contain important **oyster** beds, and are a prime breeding ground for the **tarpon** (*Megalops atlanticus*), one of the world's most primitive bony fish and the mainstay of the Costa Rican sport-fishing industry. Birding is also excellent here, particularly for wading birds.

Note: Stay away from the Panamanian side of the river as there have been some reports of hassles with Panamanian border police. Make it clear with whoever you go with that under no circumstances do you want to stop anywhere on the south side of the river.

HITOY-CERERE BIOLOGICAL RESERVE

Size: 9,154 hectares
Distance from San José: 219 kilometers
Camping: Not permitted
Trails: Yes, although most of the reserve is accessible only by following rivers and other watercourses
Map: 1:200,000 Limón; 1:200,000 Talamanca; 1:50,000 Estrella; 1:50,000 Telire
Dry season: None
Transportation: Bus from Limón to Valle de Estrella; call the ICT at 222-1090 for the latest schedules

Hitoy-Cerere derives its name from two words in a local indigenous language. *Hitoy* means "woolly," a reference to the green blanket of mosses and epiphytes that covers everything that's not moving. *Cerere* means "water," a reference to the reserve's abundance of streams and rivers. Hitoy-Cerere has been little studied and is not often visited, perhaps because of its precipitous terrain and wet climate (with more than 3,500 millimeters of rain per year, it is one of the wettest in the country), but these same two factors have produced a biological diversity that may prove to be one of the richest in Costa Rica.

The 1991 earthquake, which had its epicenter in the nearby Valle de Estrella, hit the reserve hard, sending a lot of trees and topsoil into the streams of the upper watershed, but early reports of Hitoy-Cerere's demise were much exaggerated. Most of the reserve is accessible only by following streambeds, and some of these are now difficult or impossible to get into, but there is much left to be explored. The temperature is consistently warm, with daytime temperatures averaging around 25 degrees Celsius. Bring your rain gear, as rain is possible any time of the year. Rubber boots are also recommended.

LOCATION AND ACCESS

The reserve is surrounded on three sides by reserves for indigenous people: Telire to the west, Talamanca to the south, and Tayní to the north. To the east and in the lowlands are the massive banana plantations of the Valle de Estrella, and it is through this area that the reserve is accessible. If you want to travel all the way to the reserve with your own vehicle, you will need one with four-wheel drive. The road is passable up to the last 4 kilometers with two-wheel drive, but the problem is that there is no place to park it.

It is a lot easier to take the Valle La Estrella bus from Limón that passes through the town of Penhurst to the town of Fortuna. In Fortuna you can usually arrange for a taxi to drop you off at the reserve and pick you up at a prearranged date. Someone in town with a four-wheel-drive pickup that can haul up to six passengers and gear can sometimes be found by calling the banana company office (558-0753; Spanish only). The fare is around 2,000 colones each way.

You could get a taxi in Cahuita, but this would cost considerably more and there are few in town that have four-wheel drive. Taking a taxi also eliminates the inevitable confusion of traversing the maze of dirt roads that veer off in all directions through almost 10 kilometers of banana plantation before you get to the road to the reserve, which is another 14 kilometers distant.

VISITOR FACILITIES

For overnight visits, you need to bring a tent or try to make arrangements to stay at the headquarters, which has room for about ten people provided that it's not being used for researchers. You can try calling the parks office in San José (257-0922) or the Limón regional office (758-3796) to see if they can make radio contact with the park's headquarters to verify whether there is room for you. Other than that, the closest accommodations are in Cahuita or Limón.

TRAILS

Espavel Trail
   Distance: 9 kilometers round trip
   Hiking time: 1 to 2 days; day hike
   Elevation gain: 1,000 meters
   Map: 1:50,000 Estrella

This trail takes you through a portion of the reserve's magnificent lowland and premontane forest, with emergent trees that tower more than 50 meters in height. Like most of the forest in the reserve, the canopy is extremely dense and loaded with epiphytes such as **bromeliads, orchids,** and **ferns.** Fallen trees, rocks, and boulders are often covered with primitive plants such as liverworts and mosses of literally hundreds of species. The conditions that create such a great profusion of plant life also make for extremely muddy hiking, so you may consider doing it in rubber boots.

The trail begins behind the headquarters building, climbing up a hill with mud deep enough to suck the boots off your feet. You walk about 0.75 kilometer through secondary growth until you reach an open area with a number of **espavel** or **wild cashew** trees (*Anacardium excelsum*), recognizable by their white and gray splotched bark. These trees are often left when an area is cleared because of

Hikers on the Río Cerere, Hitoy-Cerere Biological Reserve

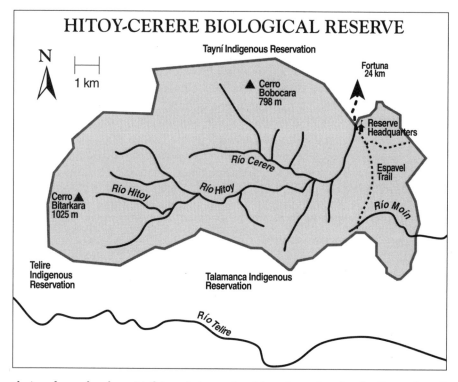

their value as lumber. At this point you should notice a sign for the Espavel Trail that leads off to your right. (The trail that heads straight is off limits; it goes a few kilometers before leaving the reserve for the indigenous people's reservation.) The Espavel Trail heads steeply up onto a ridge and then follows it for a while before descending steeply to its end at the Río Moín, 4.5 kilometers from the trailhead.

Río Cerere

    Distance: 6 to 50 kilometers, or more
    Hiking time: A few hours to many days
    Elevation gain: Almost none
    Map: None

River walking here is a wet undertaking, and the best footgear might be a pair of tight-fitting, waterproof sandals or a pair of shoes that you don't mind getting wet. To get to the Río Cerere, follow an obvious, short path from the front of the headquarters building. You could spend many days exploring the side creeks that flow into the principal rivers, the Hitoy and Cerere, but remember that stream hiking can be treacherous due to slippery rocks and fallen trees that you'll need to get around, over, or under. The upper reaches of the reserve are extremely remote; in fact, much of the reserve has probably never been visited by nonindigenous people. Camp as high out of the riverbeds as you can get, as the water level does fluctuate with heavy storms.

APPENDICES

1. Recommended Resources

All addresses and telephone numbers are for Costa Rica unless noted otherwise.

Asociación Talamanqueña de Ecoturismo y Conservación (ATEC) (Talamanca Association for Ecotourism and Conservation). ATEC is an excellent source of information for the Talamanca region and can arrange guides for many of the region's more remote areas, including indigenous reservations. Address: Puerto Viejo de Limón, Costa Rica. Telephone: 750-0191. Telephone/fax: 750-0188. E-mail: atecmail@sol.racsa.co.cr.

Dirección Forestal (Forestry Directorate). Manages the forest reserve system, but is not terribly amenable to providing information to visitors. Address: Calle 25, Avenidas 8/10, San José. Telephone: 221-9535.

Dirección de Transito (Transit Directorate), San José. Report all traffic accidents to this agency by dialing 911.

Fundación de Parques Nacionales (National Parks Foundation). Source of up-to-date information about the parks, but generally does not have maps. Location: Avenida 15 east of Calle 23 near the Santa Teresita Church in San José. Telephone: 257-2239, 222-4732, 220-1744.

Horizontes Tours. One of the best tour companies in Costa Rica. Offers regular trips to many parks and protected areas and can develop custom itineraries. Location: Calle 28 between Avenidas 1 and 3 in San José. Address: P.O. Box 1780-1002, San José. Telephone: 222-2022, 255-4513. Fax: 222-2022.

Instituto Costarricense de Tourismo (ICT) (Costa Rican Tourism Bureau). Provides information about bus schedules and private reserves, although the information on national parks is often out of date. The staff speaks English. Address: Plaza de la Cultura, Avenidas Central/2, Calle 5, San José. Telephone: 222-1090.

Instituto Geographico Nacional (IGN) (National Geographic Bureau). Supplies topographic maps. Address: Avenida 20, Calles 5/7, San José. No telephone. The IGN and Librería Lehmann at Calle 3, Avenida Central, San José, are the best sources for maps in the country.

Instituto Nacional de Biodiversidad (National Institute of Biodiversity). Specialized information on scientific research being conducted in the parks and preserve system can be accessed through the Conservation Data Center, Instituto Nacional de Biodiversidad in Santo Domingo de Heredia. Telephone: 236-4269.

Organization for Tropical Studies (OTS). A scientific research organization that operates field stations in La Selva, Palo Verde, and Las Cruces. Address: Apdo. 676-2050, San José, Costa Rica. Telephone: 240-6696. Fax: 240-6783. For reservations at OTS facilities, contact Annie Simpson at e-mail address asgamboa@ns.ots.ac.cr.

National Wildlife Directorate. Administers the country's national wildlife refuges. The office is located at Calle 25 and Avenidas 8/10, San José. The telephone numbers are 233-8112 and 222-9533.

Proyecto Campanario. A private reserve that is an excellent base for trips into the northern part of Corcovado National Park. The staff can arrange trips to Isla del Caño. Telephone: 282-5898. Fax: 282-8750. E-mail: campanar@sol.racsa.co.cr. Internet: www.edenia.com/campanar.

Selvamar. Provides support for small-scale ecotourism operations in the southwest part of the country and supplies information about the area. Contact: Walter Odio and Pérez Zeledón, Apdo. 215-8000, San Isidro de El General. Telephone: 771-4582. Fax: 771-8841. E-mail: selvamar@sol.racsa.co.cr.

Servicio de Parques Nacionales (SPN) (National Parks Directorate). The directorate has two offices in San José. The public information office is located at SPN headquarters in the Ministry of Natural Resources and Mines. It is open Monday through Friday, 8 A.M.–4 P.M. Location: Calle 25, Avenidas 8/10. Address: MIRENEM, Apdo. 10094, San José 1000. There is a three-digit, toll-free number, 192, which may or may not be functional; otherwise call 257-0922 for assistance. If you need to arrange meals, accommodations, or guides with local parks offices that don't have a telephone, call the radio communications office at 233-4160. Another public information office is at the Parque Bolívar Zoo. Location: Calle 7, Avenida 11. The staff at this office generally doesn't speak English.

U.S. Centers for Disease Control. Federal organization provides information on diseases, including international outbreaks, such as malaria and cholera. Address: 1600 Clifton Road, Atlanta, Georgia 30333. Telephone: 404-639-3311. Internet: www.cdc.gov.

Wildlife Directorate. Location: Calle 25, Avenidas 8/10, San José. Telephone: 233-8112, 222-9533. Radio operator: 333-4070.

2. Conservation Organizations

ABCONA. This organization specializes in investigating environmental infringements and initiates legal action. It needs volunteers with a background in law and environmental sciences. Donations, which are also needed, can be made through the World Wildlife Fund, 1250 24th St. NW, Washington, D.C. 20037. Address in Costa Rica: Apdo. 8-3790, San José 1000.

Asociación Costarricense para la Conservación de la Naturaleza (ASCONA). Works with local communities on conservation projects. Contact: Leon Gonzalez. Address: Apdo. 8-3790, San José 1000. Telephone: 222-2296, 222-2288.

Asociación de los Nuevas Alquimistas (ANAI). Created by people formerly associated with the New Alchemy Institute in the U.S. Their focus is the Gandoca-Manzanillo National Wildlife Refuge. U.S. address: 1176 Bryson

City Road, Franklin, NC 28734. Costa Rica address: Apdo. 170-2070, Sabanilla. Costa Rica telephone: 246-0990.

Asociación Talamanqueña de Ecoturismo y Conservación (ATEC) (Talamanca Association for Ecotourism and Conservation). Has a good working definition of socially responsible ecotourism. See Recommended Resources for contact information.

Asociación de Voluntarias de Parques Nacionales (Association of National Parks Volunteers). Provides volunteer opportunities for working in national parks. Prospective volunteers should be at least 18 years old. Address: Stanley Arguedas, Asociación de Voluntarias de Parques Nacionales, Apdo. 10104, San José 1000.

Association for the Protection of Trees (ARBOFILA). Grassroots organization for forest protection and reforestation. Jungle Trails works with ARBOFILA to offer a trip to reforestation sites near Carara Biological Reserve. Can be contacted through Jungle Trails. Address: Apdo. 243-1000, San José. Telephone: 555-3486.

Canadian Organization for Tropical Education and Rainforest Conservation (COTERC). They operate a field station in Barra del Colorado National Wildlife Refuge. Canada address: P.O. Box 335, Pickering, ON L1V 2R6 Canada. Canada telephone: 416-683-2116.

CEDARENA. Legal action group specializing in environmental issues. Needs volunteers with appropriate backgrounds. Address: Apdo. 134, San Pedro 2450.

Friends of Lomas Barbudal. U.S. support group for Lomas Barbudal Biological Reserve. U.S. address: 691 Colusa Avenue, Berkeley, CA 94707-1517.

Fundación Neotropica. Runs a gift shop at the visitor center in Poás National Park. Location: Calle 20, Avenida 3. Address: Apdo. 236, San José 1002. Telephone: 330-0003. Fax: 330-6617.

Fundación de Parques Nacionales. Conservation and environmental education in the park system. Address: Apdo. 236-1002, San José. Telephone: 222-4921, 223-8437.

Jardin Gaia. This group operates the first wildlife sanctuary and rehabilitation center to be officially recognized by the government in Costa Rica. They have 300 animals and could use volunteer help. Address: Apartado 182-6350, Quepos, Costa Rica. Telephone/fax: 777-1004. E-mail: wildlife@cariari.ucr.ac.cr.

Monteverde Conservation League. Conservation, reforestation, and environmental education. Volunteer possibilities. Has an office in the village of Monteverde. Address: Apdo. 10581-1000, San José. Telephone: 645-5003, 645-5200, and 645-5305. Fax: 645-5104. E-mail: acmmcl@sol.racsa.co.cr.

The Nature Conservancy, International Program. U.S. organization funds and does consulting work for conservation projects in Costa Rica. U.S. address: 1785 Massachusetts Avenue NW, Washington, DC 20036. U.S. telephone: 202-841-5300.

Organization for Tropical Studies (OTS). A consortium of U.S. and Costa Rican universities and research institutions dedicated to training, research, and wise use of resources. Operates a field station in Palo Verde National Park, Las Cruces Biological Station, and La Selva Biological Station. Address: Apdo. 676-2050, San José. Telephone: 240-6696. Fax: 240-6783.

World Wildlife Fund. Provides funding for conservation projects in Costa Rica. U.S. address: 1601 Connecticut Avenue, Washington, D.C. 20009. Telephone: 202-387-0800.

3. Suggested Reading

Costa Rican Natural History. Daniel H. Janzen. University of Chicago Press, 1983.

A Guide to the Birds of Costa Rica. F. Gary Stiles and Alexander F. Skutch. Cornell University Press, 1989.

A Neotropical Companion. John C. Kricher. Princeton University Press, 1997.

Neotropical Rainforest Mammals: A Field Guide. Louise H. Emmons. University of Chicago Press, 1990.

The Rivers of Costa Rica: A Canoeing, Kayaking and Rafting Guide. Michael W. Mayfield and Rafael E. Gallo. Menasha Ridge Press, 1988.

Tropical Nature. Adrian Forsyth and Ken Miyata. Charles Scribner's Sons, 1984.

INDEX

ABOUT THE AUTHOR

Joe Franke is a biologist, writer, and consultant on natural resource issues, based in Portland, Oregon.

THE MOUNTAINEERS, founded in 1906, is a nonprofit outdoor activity and conservation club, whose mission is "to explore, study, preserve, and enjoy the natural beauty of the outdoors . . . . " Based in Seattle, Washington, the club is now the third-largest such organization in the United States, with 15,000 members and five branches throughout Washington State.

The Mountaineers sponsors both classes and year-round outdoor activities in the Pacific Northwest, which include hiking, mountain climbing, ski-touring, snowshoeing, bicycling, camping, kayaking and canoeing, nature study, sailing, and adventure travel. The club's conservation division supports environmental causes through educational activities, sponsoring legislation, and presenting informational programs. All club activities are led by skilled, experienced volunteers, who are dedicated to promoting safe and responsible enjoyment and preservation of the outdoors.

If you would like to participate in these organized outdoor activities or the club's programs, consider a membership in The Mountaineers. For information and an application, write or call The Mountaineers, Club Headquarters, 300 Third Avenue West, Seattle, Washington 98119; (206) 284-6310.

The Mountaineers Books, an active, nonprofit publishing program of the club, produces guidebooks, instructional texts, historical works, natural history guides, and works on environmental conservation. All books produced by The Mountaineers are aimed at fulfilling the club's mission.

Send or call for our catalog of more than 300 outdoor titles:

The Mountaineers Books
1001 SW Klickitat Way, Suite 201
Seattle, WA 98134
1-800-553-4453
mbooks@mountaineers.org
www.mountaineersbooks.org

Other titles you may enjoy from The Mountaineers:

SOUTH AMERICA'S NATIONAL PARKS: A Visitor's Guide
William C. Leitch
Guide to 32 parks in 7 countries, with directions for specific trails and information on park facilities, special attractions and recreational opportunities.

LATIN AMERICA BY BIKE™: A Complete Touring Guide
Walter Sienko
Recommended tours in 13 countries from Mexico to Patagonia, with tips on accommodations and camping and local culture and history.

MEXICO: A Hiker's Guide to Mexico's Natural History
Jim Conrad
Offers 20 day hikes throughout Mexico's diverse landscape, including Baja, the Gulf Coast, Yucatan Peninsula, Chiapas, and the Mexican Plateau.

TREKKING IN BOLIVIA: A Traveler's Guide
Yossi Brain, Andrew North, and Isobel Stoddart
Guide to day trips and multi-day mountain treks, plus advice on where to buy and hire gear and services.

THE POCKET DOCTOR: A Passport to Healthy Travel, 3rd Edition
Stephen Bezruchka, M.D.
Classic reference for international travelers. Includes new information about emerging diseases such as hantavirus.

WILDERNESS NAVIGATION: Finding Your Way Using Map, Compass, Altimeter, and GPS
Bob Burns and Mike Burns
Complete guide to navigating on- and off-trail in the backcountry, with 30 practice problems and up-to-date declination maps.

BACKPACKER'S EVERYDAY WISDOM: 1001 Expert Tips for Hikers
Karen Berger
Expert tips and tricks for hikers and backpackers selected from one of the most popular *BACKPACKER* magazine columns.

ACONCAGUA: A Climbing Guide, 2nd Edition
R.J. Secor
Presenting 27 routes from the three major approaches, this is the only English-language guidebook available for South America's highest peak.